Expert Angular

Build deep understanding of Angular to set you apart from the developer crowd

Mathieu Nayrolles
Rajesh Gunasundaram
Sridhar Rao

BIRMINGHAM - MUMBAI

Expert Angular

First published: July 2017

Production reference: 1310717

Published by Packt Publishing Ltd.

Livery Place

35 Livery Street

Birmingham

B3 2PB, UK.

ISBN 978-1-78588-023-0

www.packtpub.com

Credits

Authors
Mathieu Nayrolles
Rajesh Gunasundaram
Sridhar Rao

Reviewers
Andrea Chiarelli
Phodal Huang

Commissioning Editor
Ashwin Nair

Acquisition Editor
Larissa Pinto

Content Development Editor
Aditi Gour

Technical Editor
Akansha Bathija

Copy Editor
Dhanya Baburaj

Project Coordinator
Devanshi Doshi

Proofreader
Safis Editing

Indexer
Mariammal Chettiyar

Graphics
Jason Monteiro

Production Coordinator
Shantanu Zagade

About the Authors

Mathieu Nayrolles was born in France and lived in a small village in Cote d'Azur for almost 15 years. He started his computer science studies in France and continued them in Montreal, Canada, where he now lives with his wife. Mathieu holds master's degrees from eXia.Cesi (Software Engineering) and UQAM (Computer Science) and he is now a PhD student at Concordia University (Electrical and Computer Engineering), Montreal, Canada, under the supervision of Dr. Wahab Hamou-Lhadj.

Despite his academic journey, Mathieu also worked for worldwide companies such as Airbus, Saint-Gobain, Ericsson, and Ubisoft, where he learned how important good technical resources are.

Mathieu worked start working with AngularJS in 2011 and moved over Angular2 when the rc1 came out. During these 6 years, he acted as an Angular coach, mentor, and consultant for various companies in Canada, USA, and France. He also gives classes on Angular to software engineering students and professionals in Montreal, Canada.

Finally, Mathieu is the co-founder and CTO of toolwatch.io (a website and companion mobile apps that allow you to measure the precision of your mechanical watches), where he uses Angular daily.

You can discover some of his works through his other books: *Xamarin Studio for Android Programming: A C# Cookbook, Mastering Apache Solr: A practical guide to get to grips with Apache Solr, Instant Magento Performances*, and *Instant Magento Performance Optimization How-to*, published by Packt.

Follow `@MathieuNls` on Twitter for even more information.

Rajesh Gunasundaram is a software architect, technical writer and blogger. He has over 15 years of experience in the IT industry, with more than 12 years using Microsoft .NET, 2 years of BizTalk Server and a year of iOS application development.

Rajesh is a founder and editor of technical blogs programmerguide.net and ioscorner.com and you can find many of his technical writings on .Net and iOS. He is also the founder and developer of VideoLens.co, a platform that analyses videos uploaded in Facebook pages and YouTube channels. Rajesh has also written other books for Packt publishing like *Learning Angular for .Net Developers, ASP.NET Web API Security Essentials,* and *CORS Essentials.*

Rajesh is also an YouTuber running channel ProgrammerGuide. Rajesh holds a master

degree in Computer Application and began his career as a software engineer in the year 2002. He worked on client premises located at various countries such as UK, Belarus and Norway. He also has experience in developing mobile applications for iPhone and iPad.

His technical strengths include Azure, Xamarin, ASP.NET MVC, Web API, WCF, .Net Framework / .Net Core, C#, Objective-C, Angular, Bot Framework, BizTalk, SQL Server, REST, SOA, Design Patterns and Software Architecture.

Rajesh is an early adopter of Angular since AngularJS. He has developed Rich interfaces using Angular, Bootstrap, HTML5 and CSS3. He has good experience in translation of designer mock-ups and wireframes into an AngularJS front-end. Good at unit testing Angular applications with Karma. Expertise in handling RESTful services in Angular. Supporting various web products developed using AngularJS and Angular.

I would like to dedicate this book to my family and my team. I am thankful to the entire team at Packt Publishing for providing me the opportunity to author this book. Thanks to **Larissa Pinto** *for having confident in me and giving me the opportunity to write this book. Thanks to* **Prachi Bisht** *who brought me into the world of authoring books. Thanks to* **Aditi Gour** *for guiding me and helping me in shaping the content of the book.*

Sridhar Rao holds Bachelor of Engineering degree in Information Technology from SGGS Nanded. Sridhar currently works as a Technical Lead at a leading MNC, where he is part of digital practice. Sridhar has over 10 years of experience primarily focused on frontend engineering. He has previously worked with Oracle India, Cognizant Technology Solutions, and Tech Mahindra.

To his credit, Sridhar has also led large teams implementing complex applications using AngularJS for a leading investment bank. He has successfully designed and developed reporting and dashboard application using hybrid AngularJS and Angular frameworks for a leading freight shipping company and a leading low-cost airline.

Sridhar has been a senior developer involved in migrating an entire business-critical application from AngularJS to Angular for a leading media giant.

He is author of the book *PHP and script.aculo.us Web 2.0 Application Interfaces*, published by Packt.

Sridhar is based in New York City, USA. His hobbies include playing the keyboard and traveling.

I would like to thank Mr Hanumantha Rao Chivukula, Mrs Sowbhagya Lakshmi, Gayatri Rao, Srikanth Rao, and finally my wife, Shaminder, for their unconditional love, support, guidance, and motivation. Special mention and love to Bhavya, Seema Sharma, Bhushan Gokhale, Pratyush, and Aaradhya!

About the Reviewers

Andrea Chiarelli has more than 20 years of experience as a software engineer and technical writer. In his professional career, he has used various technologies for the projects he has been involved in, from C# to JavaScript, from Angular to React, from ASP.NET to PhoneGap/Cordova.

He has contributed to many online and offline magazines and has been the author of a few books published by Wrox Press. His latest book, *Mastering JavaScript OOP,* was published by Packt Publishing.

Currently, he is a senior software engineer at the Italian office of Apparound Inc. and a regular contributor to HTML.it, an Italian online magazine focused on web technologies.

Phodal Huang is a developer, creator, and an author. He currently works for ThoughtWorks as a consultant. He now focuses on IoT and frontend development. He is the author of *Design Internet of Things and Growth: Thinking in Full Stack* (in publishing) in Chinese.

He is an open source enthusiast and has created a series of projects in GitHub. After a day's work, he likes to reinvent some wheels for fun. He created the application Growth with Ionic 2 and Angular 2, which is about coaching newbies how to learn programming, and rewriting with React Native. He loves designing, writing, hacking, and traveling.

He has worked on books such as *Learning IoT, Smart IoT Projects, Angular Services*, and *Getting Started with Angular.*

www.PacktPub.com

For support files and downloads related to your book, please visit www.PacktPub.com.

Did you know that Packt offers eBook versions of every book published, with PDF and ePub files available? You can upgrade to the eBook version at www.PacktPub.com and as a print book customer, you are entitled to a discount on the eBook copy. Get in touch with us at service@packtpub.com for more details.

At www.PacktPub.com, you can also read a collection of free technical articles, sign up for a range of free newsletters and receive exclusive discounts and offers on Packt books and eBooks.

https://www.packtpub.com/mapt

Get the most in-demand software skills with Mapt. Mapt gives you full access to all Packt books and video courses, as well as industry-leading tools to help you plan your personal development and advance your career.

Why subscribe?

- Fully searchable across every book published by Packt
- Copy and paste, print, and bookmark content
- On demand and accessible via a web browser

Customer Feedback

Thanks for purchasing this Packt book. At Packt, quality is at the heart of our editorial process. To help us improve, please leave us an honest review on this book's Amazon page at `https://www.amazon.com/dp/1785880233`.

If you'd like to join our team of regular reviewers, you can e-mail us at `customerreviews@packtpub.com`. We award our regular reviewers with free eBooks and videos in exchange for their valuable feedback. Help us be relentless in improving our products!

Table of Contents

Preface

Learn how to build great applications with the Angular framework for any deployment target--be it mobile, desktop, or native apps.

The book covers everything that is required to write modern, intuitive, and responsive applications.

The book covers concepts and fundamentals along with detailed code snippets and examples that will help you jump-start and open up new ideas by learning the Angular framework.

The chapters in the book cover topics that will help any developer pick up Angular programming skills easily. At the same time, experienced and seasoned developers will learn master the skillset of migrating from the existing AngularJS framework and also learn advanced techniques and best practices covered throughout the book.

Along with great functionality, any application heavily relies on design aspects as well. The book will introduce you to and help you sharpen your design skills with Material Design and Bootstrap CSS.

Learn how to write and create reusable, testable, and maintainable services, forms, pipes, async programming, animations, routing, and much more.

Did we say testable? You bet. The book introduces you to Jasmine and the Protractor framework. While learning about the frameworks, we will learn to write unit test scripts using Jasmine and also end-to-end test scripts using the Protractor framework.

The journey of learning and mastering Angular skills will be fun, thought-provoking, and above all easy. Step-by-step guides helps users to implement the concepts in your applications and projects.

What this book covers

Chapter 1, *Architectural Overview and Building a Simple App in Angular*, explains Angular architecture, the basics of TypeScript, and also how to create a simple Angular application.

Chapter 2, *Migrating AngularJS App to Angular App*, shows how to migrate an AngularJS application to Angular 4, and we will also discuss best practices in migrating the application.

Chapter 3, *Using Angular CLI to Generate Angular Apps with Best Practices,* shows how to use Angular command-line interface to generate boilerplate code for an Angular application.

Chapter 4, *Working with Components,* discusses the life cycle of components. We will learn how to implement multiple and container components and also the interactions between different components.

Chapter 5, *Implementing Angular Routing and Navigation,* shows how to create routing strategies and routes for our Angular applications. We will learn the building blocks of routing, create routes, child routes, and secure routes using route guards. States are an important aspect in routing. We will implement states to make secure, multi-state application routes.

Chapter 6, *Creating Directives and Implementing Change Detection,* explains directives, different types of directive provided by Angular, and also how to create custom user-defined directives. We will deep dive into learning how Angular handles change detection and how we can utilize change detection in our apps.

Chapter 7, *Asynchronous Programming Using Observables,* shows how to take advantage of asynchronous programming with Angular by using Observable and Promises. In addition, we learn how to built a basic yet extensible asynchronous JSON API for querying the Marvel cinematic universe.

Chapter 8, *Template and Data Binding Syntax,* discusses the template syntax for writing expressions, operators, attributes, and attaching events to elements. Data binding is one of the key features that allows data mapping from data source to view target and vice versa. Additionally, we will also learn different ways of data binding and create lot of examples along.

Chapter 9, *Advanced Forms in Angular,* explains how to use and master reactive forms. We tackle the reactive part of reactive forms by emphasizing the relationship between your HTML models and your NgModels so every change on a given form is propagated to the model.

Chapter 10, *Material Design in Angular,* discusses Material Design, which is a new hype regarding design. In this chapter, we learn how to integrate material design with Angular. In addition, we learn how to use useful components such as grid and button.

Chapter 11, *Implementing Angular Pipes,* explain that transforming data in the views is one of the most common rituals we have to do it in our applications. We will learn how to transform values using various built-in pipes and create our own pipes. Additionally, we will learn how to pass parameters and customize pipes based on our needs.

Chapter 12, *Implementing Angular Services*, discusses services and factories, creating Angular services, accessing data from components using services, and creating asynchronous services.

Chapter 13, *Applying Dependency Injection*, explains how to create injectables, services, and provider classes that can be used as shared resources between various components. Additionally, we will learn how to create and use the objects created dynamically just-in-time using Inject, Provider, `useClass`, and `useValue`.

Chapter 14, *Handling Angular Animation*, show that animations are key to designing and building beautiful user experiences with smooth transitions and effects. We will learn and implement examples using animations, transitions, states, and keyframes.

Chapter 15, *Integrating Bootstrap with Angular Application*, discusses Bootstrap, which is arguably the most popular frontend framework out there and, in this chapter, we learn what it means to have an Angular x Bootstrap application.

Chapter 16, *Testing Angular Apps Using the Jasmine and Protractor Frameworks*, teaches the use of arguably the most important aspect of the software development process - testing Angular applications using the Jasmine and Protractor frameworks. We will start with an overview of each of the frameworks and then move on to the testing utilities provided by Angular. We will also create sample test scripts for testing Angular components and services.

Chapter 17, *Design Patterns in Angular*, discusses Typescript, is object-oriented programming language with which, we can leverage decades of knowledge on object-oriented architecture. In this chapter, we explore some of the most useful object-oriented design patterns and learn how to apply them in an Angular way.

What you need for this book

You will need the following list of softwares:

- NodeJS 6.10 or latest version
- NPM 3.10 or later
- Good editor such as Visual Studio Code or Sublime Text
- Browser such as chrome or firefox or edge
- Internet connection to download and install node packages

Who this book is for

This book is for JavaScript developers with some prior exposure to Angular. We assume that you ve got a working knowledge of HTML, CSS, and JavaScript.

Conventions

In this book, you will find a number of text styles that distinguish between different kinds of information. Here are some examples of these styles and an explanation of their meaning. Code words in text, database table names, folder names, filenames, file extensions, pathnames, dummy URLs, user input, and Twitter handles are shown as follows: "Then, we go into the `advanced-forms` folder and prune everything that is not inside the `chap7/angular-promise` subdirectory."

A block of code is set as follows:

```
@Component({ selector: 'app-root',
 templateUrl: './app.component.html',
 styleUrls: ['./app.component.css']
  })
```

Any command-line input or output is written as follows:

```
npm install -g typescript
tsc mytypescriptcodefile.ts
```

 Warnings or important notes appear in a box like this.

 Tips and tricks appear like this.

Reader feedback

Feedback from our readers is always welcome. Let us know what you think about this book-what you liked or disliked. Reader feedback is important for us as it helps us develop titles that you will really get the most out of. To send us general feedback, simply e-mail feedback@packtpub.com, and mention the book's title in the subject of your message. If there is a topic that you have expertise in and you are interested in either writing or contributing to a book, see our author guide at www.packtpub.com/authors.

Customer support

Now that you are the proud owner of a Packt book, we have a number of things to help you to get the most from your purchase.

Downloading the example code

You can download the example code files for this book from your account at http://www.packtpub.com. If you purchased this book elsewhere, you can visit http://www.packtpub.com/support and register to have the files e-mailed directly to you. You can download the code files by following these steps:

1. Log in or register to our website using your e-mail address and password.
2. Hover the mouse pointer on the **SUPPORT** tab at the top.
3. Click on **Code Downloads & Errata**.
4. Enter the name of the book in the **Search** box.
5. Select the book for which you're looking to download the code files.
6. Choose from the drop-down menu where you purchased this book from.
7. Click on **Code Download**.

Once the file is downloaded, please make sure that you unzip or extract the folder using the latest version of:

- WinRAR / 7-Zip for Windows
- Zipeg / iZip / UnRarX for Mac
- 7-Zip / PeaZip for Linux

The code bundle for the book is also hosted on GitHub at `https://github.com/PacktPubl ishing/Expert-Angular`. We also have other code bundles from our rich catalog of books and videos available at `https://github.com/PacktPublishing/`. Check them out!

Downloading the color images of this book

We also provide you with a PDF file that has color images of the screenshots/diagrams used in this book. The color images will help you better understand the changes in the output. You can download this file from `https://www.packtpub.com/sites/default/files/down loads/ExpertAngular_ColorImages.pdf`.

Errata

Although we have taken every care to ensure the accuracy of our content, mistakes do happen. If you find a mistake in one of our books-maybe a mistake in the text or the code-we would be grateful if you could report this to us. By doing so, you can save other readers from frustration and help us improve subsequent versions of this book. If you find any errata, please report them by visiting `http://www.packtpub.com/submit-errata`, selecting your book, clicking on the **Errata Submission Form** link, and entering the details of your errata. Once your errata are verified, your submission will be accepted and the errata will be uploaded to our website or added to any list of existing errata under the Errata section of that title. To view the previously submitted errata, go to `https://www.packtpub.com/book s/content/support`and enter the name of the book in the search field. The required information will appear under the **Errata** section.

Piracy

Piracy of copyrighted material on the Internet is an ongoing problem across all media. At Packt, we take the protection of our copyright and licenses very seriously. If you come across any illegal copies of our works in any form on the Internet, please provide us with the location address or website name immediately so that we can pursue a remedy. Please contact us at `copyright@packtpub.com` with a link to the suspected pirated material. We appreciate your help in protecting our authors and our ability to bring you valuable content.

Questions

If you have a problem with any aspect of this book, you can contact us at `questions@packtpub.com`, and we will do our best to address the problem.

1
Architectural Overview and Building a Simple App in Angular

It doesn't matter if you are new to AngularJS or new to Angular. If you want to quickly develop great web apps with rich UIs and with the features of Angular components, templates, and services, you need to master Angular, and this book is for you.

Angular is a JavaScript framework that enables developers to build web and mobile applications. Applications built with Angular can target any device, such as mobiles, tablets, and desktops. Angular is not an incremental version of AngularJS. It was completely rewritten with improved Dependency Injection, dynamic loading, and simpler routing, and recommends that developers use TypeScript and leverage OOPS, static typing, generics, and lambdas.

In this chapter, we will cover the following topics:

- Angular architecture
- Basics of TypeScript
- Building a simple application

Angular architecture

Before we discuss architecture, let's see what's new in Angular. The primary focus of Angular is mobiles, as it is important to consider the performance and loading time of the application on a mobile phone. Many modules are decoupled from the Angular core, leaving only the modules that are definitely core; removing unwanted modules from Angular core leads to better performance.

Angular targets ES6 and leverages TypeScript as a development script language that enables compile time checks for types, rather than at runtime. TypeScript provides additional information about classes when instantiating them by annotating metadata to the classes. You can also use ES5 and Dart as the development language. There is an improved version of Dependency Injection that supports child injectors and instance scope. Router was rewritten completely and the component router was introduced. The Component Directive, the Decorator Directive, and the Template Directive are supported in Angular. The $scope has been completely removed from Angular.

The architecture of Angular comprises **Modules**, **Components**, **Templates**, **Metadata**, **Directives**, and **Services**:

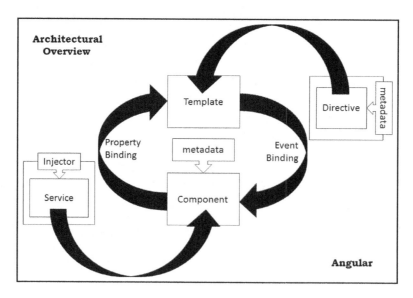

NgModules

Angular framework has various libraries that are grouped as modules in order to build an application. Angular applications are modular in nature and are constructed by assembling various modules. Modules may have components, services, functions, and/or values. Some modules may have a collection of other modules and are known as library modules.

Angular packages, such as `core`, `common`, `http`, and `router` that are prefixed with `@angular` comprise many modules. We import what our application needs from these library modules as follows:

```
import {Http, Response} from @angular/http';
```

Here, we import `Http` and `Response` from the library module, `@angular/http`. `@angular/http` refers to a folder in the Angular package. Any module defined to be exported can be imported into another module by referring to the filename of the module.

 Note: this import statement was introduced in ES2015 and is used to import objects or function that are exported from other modules or scripts

However, we can also refer to the folder as we referred to `@angular/http`. This can be achieved by adding an `index.ts` file to the folder and adding the code to export modules from the folder. This is a best practice suggested by Angular's style guide and is called the barrel technique:

```
export * from './http';
```

This is the export statement in the `index.ts` found in `@angular/http`. The statement means that it exports all the modules in HTTP and that they can be imported to our application wherever needed.

When we write an Angular application, we start by defining an `AppComponent` (not necessarily with the same name) and exporting it.

Components

A component is a class that has properties and methods to be used in the view. These properties and methods exposed to view enable the view to interact with components. We code logic that supports the view in the component class:

```
Component
{}
```

For example, next is a component class book that has a `properties` title and author and a `getPubName` method that returns the name of the book:

```
export class BookComponent {
  title: string;
  author: string;
  constructor() {
      this.title = 'Learning Angular for .Net Developers';
      this.author = 'Rajesh Gunasundaram';
  }
  getPubName() : string {
    return 'Packt Publishing';
  }
}
```

 Note: We will be using TypeScript in all our examples in this book.

The life cycle of a component is managed by Angular according to user interactions with the application. We can also add an `event` method that will be fired according to the state changes of the component. These `event` methods are known as life cycle hooks and are optional.

We will learn in detail about components in Chapter 5, *Implementing Angular Routing and Navigation*.

Templates

Templates can be thought of as a representation of a component that is visualized according to the UI/UX needs of an application. A component will have a template associated with it. The template is responsible for displaying and updating data according to user events:

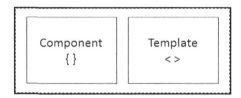

Here is a simple template that displays the title and author of a book:

```
<h1>Book Details</h1>
<p>Title of the Book: {{title}}</p>
<p>Author Name : {{author}}</p>
```

Here, the title and author values wrapped in curly braces will be supplied by the associated component instance.

We will discuss templates and their syntax in detail in Chapter 8, *Template and Data Binding Syntax*.

Metadata

A class can be turned into a component by annotating it with @Component and passing the necessary metadata, such as selector, template, or templateUrl. Angular considers a class as a component only after attaching metadata to it:

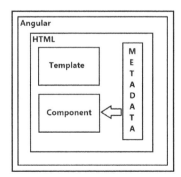

Let's revisit the `BookComponent` class we defined earlier. Angular does not consider this class as a component unless we annotate it. TypeScript leverages the ES7 feature by providing a way to decorate a class with metadata as follows:

```
@Component({
    selector:    'book-detail',
    templateUrl: 'app/book.component.html'
})
export class BookComponent { ... }
```

Here, we have decorated the `BookComponent` class with `@Component` and attached metadata selector and `templateUrl`. It means that, wherever Angular sees the special `<book-detail/>` tag in the view, it will create an instance of `BookComponent` and render the view assigned to `templateUrl`, which is `book.component.html`.

A decorator provided by TypeScript is a function that takes configuration parameters that are used by Angular to create an instance of the component and render the associated view. Configuration parameters may also have information about directives and providers, which will be made available by Angular when the component is created.

Data Binding

Data Binding is one of the core responsibilities of developers when writing code to bind data to the user interface and update changing data according to user interactions with the user interface. Angular has reduced the burden of writing large amounts of code to handle Data Binding:

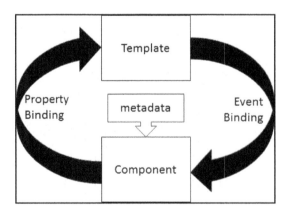

Angular handles Data Binding by coordinating with templates and components. The templates provide instructions to Angular on how and what to bind. There are two types of binding in Angular: globally One-way Data Binding and Two-way Data Binding. One-way Data Binding deals with either binding data from the component to the DOM or from the DOM to the component. Two-way Data Binding deals with both sides of communication, that is, the component to the DOM and the DOM to the component.

```
<div>Title: {{book.title}}<br/>
  Enter Author Name: <input [(ngModel)]="book.author">
</div>
```

Here, `book.title` wrapped in double curly braces deals with One-way Data Binding. The value of book title, if available in the component instance, will be displayed in the view. `book.author`, assigned to the `ngModel` property of the input element, deals with Two-way Data Binding. If the component instance has a value in the author property, then it will be assigned to the input elements, and if the value is changed by the user in the input control, then the updated value will be available in the component instance.

We will learn in detail about Data Binding in `Chapter 8`, *Template and Data Binding Syntax*.

Directives

A directive is instructions or guidelines for rendering a template. A class decorated with `@Directive` to attached metadata is called a directive. There are three types of directive supported by Angular, namely Component Directive, Structural Directive, and Attribute Directive:

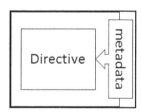

A component is one form of a directive with a template that is decorated with `@Component`: it is actually an extended `@Directive` with a template feature:

```
<book-detail></book-detail>
```

Structural Directives manipulate the DOM elements and alter their structure by adding, removing, and replacing DOM elements. The following code snippet uses two Structural Directives:

```
<ul>
<li *ngFor="let book of books">
    {{book.title}}
</li>
</ul>
```

Here, the `div` element has a `*ngFor` directive that iterates through the books collection object and replaces the title of each book.

An Attribute Directive helps to update the behavior or the appearance of an element. Let's use the Attribute Directive to set the font size of a paragraph. The following code snippet shows an HTML statement implemented with an Attribute Directive:

```
<p [myFontsize]>Fontsize is sixteen</p>
```

We need to implement a class annotated with `@Directive` along with the selector for the directive. This class should be implemented with the instructions on the behavior of the directive:

```
import { Directive, ElementRef, Input } from '@angular/core';
@Directive({ selector: '[myFontsize]' })
export class FontsizeDirective {
    constructor(el: ElementRef) {
        el.nativeElement.style.fontSize = 16;
    }
}
```

Here, Angular will look for elements with the `[myFontsize]` directive and sets the font size to `16`.

It is necessary to pass the `myFontSize` directive to the declarations metadata of `@NgModule` as follows:

```
import { NgModule } from '@angular/core';
import { BrowserModule } from '@angular/platform-browser';
import { AppComponent } from './app.component';
import { FontsizeDirective } from './fontsize.directive';
@NgModule({
  imports: [ BrowserModule ],
  declarations: [
    AppComponent,
    FontsizeDirective
  ],
```

```
    bootstrap: [ AppComponent ]
})
export class AppModule { }
```

We will discuss directives in detail in Chapter 6, *Creating Directives and Implementing Change Detection.*

Services

Services are user-defined classes used to solve problems. Angular recommends only having template-specific codes in components. A component's responsibility is to enrich the UI/UX in the Angular application and delegate business logic to services. Components are consumers of services:

Application-specific or business logic such as persisting application data, logging errors, and file storage should be delegated to services, and components should consume the respective services to deal with the appropriate business or application-specific logic:

For example, we can have a service called BookService that deals with inserting new books, editing or deleting existing books, and fetching a list of all the books available.

We will see more about services in Chapter 11, *Implementing Angular Pipes.*

Dependency Injection

When an instance of a class is created, supplying the required dependencies of that class for it to function properly is called Dependency Injection. Angular provides a modern and improved version of Dependency Injection:

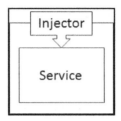

In Angular, the injector maintains the containers to hold the instances of the dependencies and serves them as and when required. If the instance of a dependency is not available in the container, then the injector creates an instance of the dependency and serves it:

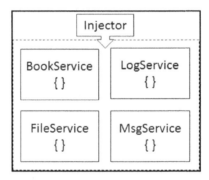

As stated earlier, components have logic that is related to templates and mostly consume services to perform business logic. So, components depend on services. When we write code for components, we create a parameter constructor that takes the service as an argument. It means that creating an instance of the component depends on the service parameter in the constructor. Angular requests that the injector provide the instance of the service in the parameter of the constructor of the component. The injector will serve the instance of the requested service, if available; otherwise, it creates a new one and serves it:

```
export class BookComponent {
  constructor(private service: BookService) { }
}
```

In this code snippet, the : symbol comes from TypeScript and is not Angular syntactical sugar. The `private` keyword is also from TypeScript and enables assigning the passed constructor to the class instance automatically. The type information is used to infer the type to be injected. The `BookComponent` has a dependency to `BookService` and is injected in the constructor. So when an instance of the `BookComponent` is created, Angular will also make sure the instance of `BookService` is readily available for the `BookComponent` instance to consume.

The injector has knowledge of the dependencies to be created from providers that are configured with the required dependency types when bootstrapping the application or when decorating the components, as follows:

```
@NgModule({
  imports: [BrowserModule],
  declarations: [AppComponent,],
  providers: [BookService],
  bootstrap: [ AppComponent ]
})
export class AppModule { }
```

The preceding code snippet adds `BookService` as a provider to the bootstrap function. The injector will create an instance of `BookService` and keep it available in the container for the entire application to inject whenever it's requested:

```
@Component({
  providers:    [BookService]
})
export class BookComponent { ... }
```

The preceding code snippet adds `BookService` as a provider in the metadata of the component. The injector will create an instance of `BookService` when it encounters a request to create an instance of `BookComponent`.

We will discuss Dependency Injection and hierarchical Dependency Injection in detail in `Chapter 12`, *Implementing Angular Services.*

Basics of TypeScript

TypeScript is a superset of JavaScript and is an open source language developed by Microsoft. Code written in TypeScript will be compiled to JavaScript and executed on any browser or server running `Node.js`. TypeScript is actually a type of JavaScript. TypeScript helps to improve the quality of code you write in JavaScript. If we use external libraries, we need to use type definition files for the imported libraries. Type definition files provide JavaScript tooling support and also enable compile time checks, code refactoring, and variable renaming support by inferring the structure of the code. TypeScript is evolving and keeps adding additional features aligned with the ES2016 specification and later.

There are various editors available on the market that write TypeScript code and compile them using a TypeScript compiler. These editors take care of compiling your TypeScript into JavaScript. Some popular editors are shown here:

- Visual Studio
- Visual Studio Code
- Sublime text
- Atom
- Eclipse
- Emacs
- WebStorm
- Vim

You can also download TypeScript as a `Node.js` package by executing the following command in the Node.js command-line tool to install TypeScript globally:

```
npm install -g typescript
```

To transpile the TypeScript code into JavaScript, you can execute the following command in the command-line tool:

```
tsc mytypescriptcodefile.ts
```

Here, `tsc` is the TypeScript compiler that converts a TypeScript file into a JavaScript file. `mytypescriptfile` is the name of your TypeScript code file and `.ts` is the extension of the TypeScript file. On executing the `tsc` command, it generates a `.js` file with the same name as the `.ts` source file.

We will be using Visual Studio Code editor for our sample code demos in this chapter. Let us see basic features of TypeScript with examples.

Basic types

Let's explore some of the basic types in TypeScript and how to use them. Basic types include primitive types such as number, string, boolean, and array in TypeScript. JavaScript only validates types during runtime, but TypeScript validates variable types during compile time and greatly reduces the possibility of typecast issues during runtime.

Number type

The number type represents floating point values. It can hold values such as decimal, binary, hexadecimal, and octal literals:

```
let decimal: number = 6;
let hex: number = 0xf00d;
let binary: number = 0b1010;
let octal: number = 0o744;
```

Boolean type

The Boolean type is a very simple type that can hold either of two values, true or false. This Boolean type is used to maintain the state in a variable:

```
let isSaved: Boolean;
isSaved = true;
```

Here, the `isSaved` variable of type Boolean is assigned with the value true.

String

The string data type can hold a sequence of characters. Declaring and initializing the string variable is very simple, as follows:

```
var authorName: string = "Rajesh Gunasundaram";
```

Here, we declared a variable named `authorName` as a string, and it is assigned the value `Rajesh Gunasundaram`. TypeScript supports surrounding the string value with either a double quotes (") or single quotes (').

Array

The array data type is meant to hold a collection of values of specific types. In TypeScript, we can define arrays in two ways, which are as follows:

```
var even:number[] = [2, 4, 6, 8, 10];
```

This statement declares an array variable of the number type using square brackets ([]) after the data type number, and it is assigned with a series of even numbers from 2 to 10. The second way to define array is as follows:

```
var even:Array<number> = [2, 4, 6, 8, 10];
```

This statement uses the generic array type, which uses the Array keyword followed by angle brackets (<>) that wrap the number data type.

Enum

The enum data type will have a named set of values. We use enumerators to give user-friendly names to constants that identify certain values:

```
enum Day {Mon, Tue, Wed, Thu, Fri, Sat, Sun};
var firstDay: Day = Day.Mon;
```

Here, we have the Day enum variable, which holds a series of values that represent each day of the week. The second statement shows how to access a particular enum value in a day and assign it to another variable.

Any

The any data type is a dynamic data type that can hold any value. TypeScript throws compile time errors if you assign a string variable to an integer variable. If you are not sure about what value a variable is going to hold and you would like to opt out of compiler-checking for the type in the assignment, you can use the any data type:

```
var mixedList:any[] = [1, "I am string", false];
mixedList [2] = "no you are not";
```

Here, we used an array of the any type so that it can hold any type, such as numbers, strings, and booleans.

Void

Void is actually nothing. It can be used as the return type of a function to declare that this function will not return any value:

```
function alertMessage(): void {
    alert("This function does not return any value");
}
```

Classes

A class is an extensible template that is used to create objects with member variables to hold the state of the object and member functions that deal with the behavior of the object.

JavaScript only supports function-based and prototype-based inheritance to build reusable components. ECMAScript 6 provides the syntactic sugar of using classes in supporting object-oriented programming. However, not all browsers understand ES6 and we need transpilers, such as TypeScript, that compile the code down to JavaScript and target ES5, which is compatible with all browsers and platforms:

```
class Customer {
    name: string;
    constructor(name: string) {
        this.name = name;
    }
    logCustomer() {
        console.log('customer name is ' + this.name;
    }
}
var customer = new Customer("Rajesh Gunasundaram");
```

This `Customer` class has three members: a name property, a constructor, and a `logCustomer` method. The last statement outside the customer class creates an instance of the customer class using the `new` keyword.

Interfaces

An interface is an abstract type that defines the behavior of a class. An interface is a contract that abstracts the implementation. An interface provides a type definition for an object that can be exchanged between clients. This enables the client to only exchange an object that is complied with the interface type definition. Otherwise, we get a compile time error.

In TypeScript, interfaces define contracts for an object within your code and the code outside your project. Let's see how to use TypeScript with an example:

```
function addCustomer(customerObj: {name: string}) {
  console.log(customerObj.name);
}
var customer = {id: 101, name: "Rajesh Gunasundaram"};
addCustomer(customer);
```

The type checker verifies the `addCustomer` method call and examines its parameter. `addCustomer` expects an object with the name property of the string type. But the client that calls `addCustomer` is passed an object with two parameters, `id` and `name`, respectively.

However, the compiler does not check the `id` property as it is not available in the parameter type of the `addCustomer` method. It only matters for the compiler that the required properties are present.

Let's rewrite the method applying `interface` as a parameter type as follows:

```
interface Customer {
  name: string;
}
function addCustomer(customerObj: Customer) {
  console.log(customerObj.name);
}
var customer = {id: 101, name: "Rajesh Gunasundaram"};
addCustomer(customer);
```

Here, we declared the `Customer` interface with the name parameter, and we modified the `addCustomer` signature to accept the parameter of the type `Customer` interface. The remaining statements are same as in the previous code snippet. The compiler only checks for the shape of the object as TypeScript implements the structural type system. It will not check whether the object we are passing implements the `Customer` interface. It only looks for the `name` property of the `string` type in the parameter and then allows it, if it's present.

Optional properties using an interface

In some scenarios, we may want to pass values only for minimal parameters. In such cases, we can define the properties in an interface as optional properties, as follows:

```
interface Customer {
  id: number;
  name: string;
  bonus?: number;
}
```

```
function addCustomer(customer: Customer) {
  if (customer.bonus) {
    console.log(customer.bonus);
  }
}
addCustomer({id: 101, name: "Rajesh Gunasundaram"});
```

Here, the bonus property has been defined as an optional property by concatenating a question mark (?) at the end of the name property.

Function type interfaces

We just saw how to define properties in interfaces. Similarly, we can also define function types in interfaces. We can define function types in interfaces by just giving the signature of the function with the return type. Note that, in the following code snippet, we have not added the function name:

```
interface AddCustomerFunc {
  (firstName: string, lastName: string): string;
}
```

Now, we have AddCustomerFunc ready. Let's define an interface variable called AddCustomerFunc and assign a function of the same signature to it as follows:

```
var addCustomer: AddCustomerFunc;
addCustomer = function(firstName: string, lastName: string) {
  console.log('Full Name: ' + firstName + ' ' + lastName);
  return firstName + ' ' + lastName;
}
```

The parameter name in the function signature can vary, but not the data type. For example, we can alter the fn and ln function parameters of the string type as follows:

```
addCustomer = function(fn: string, ln: string) {
  console.log('Full Name: ' + fn + ' ' + ln);
}
```

So, if we change the data type of the parameter or the return type of the function here, the compiler will throw an error about the parameter not matching or the return type not matching with the AddCustomerFunc interface.

Array type interfaces

We can also define an interface for array types. We can specify the data type for the index array and the data type to the array item as follows:

```
interface CutomerNameArray {
  [index: number]: string;
}
var customerNameList: CutomerNameArray;
customerNameList = ["Rajesh", "Gunasundaram"];
```

TypeScript supports two types of index: number and string. This array type interface also stipulates that the return type of the array should match the declaration.

Class type interfaces

Class type interfaces define the contract for classes. A class that implements an interface should meet the requirement of the interface:

```
interface CustomerInterface {
    id: number;
    firstName: string;
    lastName: string;
    addCustomer(firstName: string, lastName: string);
    getCustomer(id: number): Customer;
}
class Customer implements CustomerInterface {
    id: number;
    firstName: string;
    lastName: string;
    constructor() { }
    addCustomer(firstName: string, lastName: string) {
        // code to add customer
    }
    getCustomer(id: number): Customer {
        return this;
    }
}
```

The class type interface only deals with public members of the class. So, it is not possible to add private members to the interface.

Extending interfaces

Interfaces can be extended. Extending an interface makes it share the properties of another interface, as follows:

```
interface Manager {
    hasPower: boolean;
}
interface Employee extends Manager {
    name: string;
}
var employee = <Employee>{};
employee.name = "Rajesh Gunasundaram";
employee.hasPower = true;
```

Here, the `Employee` interface extends the `Manager` interface and shares its `hasPower` with the `Employee` interface.

Hybrid type interfaces

Hybrid type interfaces are used when we want to use the object both as a function and an object. We can call an object like a function if it implements a hybrid type interface, or we can use it as an object and access its properties. This type of interface enables you to use an interface as an object and a function, as follows:

```
interface Customer {
    (name: string);
    name: string;
    deleteCustomer(id: number): void;
}
var c: Customer;
c('Rajesh Gunasundaram');
c.name = 'Rajesh Gunasundaram';
c.deleteCustomer(101);
```

Inheritance

Inheritance is the concept of inheriting behaviors from another class or object. It helps to achieve code reusability and build a hierarchy in relationships of classes or objects. Also, inheritance helps you to cast similar classes.

JavaScript, by targeting ES5, doesn't support classes, and so class inheritance is impossible to implement. However, we can implement prototype inheritance instead of class inheritance. Let's explore inheritance in ES5 with examples.

First, create a function named `Animal` as follows:

```
var Animal = function() {
    this.sleep = function() {
        console.log('sleeping');
    }
    this.eat = function() {
        console.log('eating');
    }
}
```

Here, we created a function named `Animal` with two methods: `sleep` and `eat`. Now, let's extend this `Animal` function using the prototype as follows:

```
Animal.prototype.bark = function() {
    console.log('barking');
}
```

Now, we can create an instance of `Animal` and call the extended function, `bark`, as follows:

```
var a = new Animal();
a.bark();
```

We can use the `Object.Create` method to clone a prototype of the parent and create a child object. Then, we can extend the child object by adding methods. Let's create an object named `Dog` and inherit it from `Animal`:

```
var Dog = function() {
    this.bark = new function() {
        console.log('barking');
    }
}
```

Now, let's clone the prototype of `Animal` and inherit all the behavior in the `Dog` function. Then, we can call the `Animal` method using the `Dog` instance, as follows:

```
Dog.prototype = Object.create(animal.prototype);
var d = new Dog();
d.sleep();
d.eat();
```

Inheritance in TypeScript

We just saw how to implement an inheritance in JavaScript using a prototype. Now, we will see how an inheritance can be implemented in TypeScript, which is basically ES6 inheritance.

In TypeScript, similar to extending interfaces, we can also extend a class by inheriting another class, as follows:

```
class SimpleCalculator {
   z: number;
    constructor() { }
   addition(x: number, y: number) {
       this.z = this.x + this.y;
   }
    subtraction(x: number, y: number) {
       this.z = this.x - this.y;
   }
}
class ComplexCalculator extends SimpleCalculator {
    constructor() { super(); }
   multiplication(x: number, y: number) {
       this.z = x * y;
   }
    division(x: number, y: number) {
       this.z = x / y;
   }
}
var calculator = new ComplexCalculator();
calculator.addition(10, 20);
calculator.Substraction(20, 10);
calculator.multiplication(10, 20);
calculator.division(20, 10);
```

Here, we are able to access the methods of `SimpleCalculator` using the instance of `ComplexCalculator` as it extends `SimpleCalculator`.

Private and public modifiers

In TypeScript, all members in a class are `public` by default. We have to add the `private` keyword explicitly to control the visibility of the members, and this useful feature is not available in JavaScript:

```
class SimpleCalculator {
    private x: number;
    private y: number;
    z: number;
    constructor(x: number, y: number) {
        this.x = x;
        this.y = y;
    }
    addition() {
        this.z = this.x + this.y;
    }
    subtraction() {
        this.z = this.x - this.y;
    }
}
class ComplexCalculator {
    z: number;
    constructor(private x: number, private y: number) { }
    multiplication() {
        this.z = this.x * this.y;
    }
    division() {
        this.z = this.x / this.y;
    }
}
```

Note that in the `SimpleCalculator` class, we defined x and y as private properties, which will not be visible outside the class. In `ComplexCalculator`, we defined x and y using parameter properties. These `Parameter` properties will enable us to create and initialize a member in one statement. Here, x and y are created and initialized in the constructor itself without writing any further statements inside it.

Accessors

We can also implement getters and setters to the properties to control accessing them from the client. We can intercept a process before setting a value to a property variable or before getting a value of the property variable:

```
var updateCustomerNameAllowed = true;
class Customer {
    private _name: string;
    get name: string {
        return this._name;
    }
    set name(newName: string) {
        if (updateCustomerNameAllowed == true) {
            this._name = newName;
        }
        else {
            alert("Error: Updating Customer name not allowed!");
        }
    }
}
```

Here, the setter for the `name` property ensures that the customer name can be updated. Otherwise, it shows an alert message to the effect that it is not possible.

Static properties

These properties are not instance-specific and are accessed by a class name instead of using the `this` keyword:

```
class Customer {
    static bonusPercentage = 20;
    constructor(public salary: number) {   }

    calculateBonus() {
        return this.salary * Customer.bonusPercentage/100;
    }
}
var customer = new Customer(10000);
var bonus = customer.calculateBonus();
```

Here, we declared a static variable called `bonusPercentage` that is accessed using the class name `Customer` in the `calculateBonus` method. This `bonusPercentage` property is not instance-specific.

Modules

JavaScript is a powerful and dynamic language. With dynamic programming in JavaScript, we need to structure and organize the code so that it will make its maintainability easier and also enable us to easily locate the code for a specific functionality. We can organize code by applying a modular pattern. Code can be separated into various modules, and relevant code can be put in each module.

TypeScript made it easier to implement modular programming using the module keyword. Modules enable you to control the scope of variables, code reusability, and encapsulation. TypeScript supports two types of module: internal and external modules.

Namespaces

We can create namespaces in TypeScript using the namespace keyword as follows. All the classes defined under namespace will be scoped under this namespace and will not be attached to the global scope:

```
namespace Inventory {
    class Product {
            constructor (public name: string, public quantity:
                number) {    }
    }
    // product is accessible
    var p = new Product('mobile', 101);
}

// Product class is not accessible outside namespace
var p = new Inventory.Product('mobile', 101);
```

To make the Product class available for access outside the namespace, we need to add an export keyword when defining the Product class, as follows:

```
module Inventory {
    export class Product {
            constructor (public name: string, public quantity: number) {
    }
        }
}

// Product class is now accessible outside namespace
var p = new Inventory.Product('mobile', 101);
```

We can also share namespaces across files by adding a reference statement at the beginning of the code in the referring files, as follows:

```
/// <reference path="Inventory.ts" />
```

Modules

TypeScript also supports modules As we deal with a large number of external JavaScript libraries, this modularity will really help us organize our code. Using the import statement, we can import modules as follows:

```
Import { inv } from "./Inventory";
var p = new inv.Product('mobile', 101);
```

Here, we just imported the previously created module, Inventory, created an instance of Product and assigned it to the variable p.

Functions

JavaScript, which follows the ES5 specs, does not support classes and modules. However, we tried to scope variables and modularity using functional programming in JavaScript. Functions are the building blocks of an application in JavaScript.

Though TypeScript supports classes and modules, functions play a key role in defining a specific logic. We can define both named functions and anonymous functions in JavaScript as follows:

```
//Named function
function multiply(a, b) {
    return a * b;
}

//Anonymous function
var result = function(a, b) { return a * b; };
```

In TypeScript, we define functions with the type of the parameters and the return type using function arrow notation, which is also supported in ES6, as follows:

```
var multiply:(a: number, b: number) => number =
        function(a: number, b: number): number { return a * b; };
```

Optional and default parameters

Say, for example, we have a function with three parameters, and sometimes we may only pass values for the first two parameters in the function. In TypeScript, we can handle such scenarios using the optional parameter. We can define the first two parameters as normal and the third parameter as optional, as given in the following code snippet:

```
function CustomerName(firstName: string, lastName: string, middleName?:
string) {
    if (middleName)
        return firstName + " " + middleName + " " + lastName;
    else
        return firstName + " " + lastName;
}
//ignored optional parameter middleName
var customer1 = customerName("Rajesh", "Gunasundaram");
//error, supplied too many parameters
var customer2 = customerName("Scott", "Tiger", "Lion", "King");
//supplied values for all
var customer3 = customerName("Scott", "Tiger", "Lion");
```

Here, `middleName` is the optional parameter, and it can be ignored when calling the `function`.

Now, let's see how to set default parameters in a function. If a value is not supplied to a parameter in the function, we can define it to take the default value that is configured:

```
function CustomerName(firstName: string, lastName: string, middleName:
    string = 'No Middle Name') {
    if (middleName)
        return firstName + " " + middleName + " " + lastName;
    else
        return firstName + " " + lastName;
}
```

Here, `middleName` is the default parameter that will have `No Middle Name` by default if the value is not supplied by the caller.

Rest parameter

Using the rest parameter, you can pass an array of values to the function. This can be used in scenarios where you are not sure about how many values will be supplied to the function:

```
function clientName(firstClient: string, ...restOfClient: string[]) {
    console.log(firstClient + " " + restOfClient.join(" "));
}
clientName ("Scott", "Steve", "Bill", "Sergey", "Larry");
```

Here, note that the `restOfClient` rest parameter is prefixed with an ellipsis (...), and it can hold an array of strings. In the caller of the function, only the value of the first parameter that is supplied will be assigned to the `firstClient` parameter, and the remaining values will be assigned to `restOfClient` as array values.

Generics

Generics are very useful for developing reusable components that can work against any data type. So, the client that consumes this component will decide what type of data it should act upon. Let's create a simple function that returns whatever data is passed to it:

```
function returnNumberReceived(arg: number): number {
    return arg;
}
unction returnStringReceived(arg: string): string {
    return arg;
}
```

As you can see, we need individual methods to process each data type. We can implement them in a single function using the any data type, as follows:

```
function returnAnythingReceived (arg: any): any {
    return arg;
}
```

This is similar to generics. However, we don't have control over the return type. If we pass a number and we can't predict whether the number will be returned or not by the function, the return type can be of any type.

Generics offers a special variable of type T. Applying this type to the function as follows enables the client to pass the data type they would like this function to process:

```
function returnWhatReceived<T>(arg: T): T {
    return arg;
}
```

So, the client can call this function for various data types as follows:

```
var stringOutput = returnWhatReceived<string>("return this");
// type of output will be 'string'
var numberOutput = returnWhatReceived<number>(101);
// type of output will be number
```

 Note that the data type to be processed is passed by wrapping it in angle brackets (<>) in the function call.

Generic interfaces

We can also define generic interfaces using the T type variable, as follows:

```
interface GenericFunc<T> {
    (arg: T): T;
}
function func<T>(arg: T): T {
    return arg;
}
var myFunc: GenericFunc<number> = func;
```

Here, we defined a generic interface and the myFunc variable of the GenericFunc type, passing the number data type for the T type variable. Then, this variable is assigned with a function named func.

Generic classes

Similar to generic interfaces, we can also define generic classes. We define classes with a generic type in angle brackets (<>) as follows:

```
class GenericClass<T> {
    add: (a: T, b: T) => T;
}
```

```
var myGenericClass = new GenericClass<number>();
myGenericClass.add = function(a, b) { return a + b; };
```

Here, the generic class is instantiated by passing the generic data type as number. So, the add function will process and add two variables of type number passed as parameters.

Decorators

Decorators enable us to extend a class or object by adding behaviors without modifying code. Decorators wrap the class with extra functionality. Decorators can be attached to a class, property, method, parameter, and accessor. In ECMAScript 2016, decorators are proposed to modify the behavior of a class. Decorators are prefixed with the @ symbol and a decorator name that resolves to a function called at runtime.

The following code snippet shows the authorize function, and it can be used as the @authorize decorator on any other class:

```
function authorize(target) {
    // check the authorization of the use to access the "target"
}
```

Class decorators

Class decorators are declared above the class declaration. Class decorators can observe, modify, and replace a class' definition that it is decorated by applying to the constructor of that class. The signature of ClassDecorator in TypeScript is as follows:

```
declare type ClassDecorator = <TFunction extends Function>(target:
    TFunction) => TFunction | void;
```

Consider a Customer class; we would like that class to be frozen. Its existing properties should not be removed or new properties should not be added.

We can create a separate class that can take any object and freeze it. We can then decorate the customer class with @freezed to prevent adding new properties or removing the existing properties from the class:

```
@freezed
class Customer {
  public firstName: string;
  public lastName: string;
  constructor(firstName : string, lastName : string) {
    this.firstName = firstName;
```

```
    this.lastName = lastName;
  }
}
```

The preceding class takes four arguments in the `firstname` and `lastname` constructors. The following are the code snippets of the function written for the `@freezed` decorator:

```
function freezed(target: any) {
    Object.freeze(target);
}
```

Here, the freezed decorator takes `target`, which is the `Customer` class that is being decorated, and freezes it when it gets executed.

Method decorators

Method decorators are declared before the method declaration. This decorator is used to modify, observe, or replace a method definition and is applied to the property descriptor for the method. The following code snippet shows a simple class with an applied method decorator:

```
class Hello {
    @logging
    increment(n: number) {
        return n++;
    }
}
```

The `Hello` class has the `increment` method that increments a number supplied to its parameter. Note that the `increment` method is decorated with the `@logging` decorator to log input and output of the increment method. The following is the code snippet of the `logging` function:

```
function logging(target: Object, key: string, value: any) {
        value.value = function (...args: any[]) {
            var result = value.apply(this, args);
            console.log(JSON.stringify(args));
            return result;
        }
    };
}
```

The method decorator function takes three arguments: `target`, `key`, and `value`. `target` holds the method that is being decorated; `key` holds the name of the method being decorated; and `value` is the property descriptor of the specified property if it exists on the object.

The logging method gets invoked when the increment method is called and it logs the value to the console.

Accessor decorators

Accessor decorators are prefixed before the accessor declaration. These decorators are used to observe, modify, or replace an accessor definition and are applied to the property descriptor. The following code snippet shows a simple class with the applied accessor decorator applied:

```
class Customer {
  private _firstname: string;
  private _lastname: string;
  constructor(firstname: string, lastname: string) {
      this._firstname = firstname;
      this._lastname = lastname;
  }
  @logging(false)
  get firstname() { return this._firstname; }
  @logging(false)
  get lastname() { return this._lastname; }
}
```

In this class, we decorate the get accessor of `firstname` and `lastname` with `@logging` and pass `boolean` to enable or disable logging. The following code snippet shows the function for the `@logging` decorator:

```
function logging(value: boolean) {
    return function (target: any, propertyKey: string, descriptor:
              PropertyDescriptor) {
        descriptor.logging = value;
    };
}
```

The `logging` function sets the Boolean value to the logging property descriptor.

Property decorators

Property decorators are prefixed to property declarations. They actually redefine the property decorated by adding extra behavior. The signature of PropertyDecorator in the TypeScript source code is as follows:

```
declare type PropertyDecorator = (target: Object, propertyKey: string |
    symbol) => void;
```

The following is a code snippet of a class with a property decorator applied to a property:

```
class Customer {
  @hashify
  public firstname: string;
  public lastname: string;
  constructor(firstname : string, lastname : string) {
    this.firstname = firstname;
    this.lastname = lastname;
  }
}
```

In this code, the firstname property is decorated with the @hashify property decorator. Now, we will see the code snippet of the @hashify property decorator function:

```
function hashify(target: any, key: string) {
  var _value = this[key];
  var getter = function () {
      return '#' + _value;
  };
  var setter = function (newValue) {
    _value = newValue;
  };
  if (delete this[key]) {
    Object.defineProperty(target, key, {
      get: getter,
      set: setter,
      enumerable: true,
      configurable: true
    });
  }
}
```

The `_value` holds the value of the property that is being decorated. Both getter and setter functions will have access to the variable `_value` and here we can manipulate the `_value` by adding extra behaviors. I have concatenated # in the getter to return a hash-tagged `firstname`. Then we delete the original property from the class prototype using the `delete` operator. A new property will be created with the original property name with the extra behavior.

Parameter decorators

Parameter decorators are prefixed to parameter declarations, and they are applied to a function for a class constructor or a method declaration. The signature of `ParameterDecorator` is as follows:

```
declare type ParameterDecorator = (target: Object, propertyKey:
    string | symbol, parameterIndex: number) => void;
```

Now, let's define the `Customer` class and use a parameter decorator to decorate a parameter in order to make it required and validate whether the value has been served:

```
class Customer {
    constructor() {   }
    getName(@logging name: string) {
        return name;
    }
}
```

Here, the name parameter has been decorated with `@logging`. The parameter decorator implicitly takes three inputs, namely `prototype` of the class that has this decorator, the `name` of the method that has this decorator, and the `index` of the parameter that is being decorated. The `logging` function implementation of the parameter decorator is as follows:

```
function logging(target: any, key : string, index : number) {
  console.log(target);
  console.log(key);
  console.log(index);
}
```

Here, `target` is the class that has the decorator, `key` is the function name, and `index` contains the parameter index. This code just logs `target`, `key`, and `index` to the console.

Building a simple application

I assume that you have installed Node.js, npm, and Visual Studio Code and are ready to use them for development. Now let us create an Angular application by cloning the Git repository and performing the following steps:

1. Open the `Node.Js` command prompt and execute the following command:

```
git clone https://github.com/angular/quickstart my-angular
```

   Open the cloned `my-angular` application using Visual Studio Code. This command will clone the Angular quickstart repository and creates an Angular application named **my-angular** for you with all the boilerplate codes required.

Folder structure of the my-angular application.

The folder structure and the boilerplate code are organized according to the official style guide in
`https://angular.io/docs/ts/latest/guide/style-guide.html`. The `src` folder has the code files related to application logic, and the `e2e` folder has the files related to end-to-end testing. Don't worry about other files in the application now. Let's focus on `package.json` for now

2. Click on the `package.json` file, and it will have information about the configurations of the metadata and project dependencies. Here is the content of the `package.json` file:

```
{
  "name":"angular-quickstart",
  "version":"1.0.0",
  "description":"QuickStart   package.json from the documentation,
        supplemented with testing support",
  "scripts":{
    "build":"tsc   -p src/",
    "build:watch":"tsc   -p src/ -w",
    "build:e2e":"tsc   -p e2e/",
    "serve":"lite-server   -c=bs-config.json",
    "serve:e2e":"lite-server   -c=bs-config.e2e.json",
    "prestart":"npm   run build",
    "start":"concurrently   \"npm run build:watch\" \"npm run
        serve\"",
    "pree2e":"npm   run build:e2e",
    "e2e":"concurrently   \"npm run serve:e2e\" \"npm run
        protractor\" --kill-others   --success first",
    "preprotractor":"webdriver-manager   update",
    "protractor":"protractor   protractor.config.js",
    "pretest":"npm   run build",
    "test":"concurrently   \"npm run build:watch\" \"karma start
        karma.conf.js\"",
    "pretest:once":"npm   run build",
    "test:once":"karma   start karma.conf.js --single-run",
    "lint":"tslint   ./src/**/*.ts -t verbose"
  },
  "keywords":[
  ],
  "author":"",
  "license":"MIT",
  "dependencies":{
    "@angular/common":"~4.0.0",
    "@angular/compiler":"~4.0.0",
    "@angular/core":"~4.0.0",
    "@angular/forms":"~4.0.0",
```

```json
        "@angular/http":"~4.0.0",
        "@angular/platform-browser":"~4.0.0",
        "@angular/platform-browser-dynamic":"~4.0.0",
        "@angular/router":"~4.0.0",
        "angular-in-memory-web-api":"~0.3.0",
        "systemjs":"0.19.40",
        "core-js":"^2.4.1",
        "rxjs":"5.0.1",
        "zone.js":"^0.8.4"
    },
    "devDependencies":{
        "concurrently":"^3.2.0",
        "lite-server":"^2.2.2",
        "typescript":"~2.1.0",
        "canonical-path":"0.0.2",
        "tslint":"^3.15.1",
        "lodash":"^4.16.4",
        "jasmine-core":"~2.4.1",
        "karma":"^1.3.0",
        "karma-chrome-launcher":"^2.0.0",
        "karma-cli":"^1.0.1",
        "karma-jasmine":"^1.0.2",
        "karma-jasmine-html-reporter":"^0.2.2",
        "protractor":"~4.0.14",
        "rimraf":"^2.5.4",
        "@types/node":"^6.0.46",
        "@types/jasmine":"2.5.36"
    },
    "repository":{
    }
}
```

3. Now we need to run the `npm install` command in a command window, navigating to the `application` folder to install the required dependencies specified in `package.json`:

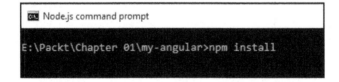

Execute the npm command to install dependencies specified in package.json.

Now, you will have all the dependencies added to the project under the `node_modules` folder, as shown in this screenshot:

Dependencies under the `node_modules` folder.

4. Now, let's run this application. To run it, execute the following command in the command window:

```
npm start
```

Running this command builds the application, starts the lite server, and hosts the application onto it.

Open any browser and navigate to `http://localhost:3000/`; and you will get the following page displayed, which is rendered through our Angular application:

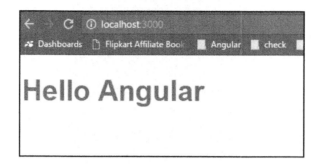

Activating the debug window in Visual Studio Code.

Let's now walk through the content of `index.html`. Here is the content of `index.html`:

```
<!DOCTYPE html>
<html>
<head>
<title>Hello Angular 4</title>
<base href="/">
<meta charset="UTF-8">
<meta name="viewport" content="width=device-width,
initial-scale=1">
<link rel="stylesheet" href="styles.css">
<!-- Polyfill(s) for older browsers -->
<script src="node_modules/core-
                js/client/shim.min.js">
    </script>
<script
        src="node_modules/zone.js/dist/zone.js">
    </script>
<script
        src="node_modules/systemjs/dist/system.src.js">
    </script>
<script src="systemjs.config.js"></script>
<script>
            System.import('main.js').catch(function(err){
            console.error(err); });
        </script>
```

```
</head>
<body>
<my-app>My first Angular 4   app for Packt
            Publishing...</my-app>
</body>
</html>
```

Notice that scripts are loaded using System.js. System.js is the module loader that loads modules during runtime.

Voila! Finally, our first Angular app is up-and-running. So far, we have seen how to create an Angular application by cloning the official quickstart repository from GitHub. We ran the application and saw it in the browser successfully.

Summary

Wow! This has been a great introduction, hasn't it? We started by learning about Angular's architecture. We discussed various artifacts of Angular's architecture. Then we dived into the basics of TypeScript. We have seen basic types with examples. We have also learned about writing classes, using interfaces, and implementing them in classes. We have also learned about inheritance.

We have learned about structuring our code by using modules and namespaces. We have also covered some advanced topics of TypeScript such as modifiers, accessors, static properties, generics, and decorators

And finally, we created a simple application using Angular and TypeScript. This chapter has equipped you with what you need to develop Angular applications using TypeScript with the syntactic sugar it has provided.

In the next chapter, we will discuss migrating AngularJS apps to Angular.

2

Migrating AngularJS App to Angular App

We all know Angular has had loads of improvements and has been designed from scratch. So, one of the most bugging questions among the Angular developers is how can we migrate existing AngularJS applications into Angular. In this chapter, we are going to discuss best practices, approaches, and tools recommended to successfully migrate existing AngularJS applications.

In this chapter, we will cover the following topics:

- Migration process
- Syntax difference
- Benefits of upgrading to Angular
- Rules for incremental upgrade to Angular
- Incremental upgrading using UpgradeAdapter
- Components migration
- Roadmap from AngularJS to Angular

Migration process

AngularJS and Angular differ syntactically and conceptually. So the migration process involves code change not only on a syntactical level but also in implementation. The Angular team made the life of the developers easier by providing built-in tools in Angular for migrating AngularJS applications to Angular. There is some preliminary process to do in our existing AngularJS applications before starting up the migration process.

The preliminary process involves decoupling the existing code and making the existing code maintainable. This preliminary process not only prepares the code for upgradation, but will also improve the performance of the existing AngularJS applications.

We can follow an incremental approach by running both AngularJS and Angular in the same application and initiate the migration process one by one starting from the components. This approach helps to migrate large applications, isolating the business from any impact and completing the upgradation over a period of time. This approach can be achieved using the Angular upgrade module.

Syntax difference between Angular and AngularJS

Angular has different syntax compared to AngularJS in many ways. Let us see few of them here.

Local variables and bindings in templates

A template is a view that deals with the UI part of an application that is written in HTML. First we will see the syntax differences for One-way Data Binding.

AngularJS:

```
<h1>Book Details:</h1>
<p>{{vm.bookName}}</p>
<p>{{vm.authorName}}</p>
```

Angular:

```
<h1>Book Details:</h1>
<p>{{bookName}}</p>
<p>{{authorName}}</p>
```

Both the code snippets show the One-way Data Binding that binds the book and author name to the UI using the double-curly braces. However, the AngularJS prefixes with the alias of controller when referring the properties of the controller to bind to the template and Angular does not use prefixes with the alias, as the view or template is associated with the component by default.

Filters and pipes in templates

AngularJS filters are now called as pipes in Angular. The filters are used after the pipe character (|) in AngularJS and there is no syntactical change in Angular. However, Angular calls the filters as pipes.

AngularJS:

```
<h1>Book Details:</h1>
<p>{{vm.bookName}}</p>
<p>{{vm.releaseDate | date }}</p>
```

Angular:

```
<h1>Book Details:</h1>
<p>{{bookName}}</p>
<p>{{releaseDate | date }}</p>
```

Notice we have applied a date pipe or filter to `releaseDate` and there is no syntactical change between AngularJS and Angular.

Local variables in templates

Let us see the example of using local variables in `ng-repeat` and `ngFor` in AngularJS and Angular, respectively.

AngularJS:

```
<tr ng-repeat="book in vm.books">
  <td>{{book.name}}</td>
</tr>
```

Angular:

```
<tr *ngFor="let book of books">
  <td>{{book.name}}</td>
</tr>
```

Notice that the local variable book is implicitly declared in AngularJS and in Angular the let keyword is used to define the local variable book.

Angular app directives

AngularJS allowed declarative bootstrapping the application using the `ng-app` directive. But, Angular doesn't support declarative bootstrapping. It supports only bootstrapping the application explicitly by calling the bootstrap function and passing the root component of the application.

AngularJS:

```
<body ng-app="packtPub">
```

Angular:

```
import { platformBrowserDynamic } from '@angular/platform-browser-dynamic';
import { AppModule } from './app/app.module';
platformBrowserDynamic().bootstrapModule(AppModule);
```

Notice that in AngularJS, the Angular module name `packtPub` has been assigned to the `ng-app` directive. However, in Angular, we pass `AppModule` to the bootstrap module as per the execution environment. Notice that `AppModule` is the `NgModule` class, which is the root module of the application that we just bootstrapped as per the execution environment.

Handling the CSS classes

AngularJS provides the `ng-class` directive to include or exclude CSS classes. Similarly, Angular has the `ngClass` directive to apply or remove CSS classes based on the expression. Class binding is another better option provided by Angular to add or remove a CSS class.

AngularJS:

```
<div ng-class="{active: isActive}">
```

Angular:

```
<div [ngClass]="{active: isActive}">
<div [class.active]="isActive">
```

Notice the class binding applied to the second `div` in Angular.

Binding click event

AngularJS provides an event based directive, `ng-click`, that can bind a `click` event to a method in an associated controller. Angular achieves the same by using native DOM elements which can be targeted with the `( )` syntax and it accomplishes this by combining One-way Data Binding with the `event` binding.

AngularJS:

```
<button ng-click="vm.showBook()">
<button ng-click="vm.showBook($event)">
```

Angular:

```
<button (click)="showBook()">
<button (click)="showBook($event)">
```

Notice that in Angular, the target event click is defined inside the parentheses and the method from the component is specified in quotes.

Controllers and components in templates

AngularJS provides the `ng-controller` directive to attach a controller to the view and ties the view to the controller related to that view. Angular doesn't support the controller and the `ng-controller` directive to associate a controller to the view. The component agrees its associated view or template and not vice versa.

AngularJS:

```
<div ng-controller="PacktBooksCtrl as vm">
```

Angular:

```
@Component({
  selector: 'packt-books',
  templateUrl:'app/packtbooks.component.html'
})
```

In AngularJS, we define controllers using **Immediately Invoked Function Expressions (IIFE)**. In Angular, we define components using TypeScript classes decorated with `@Component`, providing the metadata such as `selector`, `templateUrl`, and others.

AngularJS:

```
(function () {
    ...
}());
```

Angular:

```
@Component({
  selector: 'packt-books',
  templateUrl:'app/packtbooks.component.html'
})
export class PacktBooks {
}
```

Benefits of upgrading to Angular

Let us see some of the benefits of upgrading to Angular:

- **Better performance**: Angular supports faster change detection, faster bootstrap time, view caching, template pre-compilation, and so on.
- **Server-side rendering**: Angular has been split up into an application layer and a render layer. This enables us to run Angular in web workers or even servers other than browsers.
- **More powerful templating**: Angular introduces new template syntax that removes many directives and integrates better with web components and other elements.
- **Better ecosystem**: The Angular ecosystem will eventually get better and more interesting in the future.

Strategies to upgrade to Angular

There are different upgrade strategies available to migrate to Angular. They are as follows:

- **One time**: Replacing the entire AngularJS app, rewriting the code in Angular starting at one point.
- **Incremental**: Upgrading the existing app one service or component at a time, running AngularJS and Angular side by side.

If the AngularJS app is small, then rewriting at one time is probably the easiest and fastest way to upgrade. If the AngularJS app is larger and can't rewrite the whole code at once, we need to rewrite step by step, component by component, service by service. This is called incremental upgrading. However, running `ng1` and `ng2` side by side has performance implications.

Rules for incremental upgrade to Angular

It will be easier to do an incremental upgrade if we adhere to the following set of rules:

- Implement one component per file; it helps to isolate the components and migrate them one by one.
- Apply modular programming and arrange the folder by features; this will enable the developers to concentrate on migrating one feature at a time.
- Use a module loader; following the preceding rules, you will end up with a large number of files in a project. This creates the hassle of organizing the files and referring them in the correct order in the HTML pages. When you use a module loader such as `SystemJS`, `Webpack`, or `Browserify`, it enables us to use TypeScript built-in module systems. This enables the developers to import or export features explicitly and share them between various parts of the application in the code.
- Install TypeScript first; it is good to bring in the TypeScript compiler before starting the actual upgrade process. This can be achieved by a simple step of installing the TypeScript compiler.
- Use Component Directives; it is good practice to use Component Directives rather than `ng-controller` and `ng-include` in the AngularJS apps so that in Angular, migrating the Component Directives will be much easier than migrating the controllers.

Incremental upgrading using UpgradeAdapter

Incremental upgrading can be done seamlessly using `UpgradeAdapter`. `UpgradeAdapter` is a service that can bootstrap and manage hybrid applications that support both Angular and AngularJS code. `UpgradeAdapter` enables you to run both AngularJS and Angular code simultaneously. `UpgradeAdapter` facilitates interoperability between components and services from one framework to another framework. The interoperability in Dependency Injection, the DOM, and change detection will be taken care of by `UpgradeAdapter`.

Injecting AngularJS dependencies to Angular

We may come across a scenario where the business logic on AngularJS services or any built-in services, such as `$location` or `$timeout`, is to be injected to Angular code. This can be handled by upgrading the AngularJS provider to Angular and injecting it into Angular code wherever required.

Injecting Angular dependencies to AngularJS

Sometimes it may be necessary to downgrade Angular dependencies in order to use them in AngularJS code. This is necessary when we have a situation to migrate existing services to Angular or create new services in Angular where the components written in AngularJS are depending on them.

Components migration

Designing AngularJS applications by component centric is good practice rather than designing them by controller centric. If you had developed your application following this practice, then it will be easier for you to migrate. Component Directives in AngularJS will have their template, controller, and binding similar to Angular components. But make sure your AngularJS application Component Directives did not use the attributes such as compile, replace, priority, and terminal. If your application implemented Component Directives with these attributes then it is not liaising with Angular architecture. If your AngularJS application was developed using AngularJS 1.5 and the components are implemented using the component API, then you might have noticed the similarities in Angular components.

Roadmap from AngularJS to Angular

It is good to follow this roadmap in migrating AngularJS to Angular:

- JavaScript to TypeScript
- Installing Angular packages
- Creating the AppModule
- Bootstrapping your application
- Upgrading your application service
- Upgrading your application component
- Adding the Angular router

Let us discuss them in detail in the following sections.

JavaScript to TypeScript

Start your migration process by introducing TypeScript, as you will be writing your code using TypeScript in Angular. Installing TypeScript into your Angular application is quite easy. Run the following command to install TypeScript from npm into your application and save the package information to package.json:

```
npm i typescript --save-dev
```

 Note: As the Angular package is only available on npm, we will be installing any new packages from npm and we will slowly phase out from the Bower package manager

We also need to configure TypeScript, instructing it on transpiling the TypeScript code into ES5 code in the tsconfig.json file.

Finally, we need to add the following commands under the scripts section of package.json that runs the TypeScript compiler in watch mode in the background so that the code will be recompiled as and when you make changes:

```
"script": {
  "tsc": "tsc",
  "tsc:w": "tsc -w",
}
```

Installing Angular packages

We need to install Angular along with the SystemJS module loader. The quickest way to do this is by cloning the quickstart application from GitHub to your development system. Then copy the dependencies related to Angular from package.json into your application package.json and also copy the SystemJS configuration file systemjs.config.js to your application root directory. Once all this is done, then run the following command to install the packages we have just added in package.json:

```
npm install
```

Add the following statement to the index.html file. This will help the relative URLs to be served from the app folder. This is important because we need to move the index.html file from the app folder to the root folder of the application:

```
<base href="/app/">
```

Now, let us add the JavaScript file references and load Angular via SystemJS. Finally, load the actual application using the System.import statement:

```
<script src="/node_modules/core-js/client/shim.min.js"></script>
<script src="/node_modules/zone.js/dist/zone.js"></script>
<script src="/node_modules/systemjs/dist/system.src.js"></script>
<script src="/systemjs.config.js"></script>
<script>
  System.import('/app');
</script>
```

Creating the AppModule

We need to create an AppModule for your application. The following AppModule class is defined with the minimum NgModule:

```
import { NgModule } from '@angular/core';
import { BrowserModule } from '@angular/platform-browser';
@NgModule({
  imports: [
    BrowserModule,
  ],
})
export class AppModule {
}
```

Here we just imported an `NgModule` from `@angular/core` and `BrowserModule` from `@angular/platform-browser`. Any simple browser-based Angular application will have such a simple `AppModule`.

Bootstrapping your application

An AngularJS application will be bootstrapped by attaching the `ng-app` directive to the `<html>` element. This will no longer work in Angular as bootstrapping an Angular application differs.

Install the Angular upgrade package by running the following command and add the mapping to `system.config.js`:

```
npm install @angular/upgrade --save
```

This statement also updates `package.json` with the reference to `@angular/upgrade`. The updated `systemjs.config.js` is shown here:

```
System.config({
    paths: {
      'npm:': '/node_modules/'
    },
    map: {
      'ng-loader': '../src/systemjs-angular-loader.js',
      app: '/app',
      '@angular/upgrade/static': 'npm:@angular/upgrade/bundles/upgrade-
static.umd.js'
    }
})
```

Now remove the `ng-app` attribute from the `<html>` element in the `index.html` file. Then we need to import `UpgradeModule` to `AppModule`. To bootstrap our AngularJS application in an Angular way, we need to override the `ngDoBootstrap` function in `AppModule` as follows:

```
import { UpgradeModule } from '@angular/upgrade/static';
@NgModule({
  imports: [
    BrowserModule,
    UpgradeModule,
  ],
})
export class AppModule {
  constructor(private upgrade:   UpgradeModule) { }
```

```
    ngDoBootstrap() {
        this.upgrade.bootstrap(document.documentElement, [yourApp']);
    }
}
```

Finally, we need to bootstrap `AppModule` in `main.ts`, which is configured as the entry point of the application in `system.config.js`. The code snippet of `main.ts` is shown here:

```
import { platformBrowserDynamic } from '@angular/platform-browser-dynamic';
import { AppModule } from './app.module';
platformBrowserDynamic().bootstrapModule(AppModule);
```

Upgrading application services

A service in an Angular application is mostly used to supply data across the application and this data will be fetched from any service. In AngularJS, we have been using `ngResource` and `%http` to communicate with services and handling the data.

As part of the migration, we need to use the Angular HTTP module wherever we used `ngResource` and `$http`. To use the Angular HTTP module, we first need to import `HttpModule` and add it to the imports array in the `NgModule` directive of `AppModule` as follows:

```
import { HttpModule } from '@angular/http';
@NgModule({
  imports: [
    BrowserModule,
    UpgradeModule,
    HttpModule,
  ],
})
export class AppModule {
  constructor(private upgrade:  UpgradeModule) { }
  ngDoBootstrap() {
      this.upgrade.bootstrap(document.documentElement, ['yourApp']);
  }
}
```

Next replace the code snippets of your `ngResource` or `$http` based services in your application with the new TypeScript class decorated with the `@Injectable` directive as follows:

```
@Injectable()
export class BookService {
```

```
/* . . . */
}
```

The decorator @Injectable will add metadata specific to Dependency Injection to the BookService class so that Angular knows about the classes that are ready for Dependency Injection. We need to inject the HTTP service to the constructor of BookService and the injected HTTP service will be used to access the data from books.json to get the list of books, as follows:

```
@Injectable()
export class BookService {
  constructor(private http: Http) { }
  books(): Observable<Book[]> {
    return   this.http.get(`data/books.json`)
      .map((res: Response) =>   res.json());
  }
}
```

The following is the Book interface that can serve as a model type for a book:

```
export interface PhoneData {
  title: string;
  author: string;
  publication: string;
}
```

This Angular service is not compatible with AngularJS and cannot be injected directly. So we need to downgrade the injectable method to plug in our BookService into AngularJS code. For that we need to use a method called downgradeInjectable in @angular/upgrade/static:

```
declare var angular:   angular.IAngularStatic;
import { downgradeInjectable } from '@angular/upgrade/static';
@Injectable()
export class BookService {
}
angular.module('core.lib')
  .factory('core.lib',   downgradeInjectable(BookService));
```

The complete code snippet of BookService is shown here:

```
import { Injectable } from '@angular/core';
import { Http, Response } from '@angular/http';
import { Observable } from 'rxjs/Rx';
declare var angular:   angular.IAngularStatic;
import { downgradeInjectable } from '@angular/upgrade/static';
import 'rxjs/add/operator/map';
```

```
export interface Book {
  title: string;
  author: string;
  publication: string;
}
@Injectable()
export class BookService {
  constructor(private http: Http) { }
  books(): Observable<Book[]> {
    return   this.http.get(`data/books.json`)
      .map((res: Response) =>   res.json());
  }
}
angular.module('core.lib')
  .factory('phone',   downgradeInjectable(BookService));
```

Finally, we need to register `BookService` as the provider under `NgModule` so that Angular will keep the instance of `BookService` ready to supply wherever it is injected across the application. The updated code snippet of `app.module.ts` is shown here:

```
import { BookService } from './book.service';
@NgModule({
  imports: [
    BrowserModule,
    UpgradeModule,
    HttpModule,
  ],
  providers: [
    BookService,
  ]
})
export class AppModule {
  constructor(private upgrade:   UpgradeModule) { }
  ngDoBootstrap() {
    this.upgrade.bootstrap(document.documentElement,   [yourApp']);
  }
}
```

Upgrading your application component

As part of upgrading the components, we need to create a downgraded Angular component so that it can be consumed by AngularJS code. The following is the code snippet of the downgraded Angular component:

```
declare var angular:   angular.IAngularStatic;
import { downgradeComponent } from '@angular/upgrade/static';
```

```
@Component({
  selector: 'book-list',
  templateUrl: './book-list.template.html'
})
export class BookListComponent {
}
angular.module('bookList')
  .directive(
    'bookList',
    downgradeComponent({component:   BookListComponent}) as
         angular.IDirectiveFactory
);
```

Here, we give an instruction to the TypeScript compiler that the directive factory is returned from downgradeComponent. Now we need to register downgradeComponent by adding it to entryComponents in AppModule, as follows:

```
import { BookListComponent } from './components/book-list.component';
@NgModule({
  imports: [
    BrowserModule,
    UpgradeModule,
    HttpModule
  ],
  declarations: [
    BookListComponent,
  ],
  entryComponents: [
    BookListComponent,
  ]
})
export class AppModule {
  constructor(private upgrade:   UpgradeModule) { }
  ngDoBootstrap() {
      this.upgrade.bootstrap(document.documentElement, ['yourApp']);
  }
}
```

And the updated template of phone-list.template.html is shown here:

```
<ul>
    <li *ngFor="let book of books">
      {{book.title}}
    </li>
</ul>
```

Here ng-repeats has been replaced with *ngFor.

Adding the Angular router

Angular has completely redefined the router. It is good practice to upgrade the router module by module. Angular has a special tag, `<router-outlet>`, that displays or loads the routed views. This should be in a template of the root component. So for your application, we need to create a root component named `AppComponent`:

```
import { Component } from '@angular/core';
@Component({
  selector: 'your-app',
  template: '<router-outlet></router-outlet>'
})
export class AppComponent { }
```

This is an instruction to load the root component into `<your-app>` if it is found in a web page. So let us replace the `ng-view` directive in `index.html` with the application element `<your-app>`:

```
<body>
  <your-app></your-app>
</body>
```

We need to create another `NgModule` for routing and the code snippet is shown here:

```
import { NgModule } from '@angular/core';
import { Routes, RouterModule } from '@angular/router';
import { HashLocationStrategy,   LocationStrategy } from '@angular/common';
import { BookListComponent }   from './components/book-list.component';
const routes: Routes = [
  { path: '', redirectTo: 'books',   pathMatch: 'full' },
  { path: 'books',              component:   BookListComponent }
];
@NgModule({
  imports: [ RouterModule.forRoot(routes)   ],
  exports: [ RouterModule ],
  providers: [
    { provide: LocationStrategy,   useClass: HashLocationStrategy },
  ]
})
export class AppRoutingModule { }
```

Here we defined single routes in a routes object and also a default route for empty or the root path of the application. Then we passed the routes object to `RouterModule.forRoot` so that `RouterModule` will take care of it. We used `HashLocationStrategy` to instruct `RouterModule` to use a hash (#) in the fragment of the URL.

Finally, let us update `AppModule` to import `AppRoutingModule` and also we have come to a stage to remove `ngDoBootstrap` as everything is Angular at this stage. The following is the updated code snippet of `AppModule`:

```
import { NgModule } from '@angular/core';
import { BrowserModule } from '@angular/platform-browser';
import { HttpModule } from '@angular/http';
import { AppRoutingModule } from './app-routing.module';
import { AppComponent }  from './app.component';
import { BookService }    from './services/book.service';
import { BookListComponent }  from './components/book-list.component';
@NgModule({
  imports: [
    BrowserModule,
    HttpModule,
    AppRoutingModule
  ],
  declarations: [
    AppComponent,
    BookListComponent
  ],
  providers: [
    BookService
  ],
  bootstrap: [ AppComponent ]
})
export class AppModule {}
```

Notice that we added `AppRoutingModule` to the imports collection of the `NgModule` attribute so that the application routing will be registered with `AppModule`.

Summary

Way to go! Loads of stuffs, isn't it?! We started learning about migration in Angular.

Then we have seen various approaches and best practices in migrating AngularJS to Angular applications.

Next we discussed incremental upgrading using the upgrade adapter.

Finally, we learned in detail about the roadmap in migrating from AngularJS to Angular.

In the next chapter, we will discuss Angular CLI, which is the command line interface for Angular.

3
Using Angular CLI to Generate Angular Apps with Best Practices

Angular CLI is a command-line interface for Angular that helps you kick-start your application development with the boilerplate code that follows all the necessary best practices. By executing the commands in Angular CLI, you can generate services, components, routes, and pipes for your application.

In this chapter, we will cover the following topics:

- Introducing Angular CLI
- Installing and setting up Angular CLI
- Generating code for new applications
- Generating components and routes
- Generating services
- Generating directives and pipes
- Creating builds targeting various environment
- Running tests for your application
- Updating Angular CLI

Introducing Angular CLI

Angular CLI is a command-line interface available as a node package. Angular CLI, introduced with Angular, helps you develop applications faster by generating the boilerplate code for a new application and adding features such as services, pipes, components, and directives to existing applications. Angular CLI is very powerful and handy in scaffolding your application easily. With the help of Angular CLI, we can create, build, test, and run our application, which will be a great relief to the developers.

Angular CLI runs under node and is dependent on many packages.

Installing and setting up Angular CLI

To install Angular CLI, we must have the latest version of node and npm installed in our system. Make sure the required packages are installed already and then start installing Angular CLI globally. The minimum required npm version is 3.x.x and the node version is 4.x.x. Sometimes, you may get an error when installing Angular CLI. In such cases, make sure you have the latest version of node.js installed. We can verify the version of node by executing the following command:

```
node --version
```

We can check the version of npm by executing the following command:

```
npm --version
```

Now, we know the versions of node and npm installed in our development machine. Let's install Angular CLI globally by executing the following command:

```
npm install -g angular-cli
```

Angular CLI has been installed and is available globally to use in our development machine.

Generating code for a new application

We have Angular CLI ready to use now. Let's generate a boilerplate code for an Angular application that displays the list of books. We will call the name of the application as BookList. Execute the following command in the node.js command:

```
ng new BookList
```

This command will create a folder named BookList and generate the boilerplate code to get started with the Angular application. The following image shows the file structure organized in the generated code:

To make sure the generated code works fine, let's run the application by executing the following commands. First navigate to the application folder by executing this statement:

```
cd BookList
```

Then, execute the following code to launch the application in the development server :

```
ng serve
```

Now, let's browse to `http://localhost:4200/` and the following page will be rendered in the browser with the default text if the generated code is fine. If you get an error, make sure the firewall is not blocking the port 4200 and Angular CLI did not throw any error while generating the boilerplate code:

Generating components and routes

A component is a logical grouping of functionalities, views, and styles applicable to the view and a class associated to the component that deals with these artifacts. Components take responsibility for rendering the view as per the business logical requirements.

We can generate code for components using Angular CLI. This tool is very handy in scaffolding the components. Let's generate a component named `booklist` for our application by executing the following statement. Navigate to the Angular project folder by executing the command here:

```
cd BookList
```

Then, execute the following Angular CLI command to generate the component `Booklist`:

```
ng generate component booklist
```

Executing the preceding statement creates the `booklist.component.css`, `booklist.component.html`, `booklist.component.spec.ts` and the `booklist.component.ts`, as shown in the following image:

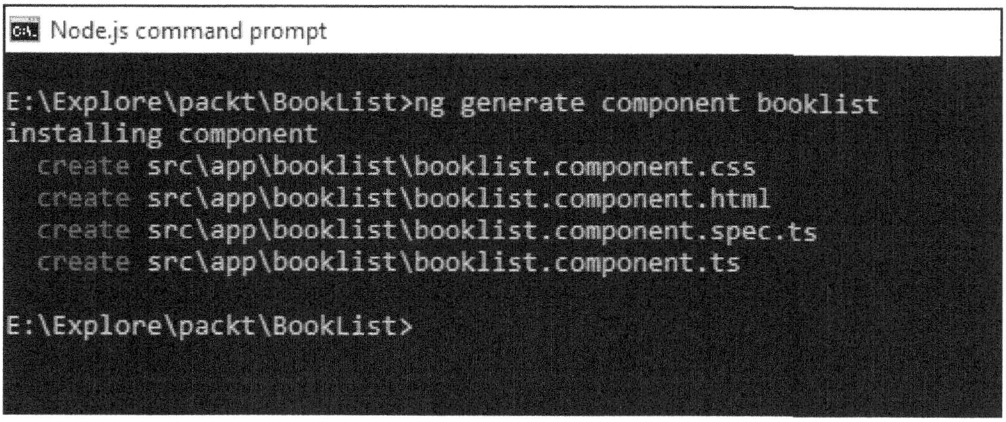

The `booklist.component.ts` file takes care of rendering the associated view according to the business logic needs. The code snippet generated by the book component is given here:

```
import { Component, OnInit } from '@angular/core';
@Component({
  selector: 'app-booklist',
  templateUrl: './booklist.component.html',
  styleUrls: ['./booklist.component.css']
})
export class BooklistComponent implements   OnInit {
  constructor() { }
  ngOnInit() {
  }
}
```

Notice that the `BooklistComponent` class is decorated with the `@Component` directive along with the metadata such as the selector, `templateUrl`, and `styleUrls`. The metadata selector enables Angular to instantiate the component `BooklistComponent` when it encounters the `app-booklist` selector.

The Angular CLI also generated the template file `booklist.component.html` with the following content. Angular will parse and render this content according to the instructions given in the component:

```
<p>
  booklist works!
</p>
```

We can also add styles specific to this template in the generated file `booklist.component.css` and the component will pick these styles, as the metadata `styleUrls` is mapped with the path of `booklist.component.css`.

`booklist.component.spec.ts` is generated to add the test methods to assert the functionalities of `BooklistComponent`. The code snippet of `booklist.component.spec.ts` is shown here:

```
/* tslint:disable:no-unused-variable */
import { TestBed, async } from '@angular/core/testing';
import { BooklistComponent } from './booklist.component';
describe('Component: Booklist', () =>   {
  it('should create an instance', ()    => {
    let component = new   BooklistComponent();
    expect(component).toBeTruthy();
  });
});
```

Routes

Routes instruct Angular on navigating the application. Routing enables Angular to load only the views specific to routes without reloading the entire page or application. At the time of writing this chapter, generating a route using Angular CLI is disabled and will be enabled soon.

Generating services

Services are user-defined classes to solve some purposes. Angular recommends having only template-specific codes in components. A component's responsibility is to enrich the UI/UX in an Angular application and it delegates business logic to services. Components are the consumers of services.

We have the component in place that helps render the `Booklist` template. Now, let's run a CLI command to generate a service to serve the list of books. Execute the following command to generate `booklist.services.ts` and `booklist.services.spec.ts`:

```
Select Node.js command prompt

E:\Explore\packt\BookList>ng g service booklist
installing service
  create src\app\booklist.service.spec.ts
  create src\app\booklist.service.ts
  WARNING Service is generated but not provided, it must be provided to be used

E:\Explore\packt\BookList>
```

The code snippet of the generated `booklist.service.ts` is shown here:

```
import { Injectable } from '@angular/core';
@Injectable()
export class BooklistService {
  constructor() { }
}
```

Notice that `BooklistService` is decorated with `@Injectible` so that this booklist service will be available to the components. Also there is a warning message, Service is generated but not provided, it must be provided to be used. It means that to consume `BooklistService`; it needs to be provided to a component that is going to consume it. Providers in Angular will be discussed in detail in the `Chapter 13`, *Applying Dependency Injection*.

Angular CLI also generated a file to write test methods to assert `BooklistService` and the code snippet of `booklist.service.spec.ts` is shown here:

```
/* tslint:disable:no-unused-variable */
import { TestBed, async, inject } from '@angular/core/testing';
import { BooklistService } from './booklist.service';
describe('Service: Booklist', () => {
  beforeEach(() => {
    TestBed.configureTestingModule({
      providers: [BooklistService]
    });
  });
  it('should ...',    inject([BooklistService], (service:
      BooklistService) => {
```

```
        expect(service).toBeTruthy();
    }));
});
```

Generating directives and pipes

A class decorated with @Directive to attach metadata is called a directive. It is an instruction or guideline to render the template.

We have seen generating components and services. Now, let's generate directives and pipes using Angular CLI. We will start with creating a directive named book. Run the following command to generate the directive:

```
ng generate directive book
```

The outcome of executing the command is shown here:

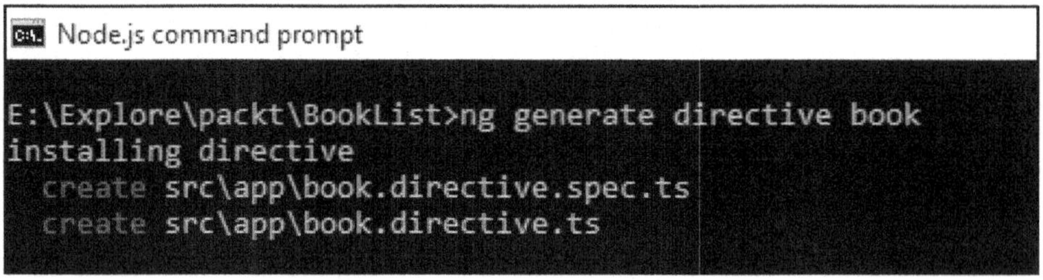

Executing this command creates two files, namely, book.directive.spec.ts and book.directive.ts respectively. Here is the code snippet of book.directive.ts:

```
import { Directive } from '@angular/core';
@Directive({
    selector: '[appBookish]'
  })
  export class BookishDirective {
      constructor() { }
  }
```

The code snippet of book.directive.spec.ts is shown here:

```
/* tslint:disable:no-unused-variable */
import { TestBed, async } from '@angular/core/testing';
import { BookDirective } from './book.directive';

describe('Directive: Book', () => {
    it('should create an instance', () =>
```

```
    { let directive = new BookDirective();
        expect(directive).toBeTruthy();
    });
  });
```

Pipes

A pipe instructs Angular in filtering or rendering the input data. A pipe transforms the input data according to the logic given in the pipe.

Now, let's generate a pipe using Angular CLI by executing the following statement:

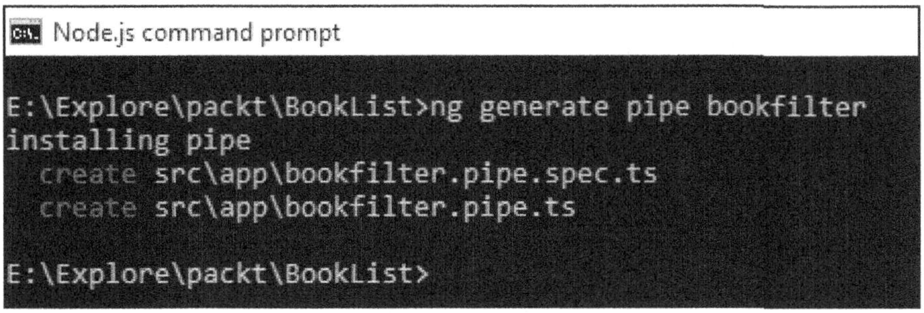

Here, I created a pipe named `bookfilter` using Angular CLI. Note that it also created a test file, `bookfilter.pipe.spec.ts`, for writing test methods to assert the pipes. The code snippet of the `bookfilter.pipe.ts` is shown here:

```
import { Pipe, PipeTransform } from '@angular/core';
@Pipe({
    name: 'bookfilter'
    })
export class BookfilterPipe implements PipeTransform {
        transform(value: any, args?: any): any {
    return null;
  }
}
```

The code snippet generated for the test file `bookfilter.pipe.spec.ts` is shown here:

```
/* tslint:disable:no-unused-variable */
import { TestBed, async } from '@angular/core/testing';
import { BookfilterPipe } from './bookfilter.pipe';
  describe('Pipe: Bookfilter', () => {
    it('create an instance', () => {
        let pipe = new BookfilterPipe();
```

```
        expect(pipe).toBeTruthy();
   });
});
```

Creating builds targeting various environments

Using Angular CLI, we can also create builds for our application targeting various environments, such as development and production. The application will be configured specific to environments. For example, an application may be configured to use staging URLs for APIs in development or staging environments and production URLs of APIs will be configured in a LIVE or production environment. Developers will be manually updating the configuration of the URL as per the environment the application is built on. Angular facilitates to automate this process of creating builds by targeting various environments.

A constant variable environment is maintained in a file named `environment.ts`. This file will help to override the default values as per the parameter passed when executing the build command.

To use the production file, we need to execute the following command:

ng build --env=prod

This command will make use of the settings in `environment.prod.ts`. The mapping to identify the environment file is instructed in `angular-cli.json`, as shown here:

```
"environments": {
  "source": "environments/environment.ts",
   "dev": "environments/environment.ts",
   "prod": "environments/environment.prod.ts"
  }
```

Running tests for your application

Testing the application is the essential process to be carried out before moving it to production. Developers can write tests to assert the behavior of the application. Writing proper tests will protect the application from deviating away from the requirement.

Jasmine is a test framework that facilitates to write tests to assert the behavior of the application and execute the tests in the browser using the HTML test runner. Karma is a test runner, which enables the developer to write unit tests simultaneously during the development phase. Once the build process is completed, tests will be executed using Karma. Protractor can be used to run end-to-end tests that assert the workflow of the application as an end-user experience.

The following command runs the tests in the application:

```
ng test
```

The end-to-end test can be executed by running the command here, and it will run successfully only when the application is served by the command ng serve. This end-to-end test is run by Protractor:

```
ng e2e
```

I am not going into detail on the content of each of files generated as there are chapters to explain in detail about them.

Updating Angular CLI

We can update the Angular CLI version in a global package and in your local project. To update the Angular CLI package globally, run the following command:

```
npm uninstall -g @angular/cli
npm cache clean
npm install -g @angular/cli@latest
```

To update the CLI in your local project folder, run the command here:

```
rm -rf node_modules dist # use rmdir /S/Q node_modules dist in Windows
  Command Prompt; use rm -r -fo node_modules,dist in Windows PowerShell
npm install --save-dev @angular/cli@latest
npm install
```

Summary

That was smooth and easy, wasn't it? Angular CLI makes the life of the developer easier by generating the boilerplate code for various artifacts of an Angular application. You started learning about the powerful tool Angular CLI and how it helps you to kick-start your application with the boilerplate code. Then, you learned to generate components, directives, pipes, routes, and services using the Angular command line interface. Finally, you also learned about building an Angular application using the Angular CLI. In the next chapter, we will discuss about working with Angular components.

4
Working with Components

In this chapter, we will discuss different techniques and strategies for working with Angular components:

- Initializing and configuring components
- Building with components
- Component life cycle
- Sharing data and communicating between components

The chapter assumes that the reader has knowledge of JavaScript and TypeScript programming fundamentals and web development in general, and is familiar with the contents of `Chapter 1`, *Architectural Overview and Building a Simple App in Angular*, from this book. All the examples from this chapter use TypeScript and can also be found on GitHub, at `https://github.com/popalexandruvasile/mastering-angular2/tree/master/Chapter4`.

> A telling sign of a successful open source project is excellent documentation, and Angular is no exception to this rule. I strongly recommend reading through all the available documentation from `https://angular.io/` and following the examples available there as well. As a general rule, all the examples from this chapter follow the format and conventions from the official documentation, and I have used a simplified version of the Angular example seed from `https://github.com/angular/quickstart` as an example. If you want to experiment or play with your own Angular creations, you can use the contents of the `Example1` folder from the code for this chapter as a starting point.

Components 101

Components are the building blocks of Angular applications, and any such application needs at least one component called the root component to be defined before it can be executed.

A basic root component

A component is defined in Angular as a class with specific metadata that associates it with an HTML template and a jQuery-like HTML DOM selector:

- The component template can be bound to any properties or functions that belong to the component class
- The component selector (similar to a jQuery selector) can target an element tag, attribute, or style class that defines the component insertion point

When executed within an Angular application, a component will usually render an HTML snippet in a specific page location that can react to user input and display dynamic data.

The component metadata is expressed as a TypeScript decorator and supports additional configuration that will be covered throughout the examples from this chapter.

 TypeScript decorators are covered in Chapter 1, *Architectural Overview and Building a Simple App in Angular*. They are essential for understanding how components are configured, and they are currently proposed to become part of the JavaScript specification (ECMAScript).

The first example from this chapter is for a basic component that is also a root component (of which any Angular app needs at least one to initialize its component tree):

```
import { Component } from '@angular/core';
@Component({
    selector: 'my-app',
    template: `
    <div class="container text-center">
      <div class="row">
        <div class="col-md-12">
          <div class="page-header">
            <h1>{{title}}</h1>
          </div>
          <p class="lead">{{description}}</p>
        </div>
      </div>
```

```
              <div class="row">
                <div class="col-md-6">
                  <p>A child component could go here</p>
                </div>
                <div class="col-md-6">
                  <p>Another child component could go here</p>
                </div>
              </div>
            </div>
            `
      })
      export class AppComponent {
        title: string;
        description: string;
        constructor(){
          this.title = 'Mastering Angular - Chapter 4, Example 1';
          this.description = 'This is a minimal example for an Angular 2
          component with an element tag selector.';
        }
      }
```

The component template relies on the Bootstrap frontend design framework
(`http://getbootstrap.com/`) for styling, and is bound to the properties of the component
class to retrieve some of its displayed text. It contains template expressions that interpolate
data from the properties of the component class, such as `{{title}}`.

The root component uses an inline template (the template content resides in the same file
with its component) and an element selector that will render the component template
within the `index.html` page, replacing the highlighted text:

```
      <!DOCTYPE html>
      <html>
        <head>
          <title>Mastering Angular example</title>
          ...
        </head>
        <body>
          <my-app>Loading...</my-app>
        </body>
      </html>
```

To view the example in action, you can run the following command line in the `Example1`
folder from the source code for this chapter:

```
npm run start
```

You can view the rendered component in the next screenshot:

Mastering Angular - Chapter 4, Example 1

This is a minimal example for an Angular component with an element tag selector.

A child component could go here   Another child component could go here

An Angular application needs at least one root module, and in the `main.ts` file, we are bootstrapping this module for our example:

```
import { platformBrowserDynamic } from '@angular/platform-browser-dynamic';
import { AppModule } from './app.module';
platformBrowserDynamic().bootstrapModule(AppModule);
```

We used the `app.module.ts` module file to define the application root module:

```
import { NgModule } from '@angular/core';
import { BrowserModule } from '@angular/platform-browser';
import { AppComponent } from './app.component';
@NgModule({
  imports:      [ BrowserModule ],
  declarations: [ AppComponent ],
  bootstrap:    [ AppComponent ]
})
export class AppModule { }
```

A module can import other modules using the `imports` property, and a module can have one or more root components defined under the `bootstrap` property. Each such root component will initialize its own component tree, which in our example consists of only one component. Any component, directive, or pipe needs to be added in the `declarations` property before being used in the module.

Defining child components

While a root component represents the container for an Angular app, you will also need other components that are direct or indirect descendants of a root component. When a root component is rendered, it will also render all its children components.

These child components can receive data from their parent component and can also send data back. Let's view some of these concepts at play in a more complex example that builds on the previous one. Note that, in the `Example1`, we suggested that a child component can be inserted within the root component template; one such child component is defined like this:

```
import { Component, Input, Output, EventEmitter } from '@angular/core';
@Component({
    selector: 'div[my-child-comp]',
    template: `
        <p>{{myText}}</p>
        <button class="btn btn-default" type="button"
(click)="onClick()">Send message</button>`
})
export class ChildComponent {
  private static instanceCount: number = 0;
  instanceId: number;
  @Input() myText: string;
  @Output() onChildMessage = new EventEmitter<string>();
  constructor(){
    ChildComponent.instanceCount += 1;
    this.instanceId = ChildComponent.instanceCount;
  }
  onClick(){
    this.onChildMessage.emit(`Hello from ChildComponent with instance
    id: ${this.instanceId}`);
  }
}
```

The first highlighted code snippet shows the component selector using a custom element attribute rather than a custom element tag. When working with the existing CSS styles and HTML markup, more often than not you need to ensure that your Angular components integrate naturally with their contextual look and feel. This is where attributes or CSS selectors prove to be really useful.

At first glance, the component class structure looks somewhat similar to the one from `Example1`--with the exception of the two new decorators in the second highlighted code snippet. The first decorator is `@Input()`, and it should be applied to any component property that can receive data from the parent component. The second decorator is `@Output()`, and it should be applied to any property that can send data to the parent component. Angular 2 defines an `EventEmitter` class that facilitates generating and consuming events using a similar approach with Node.js `EventEmitter` or jQuery events. The output event of the `string` type is generated in the `onClick()` method, and any parent component can subscribe to this event to receive data from the child component.

The EventEmitter class extends the RxJS Subject class, which in turn is a special type of RxJS Observable that allows multicasting. Further details about observables, subscribers, and other reactive programming concepts can be found in `Chapter 7`, *Asynchronous Programming Using Observables*.

We took advantage of the `static` class properties in TypeScript to generate a unique instance identifier, `instanceId`, that is used in the message sent by the child component via the `onChildMessage` output property. We will use this message to make it obvious that each child component instance sends a unique message to its subscribers, which is the `AppComponent` root component in our example:

```
@Component({
    selector: 'div.container.my-app',
    template: `
    <div class="container text-center">
      <div class="row"><div class="col-md-12">
          <div class="page-header"><h1>{{title}}</h1></div>
          <p class="lead">{{description}}</p>
      </div></div>
      <div class="row">
        <div class="col-md-6" my-child-comp myText="A child component
        goes here" (onChildMessage)="onChildMessageReceived($event)">
        </div>
        <div class="col-md-6" my-child-comp
          [myText]="secondComponentText"
          (onChildMessage)="onChildMessageReceived($event)"></div>
        </div>
      <div class="row"><div class="col-md-12"><div class="well well-
        sm">
          <p>Last message from child components: <strong>
            {{lastMessage}}</strong>
          </p>
        </div></div></div>
    </div>
})
export class AppComponent {
  title: string;
  description: string;
  secondComponentText: string;
  lastMessage: string;
  constructor(){
    this.title = 'Mastering Angular - Chapter 4, Example 2';
    this.description = 'This is an example for an Angular 2 root
    component with an element and class selector and a child component
    with an element attribute selector.';
    this.secondComponentText = 'Another child component goes here';
  }
```

```
    onChildMessageReceived($event: string)
    {
      this.lastMessage = $event;
    }
  }
```

The highlighted code shows how the root component is referencing and binding the `ChildComponent` elements. The `onChildMessage` output property is bound to an `AppComponent` method using the same parenthesis notation that Angular 2 uses to bind native HTML DOM events; for example, `<button (click)="onClick($event)">`.

The input property is simply assigned to a static value for the first `ChildComponent` instance and is bound via the bracket notation to the `AppComponent secondComponentText` property. The bracket notation is not required when we are simply assigning fixed values, and it is also used by Angular 2 when binding to native HTML element properties; for example, `<input type="text" [value]="myValue">`.

> If you are not yet familiar with how Angular binds to a native HTML element properties and events, you can refer to Chapter 6, *Creating Directives and Implementing Change Detection*, for further reference.

For both the `ChildComponent` instances, we used the same `AppComponent onChildMessageReceived` method to bind to the `onChildMessage` event using a simple event handling approach that will display the last child component message on the application page. The root component selector was changed to use an element tag and CSS class selector, and this approach leads to a simpler structured `index.html` file.

We had to modify the `AppModule` definition to ensure that `ChildComponent` can be referenced by `AppComponent` and any other component from the same module:

```
@NgModule({
  imports:      [ BrowserModule ],
  declarations: [ AppComponent, ChildComponent ],
  bootstrap:    [ AppComponent ]
})
export class AppModule { }
```

You can find this example in the `Example2` folder from the code for this chapter. The concepts covered here, such as component properties and events, component data flow, and component composition, can go a long way in building a relatively complex application, and we will explore them further throughout this chapter.

Alongside components, Angular has the concept of directives, which can also be found in Angular 1. Each Angular component is also a directive, and we can roughly define a directive as a component without any template. The @Component decorator interface extends the @Directive decorator interface, and we will discuss more about directives in Chapter 6, *Creating Directives and Implementing Change Detection*.

Component life cycle

Each component rendered by Angular has its own life cycle: it is initialized, checked for changes, and destroyed (among other events). Angular provides a hook method, where we can insert application code to participate in the component life cycle. These methods are available through TypeScript function interfaces that can be optionally implemented by the component class, and they are as follows:

- ngOnChanges: This is called once data-bound component properties get initialized before ngOnInit and each time data-bound component properties are changed. It is also part of the directive life cycle (the convention is that the interface implementation function name has the ng prefix added to the interface name; for example, ngOnInit and OnInit).
- ngOnInit: This is called once after the first ngOnChanges and when data-bound component properties and input properties are all initialized. It is also part of the directive life cycle.
- ngDoCheck: This is called as part of the Angular change detection process and should be used to execute custom change detection logic. It is also part of the directive life cycle.
- ngAfterContentInit: This is called once after the first call to ngDoCheck, and when the component template is fully initialized.
- ngAfterContentChecked: This is called once after ngAfterContentInit and after every ngDoCheck call, when the component contents are verified.
- ngAfterViewInit: This is called once after the first ngAfterContentChecked and when all the component views and their children views are initialized.
- ngAfterViewChecked: This is called once after ngAfterViewInit and after every ngAfterContentChecked call, when all the component views and their children views are verified.
- ngOnDestroy: This is called when the component is about to be destroyed and should be used for cleanup operations; for example, unsubscribing from observables and detaching from events.

We will adapt our earlier example to showcase some of these life cycle `hooks`, and we will use a parent and a child component that either displays or logs all their life cycle events to the console. The events triggered until a component is fully loaded are displayed/logged distinctly from the events that occur after the initial load, as per the following screenshot:

The code for the parent component is pretty similar to the code for the child component, and the child component has a button that sends a message to the parent component on demand. When a message is sent, both the `child` component and the parent component respond to life cycle events that are generated by the change detection mechanism from Angular. You can see the code for the child component in the `child.component.ts` file found in the `Example3` folder from the source code for this chapter:

```
import {Component, Input, Output, EventEmitter, OnInit, OnChanges, DoCheck,
AfterContentInit, AfterContentChecked, AfterViewInit, AfterViewChecked}
from '@angular/core';
@Component({
  selector: 'div[my-child-comp]',
  template: `
  <h2>These are the lifecycle events for a child component:</h2>
  <p class="lead">Child component initial lifecycle events:</p>
  <p>{{initialChildEvents}}</p>
  <p class="lead">Child component continuous lifecycle events:</p>
  <p>{{continuousChildEvents}}</p>
  <button class="btn btn-default" type="button" (click)="onClick()">Send
```

```
message from child to parent</button>`
})
export class ChildComponent implements OnInit, OnChanges, DoCheck,
AfterContentInit, AfterContentChecked, AfterViewInit, AfterViewChecked {
  initialChildEvents: string[];
  continuousChildEvents: string[];
  @Output() onChildMessage = new EventEmitter<string>();
  private hasInitialLifecycleFinished: boolean = false;
  private ngAfterViewCheckedEventCount: number = 0;
  constructor() {
    this.initialChildEvents = [];
    this.continuousChildEvents = [];
  }
  private logEvent(message: string) {
      if (!this.hasInitialLifecycleFinished) {
          this.initialChildEvents.push(message);
      } else {
          this.continuousChildEvents.push(message);
      }
  }
  ngOnChanges(): void {
    this.logEvent(` [${new Date().toLocaleTimeString()}]-ngOnChanges`);
  }
  ngOnInit(): void {
    this.logEvent(` [${new Date().toLocaleTimeString()}]-ngOnInit`);
  }
  ngDoCheck(): void {
    this.logEvent(` [${new Date().toLocaleTimeString()}]-ngDoCheck`);
  }
  ngAfterContentInit(): void {
    this.logEvent(` [${new Date().toLocaleTimeString()}]-
    ngAfterContentInit`);
  }
  ngAfterContentChecked(): void {
    this.logEvent(` [${new Date().toLocaleTimeString()}]-
    ngAfterContentChecked`);
  }
  ngAfterViewInit(): void {
    console.log(`child: [${new Date().toLocaleTimeString()}]-
    ngAfterViewInit`);
  }
  ngAfterViewChecked(): void {
    this.ngAfterViewCheckedEventCount += 1;
    if (this.ngAfterViewCheckedEventCount === 2) {
      this.hasInitialLifecycleFinished = true;
    }
    console.log(`child: [${new Date().toLocaleTimeString()}]-
    ngAfterViewChecked`);
```

```
  }
  onClick() {
    this.onChildMessage.emit(`Hello from ChildComponent at: ${new
    Date().toLocaleTimeString()}`);
  }
}
```

All the methods starting with `ng` are component life cycle hooks and when triggered, most of them log events that are stored in the component and displayed via data binding (see the highlighted code snippets from the previous code listing). Two of the life cycle hooks--`ngAfterViewInit` and `ngAfterViewChecked`--log events to the console instead of storing them as component data because any change in the component state at that point in the component life cycle will generate an exception in the Angular application. For example, let's change the `ngAfterViewInit` method body with the following:

```
ngAfterViewInit(): void {
    this.logEvent(` [${new Date().toLocaleTimeString()}]-
    ngAfterViewInit);
}
```

If you look at the application page browser console, you should see this error message after making the change:

Expression has changed after it was checked.

On the initial run of the example, the `ngDoCheck` and `ngAfterContentChecked` methods (and `ngAfterViewChecked` if you look at the browser console output) were triggered twice already for each component before any user interaction. Also, each time we press the example button, the same three methods get triggered, once for each component. In practice, you may rarely use these life cycle hooks apart from `ngOnChanges`, `ngOnInit`, and `ngAfterViewInit` unless you are writing more advanced components or a library of components. We will revisit these core life cycle hooks in Chapter 6, *Creating Directives and Implementing Change Detection*, as they are really useful in the context of forms and other interactive components.

Communicating and sharing data between components

We already used the simplest way to communicate and share data between components: the Input and Output decorators. Properties decorated with the Input decorator initialize a component by passing through data, and the Output decorator can be used to assign event listeners that will receive data out of the component. This approach can be observed with the components found in the Example2 folder from the source code for this chapter.

Referencing child components from a parent component

We can bypass the declarative binding to component properties and events using a template reference variable or by injecting the target component into the parent component via the ViewChild and ViewChildren property decorators. In both the scenarios, we get a reference to the target component and can assign its properties or invoke its methods programmatically. To demonstrate these capabilities in action, we will slightly alter the ChildComponent class from Example2 and ensure that the myText property has a default text set. This can be seen in the highlighted code snippet within the child.component.ts file found in the Example4 folder from the source code for this chapter:

```
...
export class ChildComponent {
  private static instanceCount: number = 0;
  instanceId: number;
  @Input() myText: string;
  @Output() onChildMessage = new EventEmitter<string>();
  constructor(){
    ChildComponent.instanceCount += 1;
    this.instanceId = ChildComponent.instanceCount;
    this.myText = 'This is the default child component text.';
  }

  onClick(){
    this.onChildMessage.emit(`Hello from ChildComponent with instance
    id: ${this.instanceId}`);
  }
}
```

We will then change the `app.component.ts` file to include the template reference approach for the first child component and the component injection approach for the second child component:

```
import { Component, ViewChildren, OnInit, QueryList } from '@angular/core';
import { ChildComponent } from './child.component';
@Component({
    selector: 'div.container.my-app',
    template: `
    <div class="container text-center">
      <div class="row"><div class="col-md-12">
          <div class="page-header"><h1>{{title}}</h1></div>
          <p class="lead">{{description}}</p>
      </div></div>
      <div class="row">
        <div class="col-md-6">
          <button class="btn btn-default" type="button"
          (click)="firstChildComponent.myText='First child component
          goes here.'">Set first child component text</button>
          <button class="btn btn-default" type="button"
  (click)="firstChildComponent.onChildMessage.subscribe(onFirstChildComp
          onentMessageReceived)">Set first child component message
          output</button>
          </div>
          <div class="col-md-6">
          <button class="btn btn-default" type="button"
          (click)="setSecondChildComponentProperties()">Set second
          child component properties</button>
          </div>
          </div>
      <div class="row">
        <div class="col-md-6 well well-sm" my-child-comp
        #firstChildComponent></div>
        <div class="col-md-6 well well-sm" my-child-comp
        id="secondChildComponent"></div>
      </div>
      <div class="row"><div class="col-md-12"><div class="well well-
      sm">
          <p>Last message from child components: <strong>
          {{lastMessage}}</strong></p>
      </div></div></div>
    </div>`
})
export class AppComponent {
  title: string;
  description: string;
  lastMessage: string;
  @ViewChildren(ChildComponent) childComponents:
```

```
QueryList<ChildComponent>;
constructor(){
  this.title = 'Mastering Angular – Chapter 4, Example 4';
  this.description = 'This is an example for how to reference
  existing components from a parent component.';
  this.lastMessage = 'Waiting for child messages ...';
}
onFirstChildComponentMessageReceived($event: string)
{
  alert($event);
}
setSecondChildComponentProperties(){
  this.childComponents.last.myText = "The second child component goes
  here.";
  this.childComponents.last.onChildMessage.subscribe( (message:
  string) => {
    this.lastMessage = message + ' (the message will be reset in 2
    seconds)';
    setTimeout( ()=>{ this.lastMessage = 'Waiting for child messages
    ...';}, 2000);
  });
}
}
```

First of all, the two child components from the third highlighted HTML snippet don't have any properties or event bindings. The first child component has a `#firstChildComponent` attribute, which represents a template reference variable.

Template reference variables

A template reference variable can be set in an Angular template against any component, directive, or DOM element and will make the reference available to the current template. In the first highlighted HTML snippet from the preceding example, we have two buttons that are using inline Angular expressions to set the `myText` property and bind to the `onChildMessage` event via the `firstChildComponent` template reference variable. When running the example, if we click on the **Set first child component text** button and then the **Set first child component message output** button, we will manipulate the first child component directly through the template reference variable, as seen in the first highlighted HTML snippet from the earlier example. This approach is suitable for initializing and reading component properties, but it proves to be cumbersome when we need to bind to component events.

A template reference variable cannot be accessed in a component class; hence, the contrived way we have is to bind to the first child component event. However, this type of variable will prove very useful when working with forms, and we will revisit them in Chapter 6, *Creating Directives and Implementing Change Detection*.

Injecting child components

For the second child component, we used a technique based on injecting components via this property declaration from the `app.component.ts` file:

```
@ViewChildren(ChildComponent) childComponents: QueryList<ChildComponent>;
```

The `ViewChildren` decorator takes a selector for the `ChildComponent` type that will identify and collect all the `ChildComponent` instances from the parent component template into a specialized list of the `QueryList` type. This list allows iterating through the child component instances, and we can get a reference for the second child component using the `QueryList.Last()` call in the `AppComponent`. `setSecondChildComponentProperties()` method. When running the code found in the `Example4` folder for the source code for this chapter, the second HTML snippet from the previous code listing will spring into action if you click on the **Set second child component properties** button.

Injecting child components is a versatile technique, and we can access the referenced components from the parent component code in a more efficient manner.

Using services with components

We will now evolve `Example2` once again and refactor some of the code that was defined at the component level into an Angular service.

A service is a TypeScript class that has a decorator called `Injectable` without any parameters that allows the service to be part of the dependency injection (DI) mechanism in Angular 2. DI will ensure that a service instance will be created only once per application, and this instance will be injected in any class that declares it as a dependency in their constructor declarations. Apart from the specific decorator, a service needs to be declared as a provider usually in a module definition, but it can also be declared in component, directive, or pipe definitions. Before jumping into our example for this section, you can find more information about services in Chapter 12, *Implementing Angular Services*.

Even if a service does not have other dependencies, it is a good practice to ensure that it is decorated with Injectable in case it has dependencies in the future and to simplify its usage when used as a dependency.

For our example, we will build upon the `Example2` code into a new example found in the `Example4` folder from the source code for this chapter. We will start by extracting most of the logic for the parent and `child` component into a new service class:

```
import {Injectable,EventEmitter} from '@angular/core';
@Injectable()
export class AppService {
  private componentDescriptions: string[];
  private componentMessages: string[];
  public appServiceMessage$ = new EventEmitter <string> ();
  constructor() {
    this.componentDescriptions = [
      'The first child component goes here',
      'The second child component goes here'
    ];
    this.componentMessages = [];
  }
  getComponentDescription(index: number): string {
    return this.componentDescriptions[index];
  }
  sendMessage(message: string): void {
    this.componentMessages.push(message);
    this.appServiceMessage$.emit(message);
  }
  getComponentMessages(): string[] {
    return this.componentMessages;
  }
}
```

The service stores the description used by the child components in the `componentDescriptions` array and provides a message handler through the `sendMessage()` method that also stores any processed message in the `AppService.componentMessages` property. The child component `onChildMessage` property of the `EventEmitter` type from `Example2` is now moved to `AppService.appServiceMessage$`, and it is available to any component or service that requires it. The `child` component definition is now greatly simplified:

```
import {Component, Input, Output, EventEmitter, OnInit} from
'@angular/core';
import {AppService} from './app.service';
```

```
@Component({
  selector: 'div[my-child-comp]',
  template: `
      <p>{{myText}}</p>
      <button class="btn btn-default" type="button"
      (click)="onClick()">Send message</button>`
})
export class ChildComponent implements OnInit {
  @Input() index: number;
  myText: string;
  constructor(private appService: AppService) {}
  ngOnInit() {
    this.myText = this.appService.getComponentDescription(this.index);
  }

  onClick() {
    if (this.appService.getComponentMessages().length > 3) {
      this.appService.sendMessage(`There are too many messages ...`);
      return;
    }
    this.appService.sendMessage(`Hello from ChildComponent with index:
    ${this.index}`);
  }
}
```

Child component messages are now sent via the AppService.sendMessage() method. Also, the only @Input() property, called index, stores the component index used to set the myText property via the AppService.getComponentDescription() method. Apart from the index property, the ChildComponent class relies solely on AppService to read and write data.

The AppComponent class now has very little logic and although it displays all the messages provided by the AppService instance, it also registers a custom subscription in the ngOnInit method that stores the last received message. The AppService.appServiceMessage$ property of the EventEmitter type provides a public subscription for any other Angular classes interested in consuming this event:

```
import { Component, OnInit } from '@angular/core';
import { AppService } from './app.service';
@Component({
    selector: 'div.container.my-app',
    template: `<div class="container text-center">
      <div class="row"><div class="col-md-12">
          <div class="page-header"><h1>{{title}}</h1></div>
          <p class="lead">{{description}}</p>
      </div></div>
```

```
      <div class="row">
        <div class="col-md-6 well" my-child-comp index="0"></div>
        <div class="col-md-6 well" my-child-comp index="1"></div>
      </div>
      <div class="row"><div class="col-md-12"><div class="well well-
        sm">
            <p><strong>Last message received:</strong>
             {{lastMessageReceived}}</p>
            <p><strong>Messages from child components:</strong>
             {{appService.getComponentMessages()}}</p>
        </div></div></div>
    </div>`
})
export class AppComponent implements OnInit {
  title: string;
  description: string;
  lastMessageReceived: string;
  constructor(private appService: AppService){
    this.title = 'Mastering Angular - Chapter 4, Example 4';
    this.description = 'This is an example of how to communicate and
    share data between components via services.';
  }
  ngOnInit(){
    this.appService.appServiceMessage$.subscribe((message:string) => {
      this.lastMessageReceived = message;
    });
  }
}
```

In this example, we started with a `ChildComponent` class that relied on the `@Input()` properties to get the data it needs; we switched to a class that needs just a key value to get its data from a service class. The two styles of writing components don't exclude each other, and using a service provides further support for writing modular components.

Summary

In this chapter, we first looked at a basic component example and then we explored parent and child components. An exposure to the component's life cycle was followed by examples of how to communicate and share data between components.

5
Implementing Angular Routing and Navigation

Application navigation is one of the core functionalities for any website or application. Along with defining the routes or path, navigation helps users to reach the application pages, explore functionalities, and is also very useful for SEO purposes.

In this chapter, you will learn all about the Angular routing and navigation. Here's a detailed list of functionalities we will learn and implement in routing and navigation.

You will learn the following aspects of routing and navigation:

- Importing and configuring the router
- Enabling the Router Outlet, `routerLink`, `routerLinkActive`, and `base href` in the view
- Custom component routes and child routes
- Custom component routes with inner child routes--same page loading
- Demo application routing and navigation

At the end of the chapter, we will able to do the following things:

- Create `app.routes` for the application and set up the required modules
- Implement and enable `RouterModule.forRoot`
- Define the Router Outlet and the `routerLink` directive for binding the route path
- Enable `RouterLinkActivated` to find the current active state
- Understand how the Route State works
- Understand and implement Route Lifecycle Hooks

- Create custom component routes and child routes
- Implement location strategy for our web applications
- Create a sample application routes and navigation

First things first, take a look at the demo application routing and navigation we will be developing as part of this chapter:

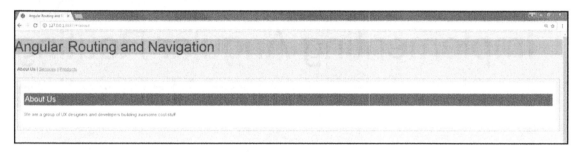

As part of the demo application, we will developing routes for **About Us**, **Services**, and **Products** components.

Services components will have inner child routes. Products component will make use of `ActivatedRoute` for getting route `params`. We will also implement navigation using the JavaScript event `onclick`.

Importing and configuring the router

In order to define and implement the navigation strategy, we will make use of router and `RouterModule`.

We need to update our `app.module.ts` file to do the following:

- Import `RouterModule` and routes from Angular router module
- Import the application components
- Define the routes with path and component details
- Import `RouterModule.forRoot` (`appRoutes`)

Each route definition can have the following keys:

- `path`: The URL we want to display in the browser address bar.
- `component`: Corresponding component that will hold the view and application logic.
- `redirectTo` (optional): This indicates the URL we want the user to get redirected from this path.
- `pathMatch` (optional): A redirect route requires `pathMatch`--it tells the router how to match a URL to the path of a route. `pathMatch` can take either value as `full` or `prefix`.

We will now import and configure the router in our `NgModule`. Take a look at the updated `app.module.ts` file with complete implementation of the router:

```
import { NgModule } from '@angular/core';
import { BrowserModule } from '@angular/platform-browser';
import { FormsModule } from '@angular/forms';
import { RouterModule, Routes } from '@angular/router';

import { AppComponent } from './app.component';
import { AboutComponent} from './about.component';
import { ServicesComponent} from './services.component';
import { ProductsComponent } from './products.component';

const appRoutes: Routes = [
 { path: 'about', component: AboutComponent },
 { path: 'services', component: ServicesComponent },
 { path: 'products', redirectTo:'/new-products', pathMatch:'full'},
 { path: '**', component: ErrorPageNotFoundComponent }
];

@NgModule({
 imports: [
 BrowserModule,
 FormsModule,
 RouterModule.forRoot(appRoutes)
 ],
 declarations: [
  AppComponent,
  AboutComponent,
  ServicesComponent,
  ProductsComponent,
 ],
 bootstrap: [ AppComponent ]
})
```

```
export class AppModule { }
```

Let's analyze the preceding code snippet:

1. We are importing `Routes` and `routerModule` from `@angular/router`.
2. We are importing the required modules `NgModule`, `BrowserModule`, and `FormsModule` from the respective Angular libraries.
3. We are importing custom defined components--`About`, `Services`, and `Products`.
4. We are defining a const `appRoutes` in which we are specifying paths for our components.
5. We are creating our routes through `appRoutes` and defining custom path for various URL router links by passing various parameters.

Now that we have learned how to import and configure our `NgModule` for implementing routes, in next section we will learn about the building blocks of router.

Building blocks of router

In this section, you will learn the important building blocks of the router. The important building blocks are `base href`, `Router Outlet`, `routerLink`, and `routerLinkActive`.

Let's now analyze each of the building blocks of the router library:

- `base href`: We must set the `base` directive in the `index.html` page. *This is a mandatory step.* Without the `base` tag, the browser may not be able to load resources (images, CSS, and scripts) when *deep linking* into the app.

  In our application, we need to define the `base href` inside the `<head>` tag in our `index.html` file:

  ```
  <base href="/">
  ```

- **Defining the** `router-outlet`: The `router-outlet` directive is the placeholder for containing the loaded data of the view. Inside the `router-outlet` directive, the component views will be loaded and displayed.
  Place the directive inside the template in the `app.component.html` to render the data:

  ```
  <router-outlet></router-outlet>
  ```

- **Using multiple** `router-outlet`: In certain cases, we will want to load data to different view containers instead of our `router-outlet`. We can easily add multiple Router Outlets to a page and assign them names so that we can render respective data inside them:

  ```
  <router-outlet></router-outlet>
  <router-outlet name="content-farm"></router-outlet>
  ```

  To load the data of the view inside the named `router-outlet`, we define the key while defining the route:

  ```
  {
    path: 'content', component: ContentFarmComponent,
    outlet: 'content- farm'
  }
  ```

- **Creating** `RouterLink`: This indicates the URL or the link address that could arrive directly from the browser address bar. Bind and associate a link path with the anchor tag: for example, `/about` or `/products`.

  The general syntax for binding and associating an anchor tag is as follows:

  ```
  <a [routerLink]="['/about']">About Us</a>
  <a [routerLink]="['/products']">Products</a>
  <a [routerLink]="['/services']">Services</a>
  ```

- `RouterLinkActive` **for active state links**: `routerLinkActive` is used to highlight the current active link. Using `routerLinkActive`, we can easily highlight the link that is currently active to better suit our applications look and feel:

  ```
  <a [routerLink]="['/about']" routerLinkActive =
      "active-state">About Us</a>
  ```

  In the style sheet, add our custom style class, `active-state`.

- **Building dynamic** `routerLink`: We can pass dynamic values or parameters by binding them with the `routerLink` directive to pass custom data. Generally, in most applications, we use a unique identifier for categorizing data-- for example, `http://hostname/product/10` will be written as follows:

```
<a [routerLink]="['/product', 10]">Product 10</a>
```

The same preceding code dynamically can be rendered in our template view:

```
<a [routerLink]="['/product', product.id]">Product 10</a>
```

- **Passing array and datasets with** `routerLink` **directive**: We can pass data arrays along with the `routerLink`:

```
<a [routerLink]="['/contacts', { customerId: 10 }]">Crisis
  Center</a>
```

About router LocationStrategy

We need to define the URL behavior of the application. Based on application preferences, we can customize how the URL should be rendered.

Using `LocationStrategy`, we can define how we want our application routing system to behave.

Angular, through `LocationStrategy`, provides two types of routing strategies we can implement in our application. Let's understand the different route strategy options we can use in our Angular applications:

- `PathLocationStrategy`: This is the default HTML style routing mechanism. Applying `PathLocationStrategy` is the common routing strategy which involves making request/calls to the server side on every change detected. Implementing this strategy will allow us to create clean URLs and also bookmark the URLs easily.

  An example of a route using `PathLocationStrategy` is given as follows:

```
http://hostname/about
```

- `HashLocationStrategy:` This is the hash URL style. In most modern web applications, we see hash URLs being used. This has a major advantage. The client doesn't make the server calls or requests when the information after # changes; hence there are fewer server calls:

    ```
    http://hostname/#/about
    ```

- Defining and setting the `LocationStrategy` in our application: In the `app.module.ts` file under `providers`, we need to pass `LocationStrategy` and tell the router to `useClass` as `HashLocationStrategy`.

    In `app.module.ts`, import and use `LocationStrategy` and mention that we want to use `HashLocationStategy`, as shown in the following code:

    ```
    @NgModule({
      imports: [
      BrowserModule,
      routing
      ],
      declarations: [
       AppComponent
      ],
      bootstrap: [
       AppComponent
      ],
      providers: [
        {provide: LocationStrategy, useClass: HashLocationStrategy }
      ]
    })
    export class AppModule { }
    ```

In the preceding code, we have injected `LocationStrategy` in our providers and we are explicitly mentioning Angular to use `HashLocationStrategy`.

By default, the Angular router implements `PathLocationStrategy`.

Handling the error state - wildcard route

We need to set up the error messages for page not found or 404 pages. We can use the `ErrorPageNotFoundComponent` component to display the page not found or error messages for paths that are unknown to the router:

```
const appRoutes: Routes = [
  { path: 'about', component: AboutComponent },
```

```
    { path: 'services', component: ServicesComponent },
    { path: 'old-products', redirectTo:'/new-products', pathMatch:'full'},
    { path: '**', component: ErrorPageNotFoundComponent },
    { path: 'content', component: ContentFarmComponent, outlet: 'content-
      farm' }
];
```

At this stage, with all the information about how to use the router with various aspects, let's add all of them to our `app.component.ts` file:

```
import { Component, ViewEncapsulation } from '@angular/core';

@Component({
 selector: 'my-app',
 template: `
 <h2>Angular2 Routing and Navigation</h2>
 <div class="">
 <p>
   <a routerLink="/about" routerLinkActive="active"> About Us</a> |
   <a routerLink="/services" routerLinkActive="active" > Services</a> |
   <a routerLink="/products" routerLinkActive="active"> Products</a>
 </p>
 <div class="app-data">
  <router-outlet></router-outlet>
 </div>
 </div>`,
  styles: [`
    h4 { background-color:rgb(63,81,181);color:#fff; padding:3px;}
    h2 { background-color:rgb(255, 187, 0);color:#222}
    div {padding: 10px;}
    .app-data {border: 1px solid #b3b3b3;}
    .active {color:#222;text-decoration:none;}
    `
   ],
 encapsulation: ViewEncapsulation.None
})
export class AppComponent {
}
```

Let's analyze the preceding code and break it down into key functionalities:

- We defined the `routerLink` attribute to enable the navigation when a user clicks on the anchor links

- The `canActivateChild` function is similar to `canActivate` with a key difference that this function protects the child routes of the component.

  The following is a sample code for using the `canActivateChild` function inside a service:

```
import {CanActivateChild} from "@angular/router";

@Injectable()
class checkCredentialsToken implements CanActivateChild {
 canActivateChild() {
 console.log("Checking for child routes inside components");
 return true;
 }
}
```

- `canDeactivate`: This handles any unsaved changes in the page--many times when a user tries to navigate away from a page having unsaved changes, we need to inform the user about the pending changes and take confirmation on whether the user wants to save their work or proceed without saving.

  That's where `canDeactivate` comes into picture. The following is the code snippet for a service, which implements the `canDeactivate` function:

```
import { CanDeactivate } from '@angular/router';

@Injectable()
export class checkCredentials {
 canDeactivate() {
 console.log("Check for any unsaved changes or value length etc");
 return true;
 }
}
```

- `Resolve`: This performs route data retrieval before route activation--`Resolve` allows us to prefetch data retrieval from the service before we activate a route and component.

  The following is the code snippet for how we can use the `Resolve` function and get the data from service before the route is activated:

```
import { Injectable } from '@angular/core';
import { Resolve, ActivatedRouteSnapshot } from '@angular/router';
import { UserService } from './shared/services/user.service';

@Injectable()
```

```
export class UsersResolve implements Resolve<any> {
  constructor(private service: UserService) {}
   resolve(route: ActivatedRouteSnapshot) {
   return this.service.getUsers();
   }
}
```

- canLoad: This guards the module even before loading the module--using canActivate, we can redirect the unauthorized user to other landing pages, but in those cases, the module gets loaded.

  We can avoid the loading of the module using the canLoad function.

In the next section, we will learn about defining the routes for components and child components. We will learn to create a multi-level hierarchy of components.

Custom component routes and child routes

In previous sections, so far we have learned about the various usage of the router; it's now time to use all our knowledge to put together a sample demo application using all the routing examples. We will now create a custom component and define its route file with child routes.

We will create an unordered list of items called **Products**, which will have linked list items that are child products. Clicking on the respective product link, the user will be displayed the product details.

The application navigation plan looks as follows:

We have in previous sections learned to define and create routes in NgModule. We can also, alternatively, define a separate app.route.ts file and place all the routing details inside it.

Create the `app.route.ts` file and add the following code snippet to the file:

```
import { productRoutes } from './products/products.routes';

export const routes: Routes = [
 {
 path: '',
 redirectTo: '/',
 pathMatch: 'full'
 },
 ...aboutRoutes,
 ...servicesRoutes,
 ...productRoutes,
 { path: '**', component: PageNotFoundComponent }
];

export const routing: ModuleWithProviders = RouterModule.forRoot(routes);
```

We import our component into the `app.routes.ts` file and then define the routes with `productRoutes`.

Now, it's time we create our `product.routes.ts` file with path definitions for our products. The following is the code for doing so:

```
import { Routes } from '@angular/router';
import { ProductsComponent } from './products.component';
import { ProductsDetailsComponent } from './products-details.component';

export const productRoutes: Routes = [
 { path: 'products', component: ProductsComponent },
 { path: 'products/:id', component: ProductsDetailsComponent }
];
```

Let's analyze the preceding code:

1. We are defining two paths in the `products.routes.ts` file.
2. The path `products` will point to `ProductsComponent`.
3. The path `products/:id` path that translates to `products/10` will be mapped to `ProductsDetailsComponent`.

Now, it's time to create our components--`ProductsComponent` and `ProductsDetailsComponent`.

Let's define the ProductsComponent class in the products.components.ts file, and add the following code:

```typescript
import { Component } from '@angular/core';
import { Routes, Router } from '@angular/router';

@Component({
 template: `
 <div class="container">
 <h4>Built with Angular2</h4>
 <p> select country specific website for more details </p>
 <ul>
 <li><a routerLink="10" routerLinkActive="disabled">Product #10</a>
   </li>
 <li><a routerLink="11" routerLinkActive="disabled">Product #11</a>
   </li>
 <li><a routerLink="12" routerLinkActive="disabled">Product #12</a>
   </li>
 </ul>

 <button (click)="navigateToServices()">Navigate via Javascript
 event</button>

 <router-outlet></router-outlet>

 </div>`,
 styles: ['.container {background-color: #fff;}']
})
export class ProductsComponent {

    constructor(private router: Router) {}

    navigateToServices(){
      this.router.navigate(['/services']);
    }
}
```

Let's analyze the preceding code in detail:

- We have created three product links with the `routerLink` directive; clicking on these links will get us mapped to the path we created in the `products.route.ts` file
- We have created a button, which has a `navigateToServices` event, and in the `ProductsComponent` class, we implement the method to navigate to the **Services** page
- We have created a `routerLink` to handle each product ID, and the respective data will be loaded in `<router-outlet>`

Now, let's create `ProductsDetailsComponent` in `products-details.components.ts` under the `products` folder using the following code:

```
import { Component, OnInit } from '@angular/core';
import { Observable } from 'rxjs/Observable';
import { ROUTER_DIRECTIVES, ActivatedRoute } from '@angular/router';

@Component({
 template: `
 <div class="container">
  <h4>Product Demo Information</h4>
  <p>This is a page navigation for child pages</p>
  showing product with Id: {{selectedId}}
  <p>
  <a routerLink="/products">All products</a>
  </p>
 </div>
 `,
 directives: [ROUTER_DIRECTIVES],
 styles: ['.container {background-color: #fff;}']
})

export class ProductsDetailsComponent implements OnInit {
  private selectedId: number;
  constructor(private route: ActivatedRoute) {}
  ngOnInit() {
   this.sub = this.route.params.subscribe(params => {
   let id = params['id'];
   this.selectedId = id;
   console.log(id);
   });
  }
}
```

Here's the analysis of the preceding code:

- When the user clicks on the product link, the `id` gets mapped and its respective product details are displayed
- We are importing the required modules, `Component` and `OnInit`, from the `@angular/core` library
- We are importing the required modules, `ROUTER_DIRECTIVES` and `ActivatedRoute` from the `angular/router` library
- We are exporting the `ProductsDetailsComponent` class
- We are injecting `ActivatedRoute` in the constructor method
- We are defining the `ngOnInit` method which will be called on the page load
- We are using the `ActivatedRoute` service which provides a `params` `Observable` which we can subscribe to get the route parameters
- We are using `this.route.params.subscribe` to map the parameters passed in the URL
- The parameter has the `id` of the selected/clicked product which we are assigning to the variable `this.selectedId`

All set so far? Great.

Now it's time to update our `app.module.ts` file with the new components and their declarations. The updated `app.module.ts` will be as follows:

```
import { NgModule } from "@angular/core";
import { BrowserModule } from "@angular/platform-browser";
import { HashLocationStrategy, LocationStrategy } from "@angular/common";

import { AppComponent } from "./app.component";
import { routing } from "./app.routes";

import { ProductsComponent } from "./products/products.component";
import { ProductsDetailsComponent } from './products/products-
  details.component';

@NgModule({
  imports: [
      BrowserModule,
      routing
    ],
  declarations: [
    AppComponent,
    ProductsComponent,
    ProductsDetailsComponent
```

```
    ],
  bootstrap: [
    AppComponent
    ],
  providers: [
      {provide: LocationStrategy, useClass: HashLocationStrategy }
    ]
  })
export class AppModule { }
```

Alright. Now, let's test drive the application we have made so far.

The following image shows how our application should behave at this stage:

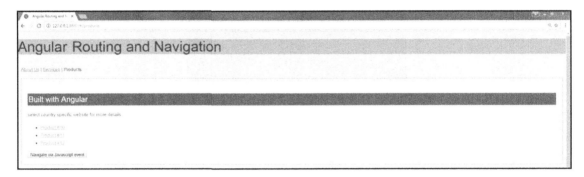

The following image shows when the user clicks on any particular product, the application will take the user to the respective product listing:

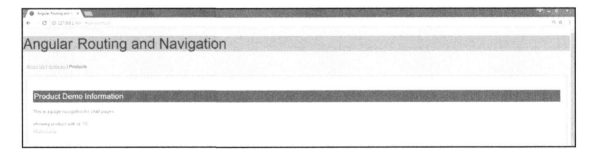

Custom component routes with inner child routes

In the preceding example, when the user clicks on product links, the user is navigated to a new path. In this example, you will learn how to create custom components and child routes and display the view inside the same path; that is, inner child routes.

Extending the same example, take a look at the application navigation plan:

```
App
    Products
        Product 1
        Product 2
        Product 3

        Services
            Web Technologies
                Angular2 Development
```

Let's start by defining the route definitions in the `service.routes.ts` file. Refer to the following code for route definitions:

```
import { Routes } from '@angular/router';

import { ServicesComponent } from './services.component';
import { ServicesChildComponent } from "./services-child.component";
import { ServicesInnerChildComponent } from "./services-inner-
    child.component";

export const servicesRoutes: Routes = [
  {
    path: 'services',
    component: ServicesComponent,
    children: [
        {
          path: '', redirectTo: 'services', pathMatch: 'full'},
          {
            path: 'web-technologies',
            component: ServicesChildComponent,
            children: [
              { path: '', redirectTo: 'web-technologies', pathMatch:
                'full'},
              { path: 'angular2', component:
                  ServicesInnerChildComponent}
            ]
```

```
        }
     ]
   }
];
```

In the preceding code snippet, we are creating path services, and inside the same path, we are creating multi-level child routes, which all belong to the same URL hierarchy.

The component navigation route definition is shown as follows:

- `/services`
- `/services/web-technologies`
- `/services/web-technologies/angular2`

Now, let's create our three new components for our services :

- `ServicesComponent`
- `ServicesChildComponent`
- `ServicesInnerChildComponent`

 Note that adding the `<router-outlet>` directive is important in parent views; otherwise, it will throw an error.

Now we need to create our Service component. For `ServicesComponent`, create a new file called `services.component.ts` and add the following code snippet to it:

```
import { Component } from '@angular/core';

@Component({
 template: `
 <div class="container">
 <h4>Services offered</h4>
 <ul>
 <li><a routerLink="web-technologies" routerLinkActive="active">Web
     Technologies Services</a></li>
 <li><a routerLink="#" routerLinkActive="disabled">Mobile Apps</a></li>
 <li><a routerLink="#" routerLinkActive="disabled">CRM Apps</a></li>
 <li><a routerLink="#" routerLinkActive="disabled">Enterprise Apps</a>
  </li>
 </ul>
 </div>
 <router-outlet></router-outlet>
 `,
```

```
  styles: ['.container {background-color:#fff;}']
})

export class ServicesComponent {
}
```

Quick notes on the preceding code follow:

1. We have defined a unordered list `<ul>` of items `<li>` inside the `ServicesComponent` template.
2. For each of the list items, we are attaching `routerLink` attribute to link the URL.
3. Inside the template, we are also adding `<router-outlet>`--this will allow the child component view template to be placed inside the parent component view.

We have our parent `ServicesComponent` created and ready. Now it's time to create the child that is the inner component: `ServicesChildComponent`.

Let's create a new file called `services-child.component.ts` and add the following code snippet to the file:

```
import {Component} from '@angular/core';

@Component({
 template: `
 <div class="container">
 <h4>Web Technologies</h4>
 <p>This is 1st level Inner Navigation</p>
 <a routerLink="angular2" routerLinkActive="active">Angular2 Services</a>
 </div>
<router-outlet></router-outlet>
 `,
 styles: ['.container {background-color: #fff;}']
})

export class ServicesChildComponent {}
```

Quick notes on the preceding code follow:

1. We have defined a title and an anchor tag `<a>` and added `routerLink` and `routerLinkActive` attributes to it.
2. For the anchor tag, we are attaching added `routerLink` and `routerLinkActive` attributes.

3. Inside the template, we are also adding `<router-outlet>`--this will allow the inner child component view template to be placed inside the child component view.

Take a look at the following hierarchy diagram, which depicts the component structure:

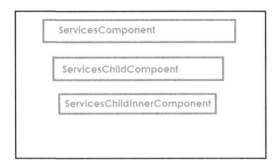

So far we have created a parent component, `ServicesComponent`, and it's child component, `ServicesChildComponent`, which have a hierarchy of parent-child relation.

It's time to create the third-level component, `ServicesInnerChildComponent`. Create a new file named `services-child.component.ts`:

```
import {Component} from '@angular/core';

@Component({
 template: `
 <div class="container">
 <h4>Angular Services</h4>
 <p>This is 2nd level Inner Navigation</p>
 <a routerLink="/services" routerLinkActive="active">View All
    Services</a>
 </div>
 `,
 styles: ['.container {background-color: #fff;}']
})

export class ServicesInnerChildComponent {}
```

Alright, now that we defined all our components and child components and their respective route definitions, it's time to see all of them in action. The following screenshots show you how the navigation routes work for the services component and child components.

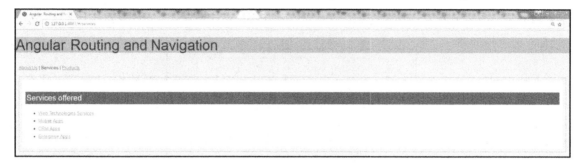

Clicking on the **Web Technologies** link will show the user child component data.

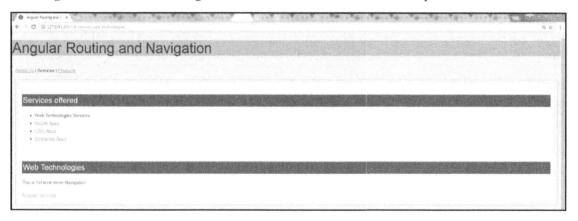

Clicking on the **Angular Services** link will show the user child component dat

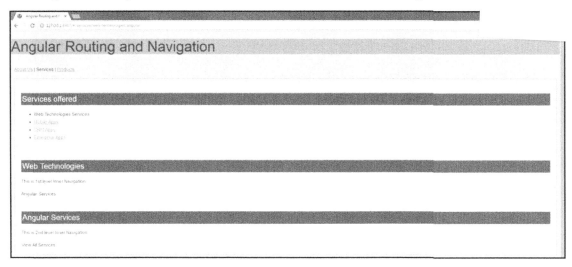

We have our components working individually very well. In next section we will integrate them all into one single working application.

Integrating all the components together

We have defined and implemented routes for the individual components, About, Services, and Products.

In this section, we will integrate them all into one single NgModule so we have all routes working together as a single page application.

Let's add all the individual routes of the About, Services, and Products components to our app.routes.ts and the updated app.route.ts file is as follows:

```
import { ModuleWithProviders } from '@angular/core';
import { Routes, RouterModule } from '@angular/router';
import { PageNotFoundComponent } from './not-found.component';

import { AboutComponent } from "./about/about.component";

import { ServicesComponent } from "./services/services.component";
import { ServicesChildComponent } from "./services/services-
  child.component";
import { ServicesInnerChildComponent } from "./services/services-inner-
  child.component";
```

```
import { ProductComponent } from "./products/products.component";
import { ProductsDetailsComponent } from './products/products-
  details.component';

import { aboutRoutes } from './about/about.routes';
import { servicesRoutes } from './services/services.routes';
import { productRoutes } from './products/products.routes';

export const routes: Routes = [
  {
    path: '',
    redirectTo: '/',
    pathMatch: 'full'
  },
  ...aboutRoutes,
  ...servicesRoutes,
  ...productRoutes,
  {
   path: '**', component: PageNotFoundComponent }
];

export const routing: ModuleWithProviders = RouterModule.forRoot(routes);
```

We have updated the `app.routes.ts` file to include all the routes of the components as well as the child components.

It's now time to update the `NgModule` to import all the components as well the updates routes.

The updated `app.module.ts` file is given as follows:

```
import { NgModule } from "@angular/core";
import { BrowserModule } from "@angular/platform-browser";
import { HashLocationStrategy, LocationStrategy } from "@angular/common";

import { AppComponent } from "./app.component";
import { routing } from "./app.routes";
import { PageNotFoundComponent } from './not-found.component';

import { AboutComponent } from "./about/about.component";
import { ServicesComponent } from "./services/services.component";
import { ServicesChildComponent } from "./services/services-
  child.component";
import { ServicesInnerChildComponent } from "./services/services-inner-
  child.component";

import { ProductsComponent } from "./products/products.component";
import { ProductsDetailsComponent } from './products/products-
```

```
     details.component';

@NgModule({
  imports: [
   BrowserModule,
   routing
    ],
  declarations: [
   AppComponent,
   ProductsComponent,
   ServicesComponent,
   AboutComponent,
   ProductsDetailsComponent,
   PageNotFoundComponent,
   ServicesChildComponent,
   ServicesInnerChildComponent
    ],
  bootstrap: [
   AppComponent
    ],
  providers: [
    {provide: LocationStrategy, useClass: HashLocationStrategy }
    ]
})
export class AppModule { }
```

Important things to note in the preceding code are:

1. We are importing all the components we created so far, namely `About`, `Services`, and `Products`.
2. We are also importing the routes `app.routes.ts` we created for each of the components.
3. We are injecting `LocationStrategy` and explicitly mentioning it to `useClass` `HashLocationStrategy`.

We have learned about `router`, `routerModule`, and utilities provided by Angular for implementing the routing mechanism of our applications. We learned about different types of `LocationStrategy` we can use to define how the URLs should be displayed.

We created components having route paths and route paths for child components, and we have learned to navigate using JavaScript events as well.

In the next section, we will stitch all the code together to make our demo application.

Demo application routing and navigation

We have come a long way in learning all about the Angular router. We have seen various tips and tricks of how to use the router module. It's now fun time as we put together all the pieces we have learned so far into a neat, clean application.

The following image shows our final application filesystem structure :

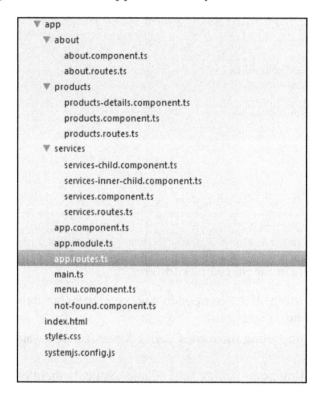

We will add the main navigation menu and some basic styling to jazz up our application in the app.component.ts file:

```
import { Component, ViewEncapsulation } from '@angular/core';

@Component({
  selector: 'my-app',
  template: `
    <h2>Angular2 Routing and Navigation</h2>
    <div class="">
    <p>
      <a routerLink="/about" routerLinkActive="active">About Us</a>|
```

```
        <a routerLink="/services" routerLinkActive="active">Services</a>|
        <a routerLink="/products" routerLinkActive="active">Products</a>
    </p>
    <div class="app-data">
        <router-outlet></router-outlet>
    </div>
  </div>`,
      styles: [`
        h4 { background-color:rgb(63,81,181);color:#fff; padding:3px;}
        h2 { background-color:rgb(255, 187, 0);color:#222}
        div {padding: 10px;}
        .app-data {border: 1px solid #b3b3b3;}
        .active {color:#222;text-decoration:none;}

      `,
      ],
  encapsulation: ViewEncapsulation.None
})

export class AppComponent {
}
```

Our final `app.routes.ts` file code is given as follows:

```
import { ModuleWithProviders } from '@angular/core';
import { Routes, RouterModule } from '@angular/router';
import { PageNotFoundComponent } from './not-found.component';

import { AboutComponent } from "./about/about.component";
import { ServicesComponent } from "./services/services.component";
import { ServicesChildComponent } from "./services/services-
    child.component";
import { ServicesInnerChildComponent } from "./services/services-inner-
    child.component";

import { ProductComponent } from "./products/products.component";
import { ProductsDetailsComponent } from './products/products-
    details.component';

import { aboutRoutes } from './about/about.routes';
import { servicesRoutes } from './services/services.routes';
import { productRoutes } from './products/products.routes';

export const routes: Routes = [
    {
      path: '',
      redirectTo: '/',
      pathMatch: 'full'
    },
```

```
   ...aboutRoutes,
   ...servicesRoutes,
   ...productRoutes,
   { path: '**', component: PageNotFoundComponent }
];

export const routing: ModuleWithProviders =
        RouterModule.forRoot(routes);
```

Our `app.module.ts` file code is given as follows:

```
import { NgModule } from "@angular/core";
import { BrowserModule } from "@angular/platform-browser";
import { HashLocationStrategy, LocationStrategy } from
    "@angular/common";
import { AppComponent } from "./app.component";
import { routing } from "./app.routes";

import { PageNotFoundComponent } from './not-found.component';
import { AboutComponent } from "./about/about.component";

import { ServicesComponent } from "./services/services.component";
import { ServicesChildComponent } from "./services/services-
   child.component";
import { ServicesInnerChildComponent } from "./services/services-inner-
   child.component";

import { ProductsComponent } from "./products/products.component";
import { ProductsDetailsComponent } from './products/products-
    details.component';

@NgModule({
 imports: [
   BrowserModule,
   routing
   ],
 declarations: [
   AppComponent,
   ProductsComponent,
   ServicesComponent,
   AboutComponent,
   ProductsDetailsComponent,
   PageNotFoundComponent,
   ServicesChildComponent,
   ServicesInnerChildComponent
 ],
 bootstrap: [
    AppComponent
```

```
    ],
    providers: [
        { provide: LocationStrategy, useClass: HashLocationStrategy }
    ]
})
export class AppModule { }
```

Our application is ready for the grand demo.

In the following screenshots, we show you the behavior of the application.

When we launch the page, we see the landing page. The landing page screenshot is as follows:

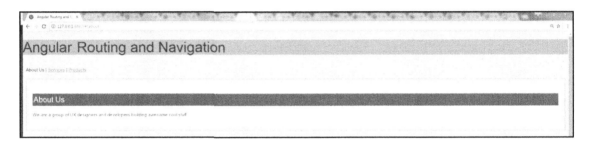

Landing page

Now let's click on the **Services** link. The `routerLink/services` will be activated, and the following screen should be displayed:

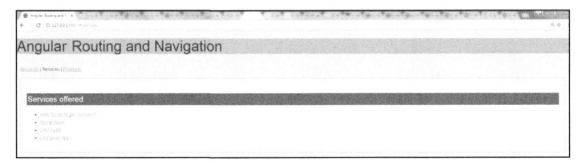

Services page.

Alright, now we are in the **Services** page. Now, click on the child component, **Web Technology Services**. The following screen should be displayed:

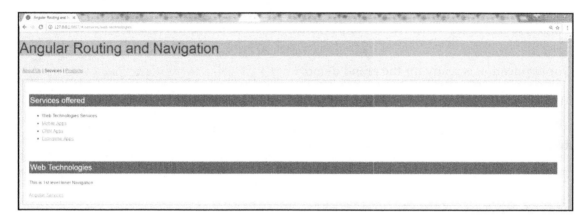

Services child page--Web Technologies.

Things are shaping up really well here.

We are now already in the child component--**Web Technology Services**, and now we click one more level down. Let's click on **Angular2 Services**. The following screen should be displayed:

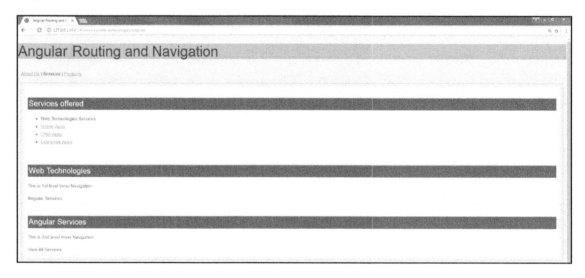

Web Technologies inner child route--Angular2.

Okay, now click on the **Products** link. The following screenshot should be displayed:

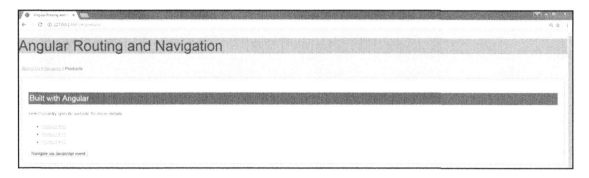

Products page.

Alight, now we are in the **Products** page. Now, click on the **All** products link and navigate to the **Services** page.
However, the navigation happened using the JavaScript event and not the `routerLink`.

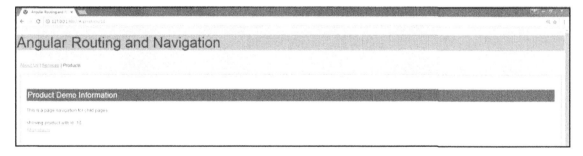

Product details page.

Summary

Angular routing is one of the core functionalities of any web application. In this chapter, we discussed, designed, and implemented our Angular routing in detail. We also discussed how to implement and enable `RouterModule.forRoot`. Additionally, we defined Router Outlet and `routerLink` directive to bind the route path and enabled `RouterLinkActivated` to find the current active state.

We focused on how route state works, and understood and implemented Route Lifecycle Hooks. We outlined how to create custom component routes and child routes and how to implement location strategy for our web applications. Finally, we created a sample application implementing routes and navigation.

In the next chapter, you will learn about creating directives and implementing change detection. You will also learn about directives, different types of directives provided by Angular, and also create custom user-defined directives.

You will deep dive into learning how Angular handles the change detection and how we can utilize change detection in our apps.

6
Creating Directives and Implementing Change Detection

In this chapter, we will learn and understand all about Angular Directives and change detection.

We will learn about different types of directives provided by Angular and also create some custom user-defined directives. We will deep dive into learning how Angular handles the change detection and how we can utilize change detection in our apps.

At the end of this chapter, you will be able to do the following things:

- Understand Angular Directives
- Understand and implement built-in Component Directives
- Understand and implement built-in Structural Directives
- Understand and implement built-in Attribute Directives
- Create custom-defined Attribute Directives
- Understand how change detection works in Angular

Angular Directives

Directives allows us to extend the behavior of the elements. We can manipulate the **Document Object Model** (**DOM**) of a HTML page using the different types of directive definitions.

Angular uses the `@Directive` metadata to tell the application about the type of directives they have and the functional capabilities defined with each directive.

The following diagram shows the different types of directives:

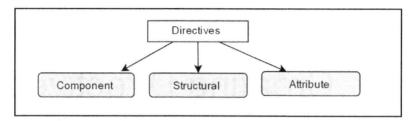

There are mainly three types of Angular Directives:

- **Component Directives**: We can define these as user-defined directives, similar to custom directives in Angular 1.x
- **Structural Directives**: Directives that alter or transform the DOM elements (one or more) on the fly
- **Attribute Directives**: Directives that extend the behavior or look and feel of an element

 In Angular 1.x, we had the A (Attribute), E (Element), C (Class), M (Matches comment) directives.

Angular comes with a lot of built-in directives, which we will be categorized in the preceding mentioned categories.

 Angular uses directives that use `ng`, hence avoid using `ng` along with custom-defined directives; it may lead to unknown issues. For example, `ng-changeColor` is an instance of bad styling.

Component Directives

Component Directives are user-defined directives to extend the functionality and create small reusable functionalities.

Think of Component Directives as directives that have a template attached to them since Components Directives have their own view or template defined with them.

In previous chapters, we have created many components. If you have mastered the art of creating components and using them in our layouts, you will already know how to create Component Directives.

A quick recap on Angular components: components are small reusable pieces of code that we can use in throughout our applications.

In the following code snippet, we will see the basic syntax of the component. Create a file named `my-template.component.ts`:

```
import {Component} from "@angular/core";

@Component({
 selector: 'my-app',
 template: `<h2>{{ title }}</h2>`
})

export class MyTemplateComponent {
 title = 'Learning Angular!!!'
}
```

Import the newly created component:

```
import {MyTemplate} from "./my-app.component"
```

Then, call the Component Directive in our `index.html` file:

```
<my-app>Loading...</my-app>
```

The following is the simplest and easiest component example you will have seen; it's as simple as this:

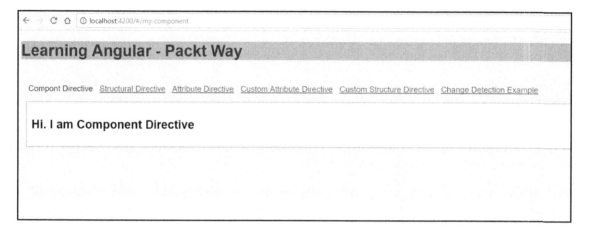

So, whatever components we have created so far are all Component Directives. If you want to deep dive into learning more and creating components, refer to `Chapter 4`, Working with Components.

Structural Directives

As the name mentions, Structural Directives alter the DOM structure by adding, appending, or removing DOM elements on the fly.

Angular Structural Directives are displayed with an (*) asterisk symbol before the directive name.

Some of the commonly used Structural Directives are as follows:

- `ngFor`: Repeater directive generally used to loop through and display a list of elements.
- `ngIf`: Shows or hides DOM elements depending on the result of expression evaluation; the result is either true or false.
- `ngSwitch`: Returns if the match expression value matches the value of the switch expression. The result returned can be any value; a conditional check is done for matching values.

Only one Structural Directive is allowed per element.

Let's learn about each of these Structural Directives in detail and create few examples using them:

ngFor directive

The ngFor directive will help us iterate the items and append them to the list on the fly.

We need to declare an array in the StructureDirectiveComponent class, and then use ngFor to loop the values and display them in the template.

The list <li> elements get appended on the fly to the <ul> element.

The following is the component snippet for the ngFor directive usage:

```
import {Component} from '@angular/core';

@Component({
    selector: 'my-app',
    template: `

    <h4>{{title}}</h4>

    <strong>Using ngFor directive</strong>
    <ul>
<li *ngFor="let language of languages">{{ language.name }}</li>
</ul>
    `
  })
export class StructureDirectiveComponent {
  title = 'Structural Directives';

 public languages = [
   { name: "PHP"},
   { name: "JavaScript"},
   { name: "Ruby"},
   { name: "Java"},
   { name: "HTML5"}
];

}
```

The output of the preceding component is shown as follows:

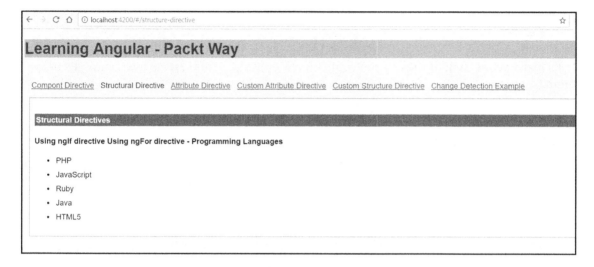

ngIf directive

The `ngIf` directive help us to evaluate the expression based on a condition very similar to the `if` statements in any programming language.

The general syntax is shown in the following code snippet :

```
<div *ngIf="!isLoggedIn">
  <p>Hello Guest user</p>
</div>
```

The preceding code snippet has a `*ngIf` condition; if `isLoggedIn` is `true`, the directive will render the statement inside; otherwise, it will skip and continue.

Let's create an example using both the `*ngFor` and `*ngIf` statements as shown in the following code:

```
import {Component} from '@angular/core';

@Component({
  selector: 'my-app',
  template: `
    <h4>{{title}}</h4>
    <strong>Using ngIf directive</strong>
    <div *ngIf="isLoggedIn">
```

```
        <p>Hello Packt Author</p>
    </div>

  <div *ngIf="!isLoggedIn">
      <p>Hello Guest user</p>
  </div>
  <strong>Using ngFor directive - Programming Languages </strong>

  <ul>
    <li *ngFor="let language of languages">{{ language.name }}</li>
  </ul>
`
})

export class StructureDirectiveComponent {
 title = 'Structural Directives';
 isLoggedIn= true;

 public languages = [
  { name: "PHP"},
  { name: "JavaScript"},
  { name: "Ruby"},
  { name: "Java"},
  { name: "HTML5"}
];

}
```

Let's analyze the preceding code snippet in detail:

1. We used *ngFor and *ngIf in the view template.
2. In the component class, we define a isLoggedIn variable with Boolean values.
3. We create an array of teams having team names in the list, which we will iterate and display in the view.

Run the app, and we should see output as shown in the following screenshot:

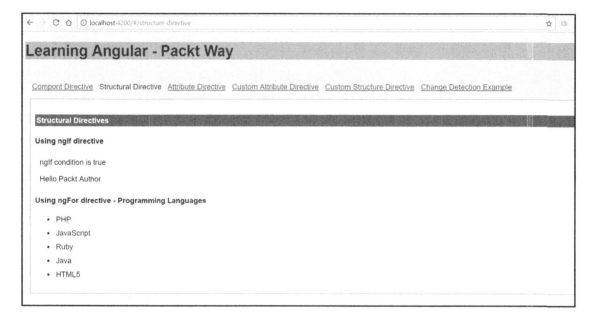

ngSwitch directive

When we have to evaluate the expression based on multiple values, we make use of `ngSwitch`. An example of `ngSwitch` is shown in the following code snippet:

```
<div [ngSwitch]="taxRate">
  <p *ngSwitchCase="'state'">State Tax</p>
  <p *ngSwitchCase="'fedral'">Fedral Tax</p>
  <p *ngSwitchCase="'medical'">Medical Tax</p>
  <p *ngSwitchDefault>Default</p>
</div>
```

Based on the value of `taxRate`, our application will decide which element to display. Let's update our example and add an `*ngSwitch` statement.

The updated example code is given as follows:

```
import {Component} from "@angular/core";
@Component({
    selector: 'structure-directive',
    templateUrl: 'structure-directive.component.html'
})

export class StructureDirectiveComponent {
 title = 'Structural Directives';

 username = "Sridhar Rao";
 taxRate = "state";
 isLoggedIn= true;

 public languages = [
   { name:  "PHP"},
   { name:  "JavaScript"},
   { name:  "Ruby"},
   { name:  "Java"},
   { name:  "HTML5"}
 ];
}
```

The output of the preceding code example is as follows:

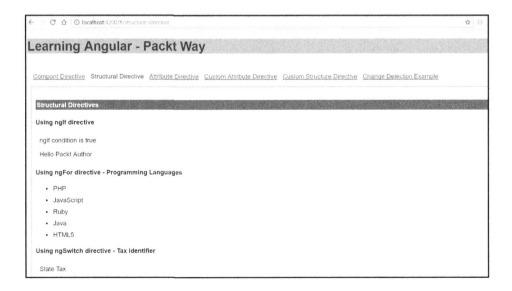

Attribute Directives

Attribute Directives extend the behavior or the look and feel of a given element. Attribute Directives are very similar to HTML attributes defined along with the element.

Attribute Directives can be of two types:

- Built-in Attribute Directive
- Custom or user-defined Attributes Directive

Let's now look at them in detail in the following sections.

Built-in Attribute Directives

As mentioned before, attributes are properties of the elements in the page. Some of the examples of the attributes for HTML elements are class, style, and so on.

Similarly Angular provides several built-in Attribute Directives. The directives include `ngModel`, `ngClass`, `ngStyle`, and so on.

Let's learn about each of these Attribute Directives by creating few examples that are shown as follows for your reference:

- `ngModel`: Using `ngModel`, we can implement a Two-way Data Binding. For learning more about Data Binding and Template Syntax, please refer to `Chapter 8`, *Template and Data Binding Syntax*.

  The `ngModel` directive is written inside a square with the parentheses of event binding `[()]`.

 Remember to import the forms Module from Angular forms or else you will get error messages.

  An example of the `ngModel` Attribute Directive is as follows:

```
<input [(ngModel)]="username">
<p>Hello {{username}}!</p>
```

- ngClass: When we want to add or remove any CSS class to a DOM element, it's preferred that we use the ngClass Attribute Directive. We can assign class names in different ways to ngClass.

    We can assign class names using a string, or an object or a component method

    An example of the ngClass Attribute Directive is as follows:

    ```
    //passing string to assign class name
    <p [ngClass]="'warning'" >Sample warning message</p>

    //passing array to assign class name
    <p [ngClass]="['error', 'success']" > Message </p>

    //Passing object to assign class name
    <p [ngClass]="{'error': true, 'success': false }"> Message</p>

    //Passing component method to assign class name
    <p [ngClass]="getClassName('error')"> </p>
    ```

> Remember to wrap the name of CSS class in a single quote; otherwise, you won't see the styling.
> Remember to include the style sheet either in index.html or in your respective component.

- ngStyle: When we want to manipulate a few style properties of any DOM element, we can use ngStyle. You can relate this to inline styling in the CSS world.

    An example of an ngStyle Attribute Directive is as follows:

    ```
    <p [ngStyle]="{ 'font-size': '13px', 'background-color':'#c5e1a5'}"
    >Sample success message</p>
    ```

Alright, now that we learned about our built-in Attribute Directives, let's put them all together in an example.

The following is a code example using ngModel, ngClass, and ngStyle:

```
import { Component} from '@angular/core';

@Component({
 selector: 'my-app',
 styleUrls: ['./attribute-directive.component.css'],
 template:`
```

```
<h4>Welcome to Built-In {{title}}</h4>

<strong>using ngModel</strong>
<div><label for="username">Enter username</label>
<input type="text" [(ngModel)]="username" placeholder="enter username"
    id="username">
<p>username is: {{username}}</p>
</div>

<strong>Notification example using ngStyle</strong>
 <p [ngStyle]="{ 'font-size': '13px', 'background-color':'#c5e1a5'}"
>Sample success message</p>

<strong>Notification example using ngClass</strong>
    <p [ngClass]="'warning'" >Sample warning message</p>
    <p [ngClass]="'error'" >Sample error message</p>

})
export class AttributeDirectiveComponent {
 title = 'Attribute Directive';
 public username="Packt Author";
}
```

Take a look at the following screenshot with the output of the preceding code example:

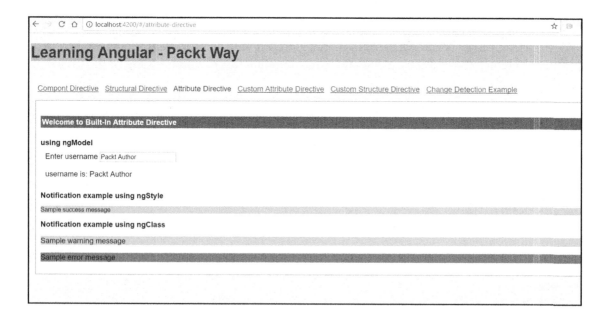

Creating custom directives - Structural and Attribute Directives

So far in previous sections, we have learned about and implemented built-in directives provided by Angular.

By creating custom user-defined directives, Angular allows us to define and extend the behavior and functionality of the elements in the page.

To create custom directives, we have to use the `@Directive` decorator and implement the logic in the class definition.

We can create custom Component, Structural, and Attribute Directives.

Any user-defined HTML tag is a component attribute (for example, `<my-app>`). We have been creating custom components all along, throughout each chapter of the book.

Angular CLI - generating the directives

We will use the Angular CLI tool to generate directives for our examples.

Navigate to the project directory and run the following `ng` command:

```
ng generate directive highlightDirective
```

We should see the output as shown in the following screenshot:

As you can see in the preceding screenshot, the newly generated directive `highlightDirective` is created and the `app.module.ts` file is updated.

Before we go ahead with implementing our directives, here's a quick recap of the Structural and Attribute Directives:

- **Structural Directive**: As the name suggests, the structural attribute affects the structure of the HTML layout since it shapes or reshapes the DOM structure. It can affect one or more elements in the page.
- **Attribute Directive**: Defines and extends the appearance or behavior of an element in the page.

We learned to generate custom directives using Angular CLI and now we clearly know what and how Structural and Attribute Directives work.

It's time to create our own custom directives. Read on.

Creating custom Attribute Directives

We will start by creating custom Attribute Directives. We will continue with the example `highlightDirective` we created in the preceding section.

As the name suggests, we will use this directive to highlight the changed text color of elements attached to this attribute.

It's time to define the functionality and behavior of our directive, `highlightDirective`.

In the `highlight-directive.ts` file, add the following lines of the code:

```
import { Directive, ElementRef } from '@angular/core';

@Directive({
  selector: '[appHighlightDirective]'
})
export class HighlightDirectiveDirective{

  constructor(private elRef: ElementRef) {
    this.elRef.nativeElement.style.color = 'orange';
  }
}
```

Let's analyze the preceding code snippet in detail:

1. We need to import the required utilities provided by Angular for working with directives.
2. We will import `Directive`, `ElementRef`, and `AfterViewInit` from `@angular/core`.

3. As mentioned earlier, we define a directive using the `@Directive` decorator and passing the name `appHighlightDirective` in the metadata selector.

4. We are exporting the `appHighlightDirective` class.

5. As mentioned earlier, the Attribute Directive is specific to an element and hence we need to create an instance of the `ElementRef` variable, `elRef`, which we will use to target and update the element attached to our custom directive.

6. In the `constructor` we are targeting the specific element by using the `nativeElement` method and updating the `style` property `color` with a value, `orange`.

Now that we have created our directive, we need to apply it to the element in the app component template `app.component.html` file:

```
<div appHighlightDirective> Custom Directive </div>
```

Now run the application and we should see the output as shown in the following screenshot:

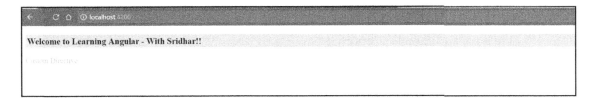

See how easy and simple it is to create a custom Attribute Directive.

If you notice carefully, it's a very basic attribute which changes the color of the text. Now what if we want to pass the value of the color dynamically instead of a statically?

We have to enable our attribute to pass values as well. Let's see what changes we need to make our directive a more suitable candidate.

Let's first edit in our component `app.component.html` template where we want to use the attribute:

```
<div appHighlightDirective highlightColor="green">Custom
    Directive</div>
```

You will see, we are now passing a value `green` through the `highlightColor` variable for our attribute `appHighlightDirective`.

Now update our `highlight-directive.ts` file and add the following lines of code to it:

```
import { Directive, ElementRef, Input, AfterViewInit } from
'@angular/core';

@Directive({
 selector: '[appHighlightDirective]'
})
export class HighlightDirectiveDirective{

 @Input() highlightColor : string;

 constructor(private elRef: ElementRef) {
   this.elRef.nativeElement.style.color = 'orange';
 }

 ngAfterViewInit(): void {
   this.elRef.nativeElement.style.color = this.highlightColor;
 }
}
```

Let's see the changes we have done in the `highlight-directive.ts` file:

1. We have additionally imported `Input` and `AfterViewInit` modules from the `@angular/core` library.
2. We are using the `@Input` decorator to tell Angular that we want the value to be passed dynamically through the variable defined as `highlightColor`.
3. In the `ngAfterViewInit` method we are creating an object instance of the element using the `ElementRef` instance, `elRef`, and using the `nativeElement` method to update the `style` property `color` of the element.
4. The `color` of the text changes to the value passed through the element's `appHighlightDirective` attribute's value passed through `highlightColor`.

Run the application and we should see the output as shown in the following screenshot:

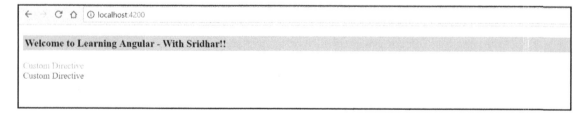

Alright, so far so good. Our attribute is rather shaping up really well.

Let's see the progress you have made so far in implementing our custom directive:

- We have created a custom Attribute Directive, `highlightDirective`
- We learned to pass values to the custom Attribute Directive using the `highlightColor` variable

This is good stuff. But what if we want to bind `Javascript` events such as `mouseover`, `mouseout`, `click`, or so on, to our attribute?

Let's make the necessary changes needed to implement events attached to our attribute. For this we will need a beautiful image and we will attach a few events along with custom Attribute Directive.

Let's add an image to the component `app.component.html` file template:

```
<img [src]="imageUrl" width="100" height="100" appHighlightDirective
    showOpacity="0.5" hideOpacity="1">
```

Important notes on the preceding code snippet:

1. We have added our custom attribute component, `appHighlightDirective`, to the element.
2. Additionally, we have added two attributes, `showOpacity` and `hideOpacity`, which will have the style property of opacity to the element.
3. We will attach `onmouseover` and `onmouseout` events to these attributes and will change the opacity of the image dynamically.

Now that we have added an image to the component view template, the updated output looks like the following screenshot:

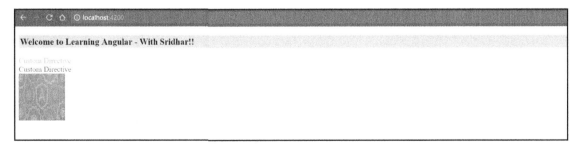

Let's move over to the custom directive `highlight-directive.directive.ts` file:

```
import { Directive, ElementRef, Input, HostListener, AfterViewInit }
  from '@angular/core';

@Directive({
 selector: '[appHighlightDirective]'
})
export class HighlightDirectiveDirective{
 @Input() highlightColor : string;
 @Input() showOpacity : string;
 @Input() hideOpacity : string;

 constructor(private elRef: ElementRef) {
   this.elRef.nativeElement.style.color = 'orange';
 }
 ngAfterViewInit(): void {
   this.elRef.nativeElement.style.color = this.highlightColor;
 }

@HostListener('mouseover') onmouseover() {
  this.elRef.nativeElement.style.opacity = this.hideOpacity;
 }

@HostListener('mouseout') onmouseout() {
  this.elRef.nativeElement.style.opacity = this.showOpacity;
 }
}
```

Let's analyze the updates we have done to the file in the preceding code:

1. We are importing the required modules `Directive`, `ElementRef`, `Input`, `HostListener`, and `AfterViewInit` from `@angular/core`.

2. Note that for binding and implementing events to elements, we especially need to import `HostListener`.

3. Using the `@HostListener` decorator, we are binding the `mouseover` and `mouseout` events to the element we are attaching the custom attribute.

4. Note that when we use `this.elRef.nativeElement`, we are referring to the element which has the custom attribute attached to it.

5. We are assigning the value of the `this.hideOpacity` variable when the user takes the mouse over the element.

6. We are assigning the value of the `this.showOpacity` variable when the user takes the mouse out of the element.

Now run the application and you should see the output as shown in the following screenshot:

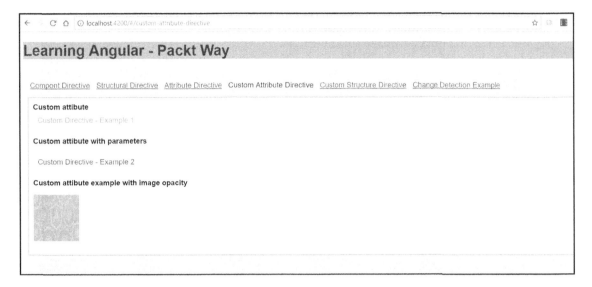

Awesome. Now let's see the progress you have made so far in implementing our custom directive:

- We have created a custom Attribute Directive, `highlightDirective`
- We learned to pass values to the custom Attribute Directive using the `highlightColor` variable
- We have learned to attach events such `mouseover` and `mouseout` to our custom attribute, `highlightDirective`

In this section, you have learned to create and use a custom Attribute Directive having attributes and methods attached to the directive.

In next section, you will learn to create custom Structural Directives.

Creating custom Structural Directives

So far you have learned and implemented built-in directives--Component, Structural, and Attribute Directives.

We also learned to generate custom directives using Angular CLI in the section *Angular CLI - generating the directives.*

In previous section, we learned and implemented custom Attribute Directives. In this section, we will learn to create Structural Directives.

Let's create a new directive using Angular CLI:

```
ng generate directive custom-structural
```

You should see the output of the preceding command as shown in the following screenshot:

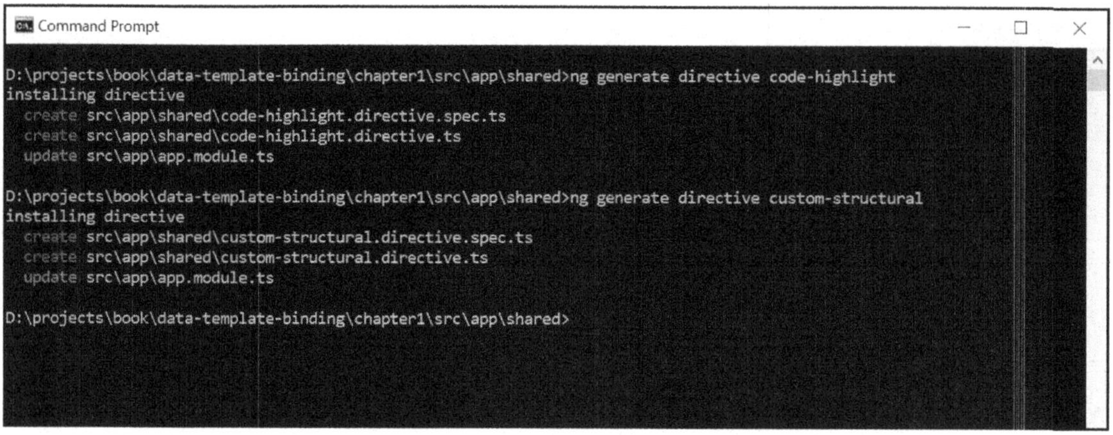

Run the preceding ng command and we should see the directive created and the app.module.ts is updated with the newly created directive.

Alright, time to create and implement our custom Structural Directive. Here's the use case we will build using our custom Structural Directive:

1. We will use our Structural Directive to loop through a list of products.
2. The directive should display elements only which have isAvailable set to true.

First let's define our products JSON in the app.component.ts file:

```
public products = [{
 productName: 'Shoes',
 isAvailable : true
 },
 {
 productName: 'Belts',
 isAvailable : true
 },
 {
```

```
productName: 'Watches',
isAvailable : false
}]
```

We just created a JSON list of products with the keys `productName` and `isAvailable`.

Nothing super-heroic, not just yet!

It's time to use the `*ngFor` loop and display the list of products in `app.component.html` file:

```
<ul *ngFor="let product of products">
  <li *appCustomStructural="product">{{product.productName}}</li>
</ul>
```

Let's quickly analyze the preceding code

1. We are using a built-in Structural Directive, `*ngFor`, for looping through the product list and displaying the name using the key `product.productName`.
2. We are defining our custom Structural Directive, `appCustomStructural`, and passing the `product` object for analysis.
3. Since we are passing the entire product object to our attribute, we can now define our custom logic in `appCustomStructural` and do transformations based on our application needs.

Time for some super-heroic work in our directive `custom-structural.directive.ts` file:

```
import { Directive, Input, TemplateRef, ViewContainerRef, AfterViewInit
     } from '@angular/core';

@Directive({
 selector: '[appCustomStructural]'
})
export class CustomStructuralDirective {
 @Input()
 set appCustomStructural(product){
  if(product.isAvailable == true)
  {
    this.viewContainerRef.createEmbeddedView(this.templateRef );
  }
 }

 constructor(
   private templateRef : TemplateRef<any>,
   private viewContainerRef : ViewContainerRef
```

```
    ) { }
}
```

Let's analyze in detail the preceding code:

1. We are importing the required modules `Directive`, `Input`, `TemplateRef`, `ViewContainerRef`, and `AfterViewInit` from `@angular/core`.

2. We are defining the CSS `selector` for our custom Structural Directive, `appCustomStructural`.

3. By using the `@Input` decorator, we are explicitly telling Angular that our custom directive will get input through `appCustomStructural`.

4. In the constructor, we are injecting the instances of `TemplateRef<any>` and `ViewContainerRef`.

5. Using `TemplateRef<any>`, we are mentioning that it's an embedded template that can be used to instantiate embedded views.

6. Since Structural Directives involve the shaping or reshaping of the DOM structure in the page, we are injecting `ViewContainerRef`.

7. We are checking if the value of `product.isAvailable` is equal to `true`.

8. If the value of `product.isAvailable` is true using the instance of `ViewContainerRef`--a container where one or more views can be attached, by using the method `createEmbeddedView`--we are appending the element to the view.

Run the application and we should see the output as shown in the following screenshot:

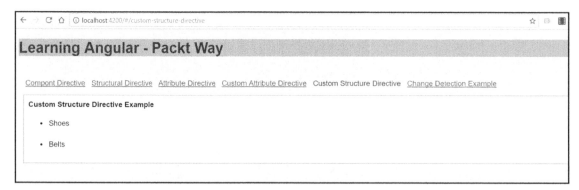

We see only **Shoes** and **Belts** being displayed since only those products have the `isAvailable` key set to true. Try changing the values of other products too and see the output display.

In this section, we have learned about the custom Structural Directive. We learned about important utilities provided by Angular--`createEmbeddedView`, `ViewContainerRef`, and `TemplateRef`.

A quick summary of things we have learned and implemented so far for our custom directives follows.

We have created a custom Attribute Directive, `highlightDirective`. We learned to pass values to the custom Attribute Directive using the `highlightColor` variable. We have learned to attach events such as `mouseover` and `mouseout` to our custom attribute `highlightDirective`.

We have learned to create a custom Structural Directive `appCustomStructural`. We have learned to use `createEmbeddedView`, `ViewContainerRef`, and `TemplateRef`.

In the next section, we will learn about change detection, an important aspect of how Angular framework works internally, and also learn to use it for our applications as well.

Implementing change detection in Angular

Change detection is the process of detecting any internal state changes in a model or component class and then reflect them back to the view, mainly by manipulating DOM.

Change detection is one of the most important changes from Angular 1.x to 2.

The application state changes happen either from model to view or vice versa. To understand better, take a look at the following diagram:

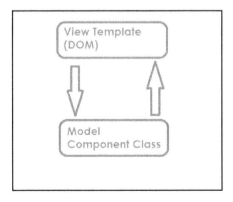

Application state changes can happen in two ways:

- From Model to View Template (DOM)
- From View (DOM) to Model (Component Class)

Now that we know that state changes happen either in a model or in DOM, let's analyze what triggers change detection.

Change detection is triggered by the following:

- JavaScript events (`click`, `mouseover`, `keyup`, and so on)
- `setTimeout()` and `setInterval()`
- Asynchronous requests

 Note that all the preceding three listed ways are async processes. So it's safe to say that in Angular, change detection happens whenever we have async methods/requests in place.

Before we jump into understanding more on change detection--how it works, how it's handled, and so on--let's quickly create an example to understand what triggers change detection.

Take a look at the following code snippet:

```
import { Component} from '@angular/core';
@Component({
  selector: 'my-app',
  template:`
  <h4>Learning Angular {{title}}</h4>

  <button (click)="toggleUser()"> Toggle User </button>
  <div *ngIf="isLoggedIn">
    <b>Hello Packt Author</b>
  </div>

  <div *ngIf="!isLoggedIn">
    <b>Hello Guest user</b>
  </div>

  ]
})
export class AppComponent {
 title = 'Change Detection';
 isLoggedIn = true;
```

```
toggleUser(){
if (this.isLoggedIn)
  this.isLoggedIn = false
else
  this.isLoggedIn = true
}
}
```

The preceding code snippet can be explained as follows:

1. We created a button with a click event calling the `toggleUser` method.
2. On the click event on `toggleUser`, the variable `isLoggedIn` value is set either to `true` or `false`.
3. Based on the variable, the value of `isLoggedIn` in the view is updated. If the value is `true`, **Hello Packt Author** is displayed, and if the value is false, `Hello Guest user` is displayed.

In the next section, we will learn about how Angular handles change detection internally and the utilities provided by Angular to help us implement better change detection.

Change detection - Angular and ZoneJS

The official site of ZoneJS describes the library as follows:

A Zone is an execution context that persists across async tasks.

Angular uses ZoneJS for detecting changes and then calls the listener methods of those events.

Angular takes advantage of zones to handle all the internal state changes and change detection. Zones understand the context of the asynchronous actions and state changes.

Angular has a built-in `ngZone`, which tracks all the completed asynchronous actions and notifies them with a `onTurnDone` event. Every component gets a change detector, which keeps track of all the bindings attached to the component in a tree structure.

We don't have `$scope.apply` or `$digest` like in the previous version of Angular.

By default, Angular change detection will always check whether the values have changed. Change detection is always performed the same from the top root component to the inner components in a tree structure.

This is done for all components through change detector objects.

Using `ngZones`, the performance of the Angular applications has increased drastically.

Change detection strategy

By default, Angular defines a change detection strategy for every component in our application--which means every time there is any change in our template, it traverses down to the last component in a tree structure check for any changes and makes the necessary updates.

This takes a performance hit!

Hence, Angular provides us with options to define explicitly which change detection strategy we want to implement for our components.

Angular provides a `ChangeDetectionStrategy` module by which we can define the change detection strategy we want to use.

There are two different values `ChangeDetectionStrategy` takes:

- `Default`
- `OnPush`

Let's analyze each of these options in detail to understand how each of these work.

ChangeDetectionStrategy - Default

This is the default mechanism that Angular implements--changes are triggered by events and the propagation of changes goes from the view template to the model. Based on the logic implemented, the DOM structure is updated.

An important thing to note here is that using this strategy, every time Angular will traverse through all the components starting from the root component to the last component for checking if the properties have to be updated throughout.

Refer the example we created in preceding section, *Implementing change detection in Angular*. We are updating the properties and Angular by default uses the `ChangeDetectionStrategy` with the `Default` value.

ChangeDetectionStrategy - OnPush

We use OnPush to improve the performance of our Angular applications. We have to explicitly mention that we want to use the OnPush value for ChangeDetectionStrategy.

Changes are triggered by events and the propagation of changes goes for the entire object that is rendered in the view template and not for each property.

When we use the OnPush value, we are forcing Angular to depend only on the inputs. We pass the objects through the @Input decorator and only the complete object and it's properties will be affected and not any individual property changed.

Advantages of ChangeDetectionStrategy - OnPush

In previous section you have learned about ChangeDetectionStrategy using both default and OnPush options.

Some of the advantages of using OnPush option over default are given:

1. It helps in increasing the performance of our Angular applications.
2. Angular doesn't have to traverse the entire component tree structure for detecting individual changes on properties.
3. Angular internally can skip the nested tree structures when inputted properties don't change.

To understand it better, let's create a use case. For that first we need to create a new component named change-detect using Angular CLI ng command.

Once the component is created, you should see the output as shown in the following screenshot:

```
Command Prompt                                                    —    □    ×
  create src\app\change-detect\change-detect.component.ts
  update src\app\app.module.ts

D:\projects\book\data-template-binding\chapter1\src\app>ng generate component change-detect
installing component
  create src\app\change-detect\change-detect.component.css
  create src\app\change-detect\change-detect.component.html
  create src\app\change-detect\change-detect.component.spec.ts
  create src\app\change-detect\change-detect.component.ts
  update src\app\app.module.ts

D:\projects\book\data-template-binding\chapter1\src\app>
```

Let's create a `class` user and with properties `userName` and `userId` in the `user.ts` file:

```
export class User {
 constructor(
 public userName: string,
 public userId: number) {}
}
```

Now let's edit the `Component` class we generated and add the following lines of code snippet:

```
import { Component, Input, ChangeDetectionStrategy  } from '@angular/core';
import { User } from '../shared/user';

@Component({
 selector: 'app-change-detect',
 template: `
 <h3>{{ title }}</h3>
 <p>
 <label>User:</label>
 <span>{{user.userName}} {{user.userId}}</span>
 </p>`,
 changeDetection: ChangeDetectionStrategy.OnPush,
 styleUrls: ['./change-detect.component.css']
})

export class ChangeDetectComponent{
 title = "Change Detection";
 @Input() user: User;
 constructor() { }
}
```

Let's analyze the preceding code in detail:

1. We are importing the required modules from `Input`, `Component`, and `ChangeDetectionStrategy` from the `@angular/core` library.
2. We are importing the newly created `User` class into the component class.
3. We are explicitly mentioning the value for `changeDetection` as `ChangeDetectionStrategy.OnPush`.
4. We are using the CSS `selector`; `app-change-detect` where we will display the output of the component.

5. Since we are telling Angular to use the `OnPush` option, we need to use `@Input` and pass object that is in our case `User`.

6. As per the template part, we are binding the user properties, `userName` and `userId`, in the `view` template.

Great. So far we have created our component and have explicitly mentioned that whenever a change is detected, the entire object that is the `user` object should be updated and not just an individual property.

Now it's time to create methods to test our logic. So an in the `AppComponent` class, add the following code:

```
changeDetectionDefault(): void {
  this.user.userName = 'Packt Publications';
  this.user.userId = 10;
}

changeDetectionOnPush(): void {
  this.user = new User('Mike', 10);
}
```

For our component, we have mentioned the `selector` to be used as `app-change-detect`. We need to use the component inside the template `app.component.html` file.

We have also mentioned that the component takes the input as `user`; hence we are passing the user object to the component.

Add the following lines of code to the `app.component.html` template file with the component `app-change-detect`.

```
<button type="button" (click)="changeDetectionDefault()">
  Change Detection: Default
</button>
<button type="button" (click)="changeDetectionOnPush()">
Change Detection: OnPush
</button>

<app-change-detect [user]="user"></app-change-detect>
```

Alright, we are all set. Run the app and you should see the output as shown in the following screenshot:

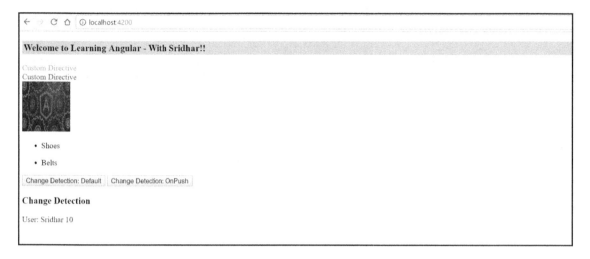

The application functionality can be summarized as follows:

1. The `app-change-detect` component is loaded into `AppComponent` template.
2. The default values passed for the object are displayed in the `view` template.
3. Click on the `Change Detection: OnPush` button and we see the updated user loaded in the view.
4. When we click on `Change Detection: Default`, unlike the previous examples we have created, we don't see any changes happening to the properties. It's because we have explicitly mentioned that any change detection should be passed through objects and not properties using the `OnPush` option of `ChangeDetectionStrategy`.

In this section, we have learned about change detection strategies provided by Angular. We have explored how we can improve the performance of our applications by using the `OnPush` option by forcing Angular to only check for objects passed as inputs and not individual properties.

Updating properties will tell Angular to traverse through the entire application component tree structure and it takes a hit on performance.

Summary

In this chapter, we learned about directives and also about different types of directives, namely Component Directives, Structural Directives, and Attribute Directives.

We implemented custom user-defined directives to understand how we can extend directives and use them more effectively.

We learned briefly about ZoneJS, and how zones can help us to handle the `async` tasks in modern applications frameworks.

Finally, we learned how Angular handles changes detection and how we can use change detection methods to improve the overall application performance.

In the next chapter, we will learn about asynchronous programming using Observables. In this chapter, we will learn how to take advantage of asynchronous programming with Angular by using Observable and Promises.

In addition, we will learn how to built a basic, yet extensible asynchronous JSON API for querying the Marvel Cinematic Universe.

7
Asynchronous Programming Using Observables

If we think about it, nothing is instantaneous. Real time is not a thing. Did I lose my mind for a second there? Now, you can push a button and feel like it's instantaneous, but, the programmer in you knows that it's not. Information has been transferred, code executed, databases fetched, and so on. During this time, as short or as long as it might be, you have waited. More precisely, your code has made your users wait. Wouldn't you rather have a code base built around this very notion of asynchronism and which can execute other things while it waits, or, at least, warn your users that we are waiting for something to happen? This is the idea on which this chapter is based. This chapter helps you to understand the concept of asynchronous programming and implementing the same using Observable in Angular.

In this chapter, we will cover the following topics:

- Observer patterns
- Asynchronous programming
- HTTP client
- Subscribing to Observables
- Promises

Observer patterns

The Observable pattern is one that allows an object, called **subject**, to keep track of other objects, called **observers**, interested in the subject state. When the subject state changes, it notifies its observers about it. The mechanics behind this are really simple.

TypeScript Observable

Let's take a look at the following Observer/Subject implementation in pure TypeScript (that is no Angular or framework of any kind, just TypeScript).

First, I defined an Observer interface that any concrete implementation will have to implement:

```
export interface Observer{
    notify();
}
```

This interface only defines the notify() method. This method will be called by the subject (that is the Object being observed by Observer) when its state changes.

Then, I have an implementation of this interface, named HumanObserver:

```
export class HumanObserver implements Observer{
    constructor(private name:string){}
    notify(){
            console.log(this.name, 'Notified');
    }
}
```

This implementation leverages the typescript property constructor, where you can define the property of your class inside the constructor. This notation is one hundred percent equivalent to the following, while being shorter:

```
private name: string;
constructor(name:string){
        this.name = name;
}
```

Following the definitions of the `Observer` interface and `HumanObserver`, we can move on to the subject. I defined a `Subject` class that manages `observers`. This class has three methods: `attachObserver`, `detachObserver`, and `notifyObservers`:

```
export class Subject{
   private observers:Observer[] = [];
   /**
   * Adding an observer to the list of observers
   */
   attachObserver(observer:Observer):void{
               this.observers.push(observer);
   }
   /**
   * Detaching an observer
   */
   detachObserver(observer:Observer):void{
      let index:number = this.observers.indexOf(observer);
      if(index > -1){
          this.observers.splice(index, 1);
        }
      else{
       throw "Unknown observer";
        }
   }
   /**
   * Notify all the observers in this.observers
   */
   protected notifyObservers(){
   for (var i = 0; i < this.observers.length; ++i) {
      this.observers[i].notify();
         }
      }
   }
```

The `attachObserver` method pushes new observers into the observer's property, while the `detachObserver` removes them.

Subject implementations are often found with attach/detach, subscribe/unsubscribe, or add/delete prefixes.

The last method is notifyObservers, which iterates over the observers and invokes their notify() method. The last class allowing us to showcase the Observable mechanic is IMDB, which extends Subject. It will notify observers when a movie gets added:

```
export class IMDB extends Subject{
    private movies:string[] = [];
    public addMovie(movie:string){
        this.movies.push(movie);
        this.notifyObservers();
    }
}
```

To make the pieces communicate with each other, we have to:

- Create a Subject
- Create an Observer
- Attach the Observer to the Subject
- Change the state of the Subject via the addMovie method

More concretely, here's an implementation of the previous list:

```
let imdb:IMDB = new IMDB();
let mathieu:HumanObserver = new HumanObserver("Mathieu");
imbd.attachObserver(mathieu);
imbd.addMovie("Jaws");
```

To speed up our development process, we will install ts-node. This node package will transpile typescript files into JavaScript and resolve the dependencies between those files.

To quickly compile and execute typescript application, I recommend the excellent ts-node package. This package will transpile the following commands:

```
$ npm install -g typescript ts-node
$ ts-node myFile.ts
```

The output is Mathieu Notified. We can test to detach mathieu and add another movie:

```
imdb.detachObserver(mathieu);
imdb.addMovie("Die Hard");
```

The output is still `Mathieu Notified`, which happens after we add the Jaws movie. The second movie addition (that is Die Hard) doesn't trigger a `Mathieu Notified` print to the console, as it has been detached.

TypeScript Observable with parameters

So, this is a basic implementation of the observer pattern. Nevertheless, it is not full-fledged, as `HumanObserver` only knows that something has changed in one of the subjects it observes. Consequently, it has to iterate over all of the subjects it observes and check their previous state against their current state to identify what has changed and where. A better way to go about this would be to modify the notify of `Observer`, so it contains more information. For example, we could add optional parameters, as follows:

```
export interface Observer{
    notify(value?:any, subject?:Subject);
}
export class HumanObserver implements Observer{
    constructor(private name:string){}
    notify(value?:any, subject?:Subject){
        console.log(this.name, 'received', value, 'from', subject);
    }
}
```

The `notify()` method now accepts an optional value parameter which characterizes the new state of the `Subject` object. We can also receive a reference to the `Subject` object itself. This is useful in case the observer observes many subjects. In such a case, we need to be able to differentiate them.

Accordingly, we have to change `Subject` and `IMDB` a bit, so they use the new `notify`:

```
export class Subject{
    private observers:Observer[] = [];
    attachObserver(oberver:Observer):void{
        this.obervers.push(oberver);
    }
    detachObserver(observer:Observer):void{
        let index:number = this.obervers.indexOf(observer);
        if(index > -1){
        this.observers.splice(index, 1);
        }else{
        throw "Unknown observer";
        }
    }
    protected notifyObservers(value?:any){
```

```
            for (var i = 0; i < this.obervers.length; ++i) {
            this.observers[i].notify(value, this);
            }
    }
}
export class IMDB extends Subject{
    private movies:string[] = [];
    public addMovie(movie:string){
            this.movies.push(movie);
            this.notifyObservers(movie);
    }
}
```

Finally, the output is as follows:

```
Mathieu received Jaws from IMDB {
  observers: [ HumanObserver { name: 'Mathieu' } ],
  movies: [ 'Jaws' ] }
```

This is way more expressive than `Mathieu Notified`.

Now, when we are used to the `Observer` patterns for asynchronous programming, what we really mean is that we ask for something, and we do not want to wait to do anything during its processing. Instead, what we do is subscribe to the response event to be notified when the response comes.

In the next sections, we will use the same pattern and mechanisms with Angular2.

 The code for this observer implementation is at `http://bit.ly/masterin g-angular2-chap7-part1`.

Observing HTTP responses

In this section, we will build a JSON API returning movies according to search parameters. Instead of simply waiting for the HTTP query to complete, we will leverage the power of the observer design pattern to let the user know we are waiting and, if need be, execute other processes.

First things first: we need a data source for our IMDB--like application. Building and deploying a server-side application able to interpret an HTTP query and send the result accordingly is relatively simple nowadays. However, this falls outside the scope of this book. Instead, what we will do is fetch a static JSON file hosted at `http://bit.ly/masteri ng-angular2-marvel`. This file contains some of the latest movies of the Marvel Cinematic Universe. It contains a JSON array describing fourteen movies as JSON objects. Here is the first movie:

```
{
    "movie_id" : 1,
    "title" : "Iron Man",
    "phase" : "Phase One: Avengers Assembled",
    "category_name" : "Action",
    "release_year" : 2015,
    "running_time" : 126,
    "rating_name" : "PG-13",
    "disc_format_name" : "Blu-ray",
    "number_discs" : 1,
    "viewing_format_name" : "Widescreen",
    "aspect_ratio_name" : " 2.35:1",
    "status" : 1,
    "release_date" : "May 2, 2008",
    "budget" : "140,000,000",
    "gross" : "318,298,180",
    "time_stamp" : "2015-05-03"
},
```

You can find classical information that an IMDB-like application would provide, such as release year, running time, and so on. Our goal is to design an asynchronous JSON API, making each one of these fields searchable.

As we are fetching a static JSON file (that is we will not insert, update, or delete any elements), acceptable API calls would be the following:

```
IMDBAPI.fetchOneById(1);
IMDBAPI.fetchByFields(MovieFields.release_date, 2015);
```

The first call simply fetches the movie with `movie_id: 1`; the second call is a more generic one that works in any field. To prevent API consumer from requesting fields that don't exist in our movie, we restrict the `field` values using an enumerator defined inside a `Movie` class.

Now, the important part here is the actual return of these calls. Indeed, they will trigger an `Observable` mechanism where the caller will attach himself to an `Observable` HTTP call. Then, when the HTTP call is complete and the results have been filtered according to the query parameter, then, the callee will notify the caller about the response. Consequently, the caller does not have to wait for the callee (`IMDBAPI`); it will be notified when the request is complete.

Implementation

Let's dive into the implementation. First, we will need to create a new Angular2 project using the Angular CLI:

```
ng new angular-observable
ng init
ng serve
```

Then, to make sure everything went well, you can browse to `localhost:4200` and see if you got something like the following:

angular-observable works!

Next, we will need a model to represent the movie concept. We will generate this class using the `ng g class` models/`Movie` command-line. Then, we can add a constructor defining all the private fields of the `Movie` models as the same as the getters and setters:

```
export class Movie {
    public constructor(
          private _movie_id:number,
          private _title: string,
          private _phase: string,
          private _category_name: string,
          private _release_year: number,
          private _running_time: number,
          private _rating_name: string,
          private _disc_format_name: string,
          private _number_discs: number,
          private _viewing_format_name: string,
          private _aspect_ratio_name: string,
          private _status: string,
          private _release_date: string,
          private _budget: number,
          private _gross: number,
```

```
            private _time_stamp:Date){
    }
    public toString = () : string => {
            return `Movie (movie_id: ${this._movie_id},
            title: ${this._title},
            phase: ${this._phase},
            category_name: ${this._category_name},
            release_year: ${this._release_year},
            running_time: ${this._running_time},
            rating_name: ${this._rating_name},
            disc_format_name: ${this._disc_format_name},
             number_discs: ${this._number_discs},
            viewing_format_name: ${this._viewing_format_name},
            aspect_ratio_name: ${this._aspect_ratio_name},
            status: ${this._status},
            release_date: ${this._release_date},
            budget: ${this._budget},
            gross: ${this._gross},
            time_stamp: ${this._time_stamp})`;
    }
    //GETTER
    //SETTER
}
export enum MovieFields{
    movie_id,
    title,
    phase,
    category_name,
    release_year,
    running_time,
    rating_name,
    disc_format_name,
    number_discs,
    viewing_format_name,
    aspect_ratio_name,
    status,
    release_date,
    budget,
    gross,
    time_stamp
}
```

Here, each field of the movie JSON definition is mapped into a private member of the
Movie class using the constructor property declaration of typescript. Also, we override
the toString method, so it prints every field. In the toString method, we take advantage
of the multi-line string provided by the back tick (`) and the ${} syntax that allows the
concatenation of strings and different variables.

Then, we have an enumerator `MovieFields`, which will allow us to restrict the searchable field.

Moving on, we need to generate the `IMDBAPI` class. As the `IMDBAPI` class will be potentially used everywhere in our program, we will make it a service. The advantage is that services can be injected into any component or directive. Moreover, we can choose whether we want Angular2 to create an instance of the `IMDBAPI` per injection or always inject the same instance. If the provider for the `IMDBAPI` is created at the application level, then the same instance of the `IMDBAPI` will be served to anyone requesting it. At the component level, however, a new instance of `IMDBAPI` will be created and served to the component each time said component is instantiated. In our case, it makes more sense to have only one instance of the `IMDBAPI`, as it will not have any particular states that are susceptible to change from component to component. Let's generate the `IMDBAPI` service (`ng g s services/IMDBAPI`) and implement the two methods we defined earlier:

```
IMDBAPI.fetchOneById(1);
IMDBAPI.fetchByFields(MovieFields.release_date, 2015);
```

Here's `IMDBAPIService` with the `fetchOneById` method:

```
import { Injectable } from '@angular/core';
import { Http }  from '@angular/http';
import { Movie, MovieFields } from '../models/movie';
import { Observable } from 'rxjs/Rx';
import 'rxjs/Rx';
@Injectable()
export class IMDBAPIService {
  private moviesUrl:string = "assets/marvel-cinematic-universe.json";
  constructor(private http: Http) { }
  /**
   * Return an Observable to a Movie matching id
   * @param   {number}          id
   * @return {Observable<Movie>}
   */
  public fetchOneById(id:number):Observable<Movie>{
   console.log('fetchOneById', id);
        return this.http.get(this.moviesUrl)
        /**
         * Transforms the result of the http get, which is observable
         * into one observable by item.
         */
        .flatMap(res => res.json().movies)
        /**
         * Filters movies by their movie_id
         */
        .filter((movie:any)=>{
```

```
        console.log("filter", movie);
        return (movie.movie_id === id)
    })
    /**
     * Map the JSON movie item to the Movie Model
     */
    .map((movie:any) => {
    console.log("map", movie);
    return new Movie(
            movie.movie_id,
            movie.title,
            movie.phase,
            movie.category_name,
            movie.release_year,
            movie.running_time,
            movie.rating_name,
            movie.disc_format_name,
            movie.number_discs,
            movie.viewing_format_name,
            movie.aspect_ratio_name,
            movie.status,
            movie.release_date,
            movie.budget,
            movie.gross,
            movie.time_stamp
    );
    });
    }
}
```

Understanding the implementation

Let's break it down chunk by chunk. First, the declaration of the service is pretty standard:

```
import { Injectable } from '@angular/core';
import { Http }  from '@angular/http';
import { Movie, MovieFields } from '../models/movie';
import { Observable } from 'rxjs/Rx';
import 'rxjs/Rx';
@Injectable()
export class IMDBAPIService {
  private moviesUrl:string = "app/marvel-cinematic-universe.json";
  constructor(private http: Http) { }
```

Services are injectable. Consequently, we need to import and add the `@Injectable` annotation. We also import `Http`, `Movie`, `MovieFields`, `Observable`, and the operators of RxJS. **RxJS** stands for **Reactive Extensions for JavaScript**. It is an API to do `Observer`, iterator, and functional programming. When it comes to asynchronism in Angular2, you rely on RxJS for the most part.

 One important thing to note is that we use RxJS 5.0, which is a complete rewrite, based on the same concept as RxJS 4.0.

The `IMDBAPIService` also has a reference to the path of our JSON file and a constructor to receive an injection of the `http` service. On the implementation of the `fetchOneById` method, we can see four distinct operations chained with each other: `get`, `flatMap`, `filter`, and `map`.

- Get returns an `Observable` onto the body of the `http` request.
- `flatMap` transforms the get `Observable` by applying a function that you specify to each item emitted by the source `Observable`, where that function returns an `Observable` that itself emits items. `flatMap` then merges the emissions of these resulting observables, emitting these merged results as its sequence. In our case, it means that we will apply the next two operations (that is `filter` and `map`) on all the items received from the `http` get.
- `filter` checks if the ID of the current movie is the one we are looking for
- `map` transforms the JSON representation of a movie into the `typescript` representation of a movie (that is the `Movie` class).

This last operation, while counter-intuitive, is mandatory. Indeed, one could think that the JSON representation and the `typescript` representation are identical, as they own the same fields. However, the `typescript` representation, also to its properties, defines functions such as `toString`, the getters, and the setters. Removing the map would return an `Object` instance--containing all the fields of a `Movie` without being one. Also, a typecast will not help you there. Indeed, the `typescript` transpiler will allow you to cast an `Object` into a `Movie`, but it still won't have the methods defined in the `Movie` class, as the concept of static typing disappears when the `typescript` is transpiled in JavaScript. The following would transpile fail at execution time with; `movie.movie_id(25)` TypeError: `movie.movie_id` is not a function at `Object.<anonymous>`.

```
movie:Movie = JSON.parse(`{
             "movie_id" : 1,
             "title" : "Iron Man",
```

```
            "phase" : "Phase One: Avengers Assembled",
            "category_name" : "Action",
            "release_year" : 2015,
            "running_time" : 126,
            "rating_name" : "PG-13",
            "disc_format_name" : "Blu-ray",
            "number_discs" : 1,
            "viewing_format_name" : "Widescreen",
            "aspect_ratio_name" : " 2.35:1",
            "status" : 1,
            "release_date" : "May 2, 2008",
            "budget" : "140,000,000",
            "gross" : "318,298,180",
            "time_stamp" : "2015-05-03"
        }`);
Console.log(movie.movie_id(25));
```

Now, if we want to use our IMDB service, further modifications are required in the code that was generated by the Angular CLI. First, we need to modify app.module.ts so it looks like this:

```
import { BrowserModule } from '@angular/platform-browser';
import { NgModule } from '@angular/core';
import { FormsModule } from '@angular/forms';
import { HttpModule } from '@angular/http';
import { IMDBAPIService } from './services/imdbapi.service';

import { AppComponent } from './app.component';

@NgModule({
  declarations: [
    AppComponent
  ],
  imports: [
    BrowserModule,
    FormsModule,
    HttpModule
  ],
  providers: [IMDBAPIService],
  bootstrap: [AppComponent]
})
export class AppModule { }
```

The lines in bold represent what have been added. We import our `IMDBAPIService` and `HTTP_PROVIDERS`. Both providers are declared at the application level, meaning that the instance that will be injected in the component or directive will always be the same.

Then, we modify the `app.component.ts` file that was generated and add the following:

```
import { Component } from '@angular/core';
import { IMDBAPIService } from './services/imdbapi.service';
import { Movie } from './models/movie';
@Component({
  selector: 'app-root',
  templateUrl: './app.component.html',
  styleUrls: ['./app.component.css']
})
export class AngularObservableAppComponent {
  title = 'angular-observable works!';
  private movies:Movie[] = [];
  private error:boolean = false;
  private finished:boolean = false;
  constructor(private IMDBAPI:IMDBAPIService){
  this.IMDBAPI.fetchOneById(1).subscribe(
    value => {this.movies.push(value); console.log("Component",
      value)},
    error => this.error = true,
    () => this.finished = true
    )
  }
}
```

Once again, the bold lines of code represent the lines that were added in comparison to the generated file. We have added several properties to the `AppComponent`: movies, error, and finished. The first property is an array of Movie that will store the result of our queries, the second and the third flag for error and termination. In the constructor, we have an injection of the `IMDBAPIService`, and we subscribe to the result of the `fetchOneById` method. The `subscribe` method expects three callbacks:

- `Observer`: Receive the value yielded by the `Observer` method. It is the RxJs equivalent of the `notify()` method we saw earlier in this chapter.
- `onError` (Optional): Triggered if the `Observer` object yields an error.
- `onComplete` (Optional): Triggered on completion.

Finally, we can modify the `app.component.html` file to map the movies property of the AppComponent **array**:

```
<h1>
  {{title}}
</h1>
<ul>
  <li *ngFor="let movie of movies">{{movie}}</li>
</ul>
```

The produced output of our code is:

angular-observable works!

- Movie {movie_id: 1, title: Iron Man, phase: Phase One: Avengers Assembled, category_name: Action, release_year: 2015, running_time: 126, rating_name: PG-13, disc_format_name: Blu-ray, number_discs: 1, viewing_format_name: Widescreen, aspect_ratio_name: 2.35:1, status: 1, release_date: May 2, 2008, budget: 140,000,000, gross: 318,298,180, time_stamp: 2015-05-03}

We can see that the first movie item has been correctly inserted into our `ul`/`li` HTML structure. What's really interesting about this code is the order in which things execute. Analyzing the log helps us to grasp the true power of asynchronism in Angular with RxJs. Here's what the console looks like after the execution of our code:

```
fetchOneById 1
:4200/app/services/imdbapi.service.js:30 filter Object
:4200/app/services/imdbapi.service.js:34 map Object
:4200/app/angular-observable.component.js:21 Component
  Movie_aspect_ratio_name: " 2.35:1"_budget:
  "140,000,000"_category_name: "Action"_disc_format_name: "Blu-
  ray"_gross: "318,298,180"_movie_id: 1_number_discs: 1_phase: "Phase
  One: Avengers Assembled"_rating_name: "PG-13"_release_date: "May 2,
  2008"_release_year: 2015_running_time: 126_status: 1_time_stamp:
  "2015-05-03"_title: "Iron Man"_viewing_format_name:
  "Widescreen"aspect_ratio_name: (...)budget: (...)category_name:
  (...)disc_format_name: (...)gross: (...)movie_id: (...)number_discs:
  (...)phase: (...)rating_name: (...)release_date: (...)release_year:
  (...)running_time: (...)status: (...)time_stamp: (...)title:
  (...)toString: ()viewing_format_name: (...)__proto__: Object
:4200/app/services/imdbapi.service.js:30 filter Object
:4200/app/services/imdbapi.service.js:30 filter Object
:4200/app/services/imdbapi.service.js:30 filter Object
:4200/app/services/imdbapi.service.js:30 filter Object
:4200/app/services/imdbapi.service.js:30 filter Object
:4200/app/services/imdbapi.service.js:30 filter Object
:4200/app/services/imdbapi.service.js:30 filter Object
:4200/app/services/imdbapi.service.js:30 filter Object
:4200/app/services/imdbapi.service.js:30 filter Object
```

```
:4200/app/services/imdbapi.service.js:30 filter Object
:4200/app/services/imdbapi.service.js:30 filter Object
:4200/app/services/imdbapi.service.js:30 filter Object
:4200/app/services/imdbapi.service.js:30 filter Object
```

As you can see, AngularObservableAppComponent was notified that a movie matching the query was found before the filter function had analyzed all the items. As a reminder, the order to the operations inside the fetchOneById by id was: get, flatMap, filter, map, and we have logging statements in the filter and map methods. So, here, the filter operation analyzes the first item, which happens to be the one we are looking for (movie_id===1) and forwards it to the map operation that transforms it into a Movie. This Movie is sent right away to AngularObservableAppComponent. We clearly see that the received object in the AngularObservableAppComponent component is from type movie, as the console gives us our overriding of the toString method. Then, the filter operation continues with the rest of the items. None of them match; consequently, we do not have any more notifications.

Let's test this further with a second method: IMDBAPI.fetchByField:

```
public fetchByField(field:MovieFields, value:any){
  console.log('fetchByField', field, value);
  return this.http.get(this.moviesUrl)
        .flatMap(res => res.json().movies)
        /**
        * Filters movies by their field
        */
        .filter((movie:any)=>{
        console.log("filter", movie);
        return (movie[MovieFields[field]] === value)
        })
        /**
        * Map the JSON movie item to the Movie Model
        */
        .map((movie:any) => {
          console.log("map", movie);
        return new Movie(
              movie.movie_id,
              movie.title,
              movie.phase,
              movie.category_name,
              movie.release_year,
              movie.running_time,
              movie.rating_name,
              movie.disc_format_name,
              movie.number_discs,
              movie.viewing_format_name,
```

```
                movie.aspect_ratio_name,
                movie.status,
                movie.release_date,
                movie.budget,
                movie.gross,
                movie.time_stamp
        );
        });
    }
```

For the `fetchByField` method, we use the same mechanisms as `fetchById`. Unsurprisingly, the operations stay the same: `get`, `flatMap`, `filter`, and `map`. The only change is in the `filter` operation, where we now have to `filter` on a `field` received as parameter `return (movie[MovieFields[field]] === value)`.

This statement can be a bit overwhelming to the TypeScript or JavaScript newcomer. First, the `MovieFields[field]` part is explained by the fact that `enum` will be transpiled into the following JavaScript function:

```
(function (MovieFields) {
  MovieFields[MovieFields["movie_id"] = 0] = "movie_id";
  MovieFields[MovieFields["title"] = 1] = "title";
  MovieFields[MovieFields["phase"] = 2] = "phase";
  MovieFields[MovieFields["category_name"] = 3] = "category_name";
  MovieFields[MovieFields["release_year"] = 4] = "release_year";
  MovieFields[MovieFields["running_time"] = 5] = "running_time";
  MovieFields[MovieFields["rating_name"] = 6] = "rating_name";
  MovieFields[MovieFields["disc_format_name"] = 7] =
        "disc_format_name";
  MovieFields[MovieFields["number_discs"] = 8] = "number_discs";
  MovieFields[MovieFields["viewing_format_name"] = 9] =
        "viewing_format_name";
  MovieFields[MovieFields["aspect_ratio_name"] = 10] =
        "aspect_ratio_name";
  MovieFields[MovieFields["status"] = 11] = "status";
  MovieFields[MovieFields["release_date"] = 12] = "release_date";
  MovieFields[MovieFields["budget"] = 13] = "budget";
  MovieFields[MovieFields["gross"] = 14] = "gross";
  MovieFields[MovieFields["time_stamp"] = 15] = "time_stamp";
  })
(exports.MovieFields || (exports.MovieFields = {}));
var MovieFields = exports.MovieFields;
```

Consequently, the value of `MovieFields.release_year` is, in fact, 4 and `MovieFields` is a static array. So, `movie[MovieFields[field]]` is interpreted as a `movie["release_year is"]` in our current example.

The next subtlety is that every object in JavaScript is represented as an associative array, where the variable name acts as a key. Therefore, `movie["release_year"]` is equivalent to `movie.release_year`. This allows us to retrieve the value of any property only by knowing its name. Modify the constructor of `AngularObservableAppComponent` to look like the following:

```
constructor(private IMDBAPI:IMDBAPIService){
  this.IMDBAPI.fetchByField(MovieFields.release_year, 2015).subscribe(
      value => {this.movies.push(value); console.log("Component",
        value)},
      error => this.error = true,
      () => this.finished = true
  )
}
```

This will have the impact shown in the following screenshot:

angular-observable works!

- Movie (movie_id: 1, title: Iron Man, phase: Phase One: Avengers Assembled, category_name: Action, release_year: 2015, running_time: 126, rating_name: PG-13, disc_format_name: Blu-ray, number_discs: 1, viewing_format_name: Widescreen, aspect_ratio_name: 2.35:1, status: 1, release_date: May 2, 2008, budget: 140,000,000, gross: 318,298,180, time_stamp: 2015-05-03)
- Movie (movie_id: 2, title: Iron Man 2, phase: Phase One: Avengers Assembled, category_name: Action, release_year: 2015, running_time: 124, rating_name: PG-13, disc_format_name: Blu-ray, number_discs: 1, viewing_format_name: Widescreen, aspect_ratio_name: 2.35:1, status: 1, release_date: May 7, 2010, budget: 200,000,000, gross: 312,057,433, time_stamp: 2015-05-03)
- Movie (movie_id: 7, title: Iron Man 3, phase: Phase Two, category_name: Action, release_year: 2015, running_time: 130, rating_name: PG-13, disc_format_name: Blu-ray + DVD, number_discs: 2, viewing_format_name: Widescreen, aspect_ratio_name: 2.35:1, status: 1, release_date: May 3, 2013, budget: 200,000,000, gross: 408,992,272, time_stamp: 2015-05-03)
- Movie (movie_id: 11, title: Avengers: Age of Ultron, phase: Phase Two, category_name: Science Fiction, release_year: 2015, running_time: 141, rating_name: PG-13, disc_format_name: Blu-ray, number_discs: 1, viewing_format_name: Widescreen, aspect_ratio_name: 2.35:1, status: 1, release_date: May 1, 2015, budget: 250,000,000, gross: 458,991,599, time_stamp: 2015-12-07)
- Movie (movie_id: 12, title: Ant-Man, phase: Phase Two, category_name: Science Fiction, release_year: 2015, running_time: 132, rating_name: PG-13, disc_format_name: Blu-ray, number_discs: 1, viewing_format_name: Widescreen, aspect_ratio_name: 1.85:1, status: 1, release_date: July 17, 2015, budget: 130,000,000, gross: 179,017,481, time_stamp: 2015-12-07)

Now we have five matches instead of one. On the analysis of the console, we can see that the notifications still come as soon as a suitable object is found, and not when they have all been filtered:

```
fetchByField 4 2015
imdbapi.service.js:43 filter Object {movie_id: 1, title: "Iron Man",
  phase: "Phase One: Avengers Assembled", category_name: "Action",
  release_year: 2015...}
imdbapi.service.js:47 map Object {movie_id: 1, title: "Iron Man",
  phase: "Phase One: Avengers Assembled", category_name: "Action",
  release_year: 2015...}
```

```
angular-observable.component.js:22 Component Movie {_movie_id: 1,
   _title: "Iron Man", _phase: "Phase One: Avengers Assembled",
   _category_name: "Action", _release_year: 2015...}
imdbapi.service.js:43 filter Object {movie_id: 2, title: "The
   Incredible Hulk", phase: "Phase One: Avengers Assembled",
   category_name: "Action", release_year: 2008...}
imdbapi.service.js:43 filter Object {movie_id: 3, title: "Iron Man 2",
   phase: "Phase One: Avengers Assembled", category_name: "Action",
   release_year: 2015...}
imdbapi.service.js:47 map Object {movie_id: 3, title: "Iron Man 2",
   phase: "Phase One: Avengers Assembled", category_name: "Action",
   release_year: 2015...}
angular-observable.component.js:22 Component Movie {_movie_id: 3,
   _title: "Iron Man 2", _phase: "Phase One: Avengers Assembled",
   _category_name: "Action", _release_year: 2015...}
imdbapi.service.js:43 filter Object {movie_id: 4, title: "Thor", phase:
   "Phase One: Avengers Assembled", category_name: "Action",
   release_year: 2011...}
imdbapi.service.js:43 filter Object {movie_id: 5, title: "Captain
   America", phase: "Phase One: Avengers Assembled", category_name:
   "Action", release_year: 2011...}
imdbapi.service.js:43 filter Object {movie_id: 6, title: "Avengers,
   The", phase: "Phase One: Avengers Assembled", category_name: "Science
   Fiction", release_year: 2012...}
imdbapi.service.js:43 filter Object {movie_id: 7, title: "Iron Man 3",
   phase: "Phase Two", category_name: "Action", release_year: 2015...}
imdbapi.service.js:47 map Object {movie_id: 7, title: "Iron Man 3",
   phase: "Phase Two", category_name: "Action", release_year: 2015...}
angular-observable.component.js:22 Component Movie {_movie_id: 7,
   _title: "Iron Man 3", _phase: "Phase Two", _category_name: "Action",
   _release_year: 2015...}
imdbapi.service.js:43 filter Object {movie_id: 8, title: "Thor: The
   Dark World", phase: "Phase Two", category_name: "Science Fiction",
   release_year: 2013...}
imdbapi.service.js:43 filter Object {movie_id: 9, title: "Captain
   America: The Winter Soldier", phase: "Phase Two", category_name:
   "Action", release_year: 2014...}
imdbapi.service.js:43 filter Object {movie_id: 10, title: "Guardians of
   the Galaxy", phase: "Phase Two", category_name: "Science Fiction",
   release_year: 2014...}
imdbapi.service.js:43 filter Object {movie_id: 11, title: "Avengers:
   Age of Ultron", phase: "Phase Two", category_name: "Science Fiction",
   release_year: 2015...}
imdbapi.service.js:47 map Object {movie_id: 11, title: "Avengers: Age
   of Ultron", phase: "Phase Two", category_name: "Science Fiction",
   release_year: 2015...}
angular-observable.component.js:22 Component Movie {_movie_id: 11,
   _title: "Avengers: Age of Ultron", _phase: "Phase Two",
```

```
    _category_name: "Science Fiction", _release_year: 2015...}
imdbapi.service.js:43 filter Object {movie_id: 12, title: "Ant-Man",
    phase: "Phase Two", category_name: "Science Fiction", release_year:
    2015...}
imdbapi.service.js:47 map Object {movie_id: 12, title: "Ant-Man",
    phase: "Phase Two", category_name: "Science Fiction", release_year:
    2015...}
angular-observable.component.js:22 Component Movie {_movie_id: 12,
    _title: "Ant-Man", _phase: "Phase Two", _category_name: "Science
    Fiction", _release_year: 2015...}
imdbapi.service.js:43 filter Object {movie_id: 13, title: "Captain
    America: Civil War", phase: "Phase Three", category_name: "Science
    Fiction", release_year: 2016...}
imdbapi.service.js:43 filter Object {movie_id: 14, title: "Doctor
    Strange", phase: "Phase Two", category_name: "Science Fiction",
    release_year: 2016...}
```

Now, the other strength of this design pattern is the ability to unsubscribe yourself. To do so, you only have to acquire a reference to your subscription and call the `unsubscribe()` method, shown as follows:

```
constructor(private IMDBAPI:IMDBAPIService){
    let imdbSubscription =
        this.IMDBAPI.fetchByField(MovieFields.release_year, 2015).
        subscribe(
          value => {
             this.movies.push(value);
             console.log("Component", value)
             if(this.movies.length > 2){
                imdbSubscription.unsubscribe();
             }
          },
        error => this.error = true,
        () => this.finished = true
        );
}
```

Here, we unsubscribe after the third notification. To add to all this, the `Observable` object will even detect that nobody's observing anymore and will stop whatever it was doing. Indeed, the previous code with `unsubscribe` produces:

```
fetchByField 4 2015
imdbapi.service.js:43filter Object {movie_id: 1, title: "Iron Man",
    phase: "Phase One: Avengers Assembled", category_name: "Action",
    release_year: 2015...}
imdbapi.service.js:49 map Object {movie_id: 1, title: "Iron Man",
    phase: "Phase One: Avengers Assembled", category_name: "Action",
    release_year: 2015...}
```

```
angular-observable.component.js:24 Component Movie {_movie_id: 1,
    _title: "Iron Man", _phase: "Phase One: Avengers Assembled",
    _category_name: "Action", _release_year: 2015...}
imdbapi.service.js:43 filter Object {movie_id: 2, title: "The
    Incredible Hulk", phase: "Phase One: Avengers Assembled",
    category_name: "Action", release_year: 2008...}
imdbapi.service.js:43 filter Object {movie_id: 3, title: "Iron Man 2",
    phase: "Phase One: Avengers Assembled", category_name: "Action",
    release_year: 2015...}
imdbapi.service.js:49 map Object {movie_id: 3, title: "Iron Man 2",
    phase: "Phase One: Avengers Assembled", category_name: "Action",
    release_year: 2015...}
angular-observable.component.js:24 Component Movie {_movie_id: 3,
    _title: "Iron Man 2", _phase: "Phase One: Avengers Assembled",
    _category_name: "Action", _release_year: 2015...}
imdbapi.service.js:43 filter Object {movie_id: 4, title: "Thor", phase:
    "Phase One: Avengers Assembled", category_name: "Action",
    release_year: 2011...}
imdbapi.service.js:43 filter Object {movie_id: 5, title: "Captain
    America", phase: "Phase One: Avengers Assembled", category_name:
    "Action", release_year: 2011...}
imdbapi.service.js:43 filter Object {movie_id: 6, title: "Avengers,
    The", phase: "Phase One: Avengers Assembled", category_name: "Science
    Fiction", release_year: 2012...}
imdbapi.service.js:43 filter Object {movie_id: 7, title: "Iron Man 3",
    phase: "Phase Two", category_name: "Action", release_year: 2015...}
imdbapi.service.js:49 map Object {movie_id: 7, title: "Iron Man 3",
    phase: "Phase Two", category_name: "Action", release_year: 2015...}
angular-observable.component.js:24 Component Movie {_movie_id: 7,
    _title: "Iron Man 3", _phase: "Phase Two", _category_name: "Action",
    _release_year: 2015...}
```

Everything stops after the third notification.

The code for this `Observer` implementation is at `http://bit.ly/masteri ng-angular2-chap7-part2`.

Promises

Promises are another useful asynchronous concept available in Angular. Conceptually, promises implement a totally different pattern. A `Promise` is a value that will be resolved or rejected in the future. Like the `Observer` pattern, they can be used to manage async programming. So, why bother to have two concepts to do the same thing? Well, the verbosity of `Observer` allows one thing that `Promise` does not: unsubscribe. The main difference that may lead to a decision about which one to use is the ability of `Observable` to catch many subsequent asynchronous events, while `Promise` can manage a single asynchronous event. To emphasise the differences between `Observer` and `Promise`, we will take the same example as before, fetching movies from a JSON API.

The `AngularObservableAppComponent` component will make an asynchronous call to the `IMDBAPIService` and, upon the answer, will update the HTML view.

Here's the `fetchOneById` method using `Promise` instead of `Observable`:

```
/** ,
 * Return a Promise to a Movie matching id
 * @param   {number}            id
 * @return {Promise<Movie>}
 */
public fetchOneById(id:number):Promise<Movie>{
 console.log('fecthOneById', id);
      return this.http.get(this.moviesUrl)
      /**
       * Transforms the result of the http get, which is observable
       * into one observable by item.
       */
      .flatMap(res => res.json().movies)
      /**
       * Filters movies by their movie_id
       */
      .filter((movie:any)=>{
      console.log("filter", movie);
      return (movie.movie_id === id)
      })
      .toPromise()
      /**
         * Map the JSON movie item to the Movie Model
       */
      .then((movie:any) => {
      console.log("map", movie);
      return new Movie(
            movie.movie_id,
            movie.title,
```

```
                movie.phase,
            movie.category_name,
             movie.release_year,
             movie.running_time,
             movie.rating_name,
             movie.disc_format_name,
             movie.number_discs,
             movie.viewing_format_name,
             movie.aspect_ratio_name,
             movie.status,
             movie.release_date,
             movie.budget,
             movie.gross,
             movie.time_stamp
         )
        });
    }
```

As shown by this code, we went from `flatMap`, `filter`, `map` to `flatMap`, `filter`, `toPromise`, and `then`. The new operations, `toPromise` and `then` create a `Promise` object that will contain the result of the `filter` operation and, on completion of the `filter` operation, the `then` operation will be executed. The `then` operation can be thought of as a map; it does the same thing. To use this code, we also have to change the way we call `IMDBAPIService` in `AngularObservableAppComponent`, to the following:

```
    this.IMDBAPI.fetchOneById(1).then(
        value => {
            this.movies.push(value);
            console.log("Component", value)
        },
        error => this.error = true
    );
```

Once again, we can see a `then` operation that will be executed when the promise from `IMDBAPIService.FetchOneById` has completed. The `then` operation accepts two callbacks: `onCompletion` and `onError`. The second callback, `onError`, is optional.

Now, `onCompletion` callback will only be executed once `Promise` has completed, as shown in the console:

```
    imdbapi.service.js:30 filter Object {movie_id: 2, title: "The
      Incredible Hulk", phase: "Phase One: Avengers Assembled",
      category_name: "Action", release_year: 2008...}
    imdbapi.service.js:30 filter Object {movie_id: 3, title: "Iron Man 2",
      phase: "Phase One: Avengers Assembled", category_name: "Action",
      release_year: 2015...}
```

```
imdbapi.service.js:30 filter Object {movie_id: 4, title: "Thor", phase:
  "Phase One: Avengers Assembled", category_name: "Action",
  release_year: 2011...}
imdbapi.service.js:30 filter Object {movie_id: 5, title: "Captain
  America", phase: "Phase One: Avengers Assembled", category_name:
  "Action", release_year: 2011...}
imdbapi.service.js:30 filter Object {movie_id: 6, title: "Avengers,
  The", phase: "Phase One: Avengers Assembled", category_name: "Science
  Fiction", release_year: 2012...}
imdbapi.service.js:30 filter Object {movie_id: 7, title: "Iron Man 3",
  phase: "Phase Two", category_name: "Action", release_year: 2015...}
imdbapi.service.js:30 filter Object {movie_id: 8, title: "Thor: The
  Dark World", phase: "Phase Two", category_name: "Science Fiction",
  release_year: 2013...}
imdbapi.service.js:30 filter Object {movie_id: 9, title: "Captain
  America: The Winter Soldier", phase: "Phase Two", category_name:
  "Action", release_year: 2014...}
imdbapi.service.js:30 filter Object {movie_id: 10, title: "Guardians of
  the Galaxy", phase: "Phase Two", category_name: "Science Fiction",
  release_year: 2014...}
imdbapi.service.js:30 filter Object {movie_id: 11, title: "Avengers:
  Age of Ultron", phase: "Phase Two", category_name: "Science Fiction",
  release_year: 2015...}
imdbapi.service.js:30 filter Object {movie_id: 12, title: "Ant-Man",
  phase: "Phase Two", category_name: "Science Fiction", release_year:
  2015...}
imdbapi.service.js:30 filter Object {movie_id: 13, title: "Captain
  America: Civil War", phase: "Phase Three", category_name: "Science
  Fiction", release_year: 2016...}
imdbapi.service.js:30 filter Object {movie_id: 14, title: "Doctor
  Strange", phase: "Phase Two", category_name: "Science Fiction",
  release_year: 2016...}
imdbapi.service.js:35 map Object {movie_id: 1, title: "Iron Man",
  phase: "Phase One: Avengers Assembled", category_name: "Action",
  release_year: 2015...}
angular-observable.component.js:23 Component Movie {_movie_id: 1,
  _title: "Iron Man", _phase: "Phase One: Avengers Assembled",
  _category_name: "Action", _release_year: 2015...}
```

While the modification of `IMDBAPIService` was minimal for the `fetchOneById` method, we will have to change `fetchByField` more consequently. Indeed, `onComplete` callback will only be executed once, so we need to return an array of `Movie`, and not only one `Movie`. Here's the implementation of the `fetchByField` method:

```
public fetchByField(field:MovieFields, value:any):Promise<Movie[]>{
    console.log('fetchByField', field, value);
    return this.http.get(this.moviesUrl)
        .map(res => res.json().movies.filter(
        (movie)=>{
            return (movie[MovieFields[field]] === value)
        })
        )
      .toPromise()
        /**
        * Map the JSON movie items to the Movie Model
        */
        .then((jsonMovies:any[]) => {
        console.log("map", jsonMovies);
        let movies:Movie[] = [];
        for (var i = 0; i < jsonMovies.length; i++) {
            movies.push(
                new Movie(
                    jsonMovies[i].movie_id,
                    jsonMovies[i].title,
                    jsonMovies[i].phase,
                    jsonMovies[i].category_name,
                    jsonMovies[i].release_year,
                    jsonMovies[i].running_time,
                    jsonMovies[i].rating_name,
                    jsonMovies[i].disc_format_name,
                    jsonMovies[i].number_discs,
                    jsonMovies[i].viewing_format_name,
                    jsonMovies[i].aspect_ratio_name,
                    jsonMovies[i].status,
                    jsonMovies[i].release_date,
                    jsonMovies[i].budget,
                    jsonMovies[i].gross,
                    jsonMovies[i].time_stamp
                )
            )
        }
        return movies;
        });
    }
```

To implement this, I trade `flatMap` for a classical map as the first operation. In the map, I acquire the reference to the JSON movie array directly and apply the `field` filter. The result is transformed into a promise and processed in the `then` operation. The `then` operation receives an array of JSON movies and transforms it into an array of `Movie`. This produces an array of `Movie` which is returned, as the promised result, to the caller. The call in `AngularObservableAppComponent` is also a bit different, as we now expect an array:

```
this.IMDBAPI.fetchByField(MovieFields.release_year, 2015).then(
    value => {
        this.movies = value;
        console.log("Component", value)
    },
    error => this.error = true
)
```

Another way to use `Promise` is through the `fork`/`join` paradigm. Indeed, it is possible to launch many processes (`fork`) and wait for all the promises to complete before sending the aggregated result to the caller (`join`). It is therefore relatively easy to supercharge the `fetchByField` method, as it can run in many fields with logic or.

Here are the three very short methods we need to implement to the logic or:

```
/**
 * Private member storing pending promises
 */
private promises:Promise<Movie[]>[] = [];
/**
 * Register one promise for field/value. Returns this
 * for chaining that is
 *
 *   byField(Y, X)
 *   .or(...)
 *   .fetch()
 *
 * @param   {MovieFields} field
 * @param   {any}         value
 * @return  {IMDBAPIService}
 */
public byField(field:MovieFields, value:any):IMDBAPIService{
  this.promises.push(this.fetchByField(field, value));
  return this;
}
/**
 * Convenient method to make the calls more readable, that is
 *
 *   byField(Y, X)
```

```
 *  .or(...)
 *  .fetch()
 *
 *  instead of
 *
 *   byField(Y, X)
 *  .byField(...)
 *  .fetch()
 *
 *  @param   {MovieFields} field
 *  @param   {any}         value
 *  @return {IMDBAPIService}
 */
public or(field:MovieFields, value:any):IMDBAPIService{
 return this.byField(field, value);
}
/**
 * Join all the promises and return the aggregated result.
 *
 * @return {Promise<Movie[]>}
 */
public fetch():Promise<Movie[]>{
 return Promise.all(this.promises).then((results:any) => {
       //result is an array of movie arrays. One array per
       //promise. We need to flatten it.
       return [].concat.apply([], results);
 });
}
```

Here, I provide two convenient methods, byfield and/or that take a MovieField and a value as an argument and create a new Promise. They both return this for chaining. The fetch method joins all the Promise together and merges their respective results. In AngularObservableAppComponent, we can now have the following:

```
this.IMDBAPI.byField(MovieFields.release_year, 2015)
            .or(MovieFields.release_year, 2014)
            .or(MovieFields.phase, "Phase Two")
            .fetch()
            .then(
                value => {
                this.movies = value;
                console.log("Component", value)
                },
                error => this.error = true
            );
```

This is very simple to read and understand while keeping all the asynchronism capability of Angular.

> The code for the promises is available here: `http://bit.ly/mastering-an gular2-chap7-part3`.

Summary

In this chapter, we took advantage of asynchronous programming with Angular by using `Observable` and `Promise`.

More specifically, we learned how to implement the `Observable` pattern in `typescript`, and then took advantage of the Angular framework, while still using the `Observable` characteristics.

Also, we saw how to take advantage of `Promises` in Angular and built a basic, yet extensible JSON API for querying the Marvel Cinematic Universe.

In the next chapter, we will build upon this example to create advanced forms. Indeed, we will create what's required to add, remove, and update movies of the Marvel Cinematic Universe. In addition, we will also learn about FormBuilder, control groups, and custom validations.

8

Template and Data Binding Syntax

In this chapter, you will learn about Template Syntax and Data Binding provided by the Angular framework. Template Syntax and Data Binding mainly focus on the UI or view aspects of the application; hence, it is a very important and crucial functionality.

In this chapter, you will learn about Template Syntax and the different ways to include a template in our components. You will also learn to create components, including child components, and use expressions and operators inside the view template. You will also focus on how to attach events, attributes, and implement directives inside the templates.

Data Binding is one of the key features of Angular and allows us to map data from the source to the view target and vice versa. You will learn about different ways of Data Binding.

In this chapter, you will learn to include view template and define Data Bindings inside templates with the help of examples we will create while learning.

You will learn and implement the following in this chapter:

- Template Syntax
- Various ways to include Template Syntax
- Template expressions in Angular
- Data Binding syntax
- Angular Two-way Data Binding
- Property bindings in the template
- Attaching events to the view in templates

- Expressions and statements inside templates
- Directives inside templates

Learning about Template Syntax

The components view is defined using a template, which tells Angular how to render the look. Inside the template, we define how the data should appear and also attach events using Data Binding.

Most HTML tags can be used inside the Angular template. We can use and define user-defined custom directives.

The general syntax of defining a template for a component is as follows:

```
import {Component, View} from "@angular/core";

@Component({
 selector: 'my-app',
 template: `<h2>{{ title }}</h2>`
})

export class MyTemplateComponent {
 title = 'Learning Angular!!!'
}
```

Let's analyze the preceding code snippet in detail:

1. We defined a component, MyTemplateComponent.
2. We defined the component view with template.
3. Inside the template, we defined a <h2> tag.
4. We defined a title variable and assigned a value.
5. Using the {{ }} interpolation, we bound the variable to the template.

Run the app, and you should see the following output:

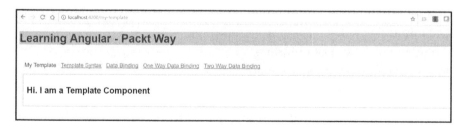

In the next section, you will learn in detail about the various ways to include templates and also about interpolation.

Various ways to include Template Syntax

In this section, you will learn about different ways to include templates in the component view. There are two ways to include Template Syntax in the component syntax:

- We can define the view template inside the `component` decorator. Using `template`, we can include the template inline in the component decorator.
- We can also include the template using `templateURL`. Using `templateUrl`, we write the template elements in a separate file and provide the path of the template to the component.

> `templateURL` is a much preferred way since it allows us to separate the code in a logical way to organize it more effectively.

Using inline Template Syntax

We discussed including templates in different ways in our component. Let's learn how to define our template inside the component.

The syntax for using templates inside the component decorator is as follows:

```
import {Component, View} from "@angular/core";

@Component({
 selector: 'my-app',
 template: `<h2> {{ title }} </h2>`
})

export class MyTemplate {
 title = 'Learning Angular!!!'
}
```

The most important things to note in the preceding code snippet are as follows:

1. We are defining the template inside the `@component` decorator.
2. The component `class` definition and template are defined in the same file.

Using templateURL to include a template

In the preceding code snippet, we created the template and component class in the same file. However, when the complexity of the component class increases in both template elements and class definitions, it will be difficult to maintain it.

We need to separate the logical class and the view so that it's easy to maintain and understand. Now, let's take a look at another way of defining the view template for the component using `templateURL`.

The syntax of using `templateURL` for viewing is as follows; let's create a file named `app-template.component.ts`:

```
import { Component } from '@angular/core';
import { FormsModule } from '@angular/forms';

@Component({
  selector: 'app-data-binding',
  templateUrl: './data-binding.component.html',
  styleUrls: ['./data-binding.component.css']
})
export class DataBindingComponent {
}
```

There will be no visual difference if we use any of the aforementioned ways to use a template. It makes sense to create separate files for HTML, CSS, and the component class, as it allows us to organize the code better and ultimately helps to maintain the codebase when it increases.

In the next section, you will learn features provided by the Angular framework for data and template binding.

Interpolation in templates

Double curly braces `{{ }}` are an interpolation in Angular. They're a way to map the text between the braces to a component property. We have already used and implemented interpolation in various examples throughout the chapters.

In the template we will write, the value is written inside double curly braces, as follows:

```
{{ test_value }}
```

Let's quickly create a simple example to understand the interpolation. In the `app.component.ts` file, let's define a variable named `title`:

```
import { Component } from '@angular/core';

@Component({
  templateUrl: './app.component.html',
  styleUrls: ['./app.component.css']
})

export class AppComponent {
  constructor() { }
  title = "Data Binding";
}
```

Now, we need to display the value of `title` in the template. Update the `app.component.html` file, and add the following line of code:

```
<p> {{ title }} </p>
```

Now, try changing the value of `title` in the class; we will see the updated value reflecting in the template automatically. That's interpolation, one of the key features we love in Angular.

Now that we know how to use interpolation, we will deal with how to add expressions inside the template in the next section.

Template expressions in Angular

We can use expressions inside the template; expressions execute and result in a value.

Just like in JavaScript, we can use expression statements with the exception of using assignments, new and chaining operators.

Let's look at some examples of template expressions:

```
<p> {{ tax+10 }} </p> // Using plus operator

<p> {{( tax*50)-10 }} </p>
```

In the preceding code snippet we are doing arithmetic operations with the variable `tax`.

If you have used any programming languages, chances are that you will find this section a cake-walk. Just like in any other language, we can make use of arithmetic operators.

Let's quickly create an example. Update the `app.component.html` file, and add the following code:

```
<h4>Template Expressions</h4>

<p> Expression with (+) Operator: <strong>{{ tax+ 10 }}</strong></p>

<p> Expression with (+ and *) Operator: <strong>{{ (tax*50) +10 }}
    </strong></p>
```

In the preceding code snippet, we used the expressions in the template. We added and did arithmetic operations with our `tax` variable.

In the update `app.component.ts` file, add the following code snippet:

```
import { Component } from '@angular/core';

@Component({
 templateUrl: './app.component.html',
 styleUrls: ['./app.component.css']
})

export class AppComponent {
 constructor() { }

 title = "Data Binding";
 tax = 10;
}
```

We are creating an `AppComponent` class and declaring two variables, `title` and `tax`. We are assigning initial values to `title` and `tax`.

Run the application, and we should see the output of the preceding code snippet, as shown in the following screenshot:

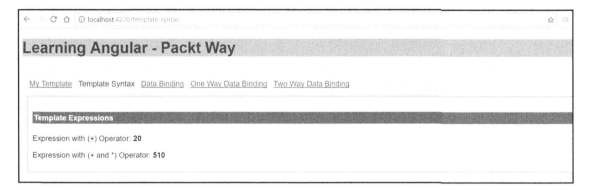

So far, you have learned about using templates in view, interpolations, and using expressions inside the template. Now, let's learn about attaching events and implementing directives inside the templates.

Attaching events to views in templates

In the previous sections, we covered how to define and include templates in our component along with interpolation and expressions inside the template.

In this section, you will learn to attach events to the elements in the template.

Events are regular JavaScript methods that are triggered based on user actions, such as `onclick` and `onmouseover`. Methods are a set of statements defined to execute a particular task.

The general syntax of attaching an event is as follows:

```
<button (click)= function_name()> Update Tax</button>
```

Let's analyze the preceding code in detail:

1. We are creating a `button` in the template.
2. We are attaching a `click` event to the button.
3. With the `click` event, we are binding the `function_name()` method.

Now, let's update our `component` file with the preceding code and see it in action.

We will first update our `app.component.html` file, and add the following code snippet:

```
<p> {{ title }} </p>
<p> {{ tax+ 10 }}</p>
<p> {{ (tax*50) +10 }} </p>
<button (click)= updateTax()> Update Tax </button>
```

Some quick notes on the preceding code snippet:

1. We added `button` to our template.
2. We attached an event called `updateTax` to the button on the `click` event.

Now, it's time to update our `app.component.ts` file with the following code:

```
import { Component } from '@angular/core';

@Component({
 templateUrl: './data-binding.component.html',
 styleUrls: ['./data-binding.component.css']
})

export class DataBindingComponent {
 constructor() { }

 title = "Data Binding and Template Syntax";
 tax = 10;

 updateTax() {
  this.tax = 20;
 }
}
```

Let's analyze the preceding code snippet:

1. We are defining and creating a component--`AppComponent`.
2. We have already defined two variables, `title` and `tax`, and assigned some values to them.
3. We are defining and creating an `updateTax` method, which when called will update the `tax` variable.
4. The updated `tax` value will be displayed in the template.

Now, run the app, and we should see the output as shown in the following screenshot; click on the **Update Tax** button, and you should see the data getting updated in the template:

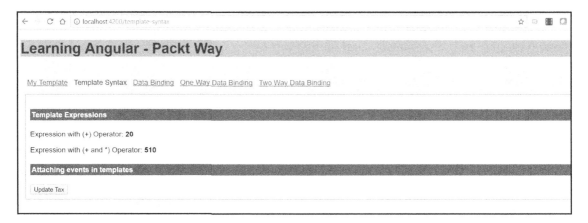

Great! So, in this section, you learned to attach events in your template and also to define methods in our component class to update the properties of the component. In the next section, you will learn to implement directives inside templates.

Implementing directives inside templates

We are making good progress in learning the Template Syntax. We discussed how to include Template Syntax, use interpolation in templates, and attach events.

Just like events, we can also implement directives and attributes inside the template. In this section, we will explain about implementing directives inside templates.

Take a look at the following code snippet:

```
<list-products></list-products>
```

Does the preceding code look similar to the way used to define custom directives in an earlier version of Angular? That's correct. Custom directives are now called components in the Angular framework.

We can create and define custom directives or tags according to the requirements of our application.

There is no relationship between the directory structure and child component, but as a good practice always keep logical parent-child relationship components under one directory; this helps in better organizing the code.

We will use the component we created in the preceding section. We created a component-data-binding.component.ts. We will now create a new component, list-products, which we will be able to bind it to the data-binding component.

Add the following code snippet to the list-products.component.ts file:

```
import { Component } from '@angular/core';

@Component({
  selector: 'list-products',
  templateUrl: './list-products.component.html',
  styleUrls: ['./list-products.component.css']
})

export class ListProductsComponent {
  constructor() { }
}
```

Let's analyze the preceding code:

1. We have created a new component, that is, the list-products component.
2. In the component definition, we mentioned selector as list-products.
3. The @Component decorator provides the Angular metadata for the component. Using the CSS selector, we can display the output of the template or the view inside the list-products tags.
4. We can give and use any name for selector, but make sure that we use the same name in the parent component, calling it as well.

Now that we have informed Angular that we need to place the output of the list-products component inside the custom tag list-products, we need to place the child component tag inside the parent component template.

We need to use the selector tag in order to identify the list-products component in the template data-binding.component.html file:

```
<list-products></list-products>
```

We are all set. Now, run the app, and we should see the output of the preceding code and the child component being displayed along with the `data-binding.component.html` template view:

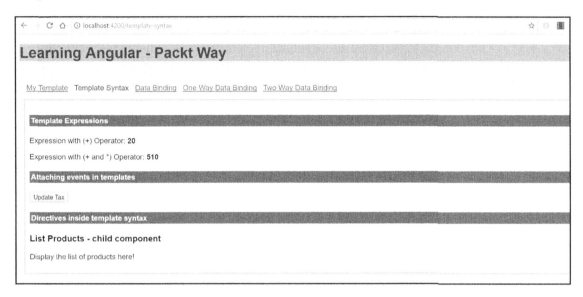

Awesome! So, you now learned how to include child components in your templates. Any Angular application will rarely be complete without using any of these. We will continue to learn and build more examples in the next section, where you will learn how to use property binding inside templates.

Bindings in the template

In this section, we will expand our example created in the preceding section. We will cover how to use property bindings in templates. Properties are attributes of the elements in the template, for example, class, ID, and so on.

The general syntax of HTML attributes is as follows:

```
<button class="myBtn" [disabled]="state=='texas'"   .
  (click)="updateTax()"></button>
```

The important points to note in the preceding code snippet are as follows:

1. We are defining an html element using the button tag.
2. We are adding the class attribute to the button tag.
3. We are attaching an on click event calling a method, updateTax to the button.
4. We have a disabled attribute; the button element will be displayed in the page and it will be disabled if the value of state is texas. if not, it will display an enabled button.

Using property binding, we can dynamically change the attribute values of disabled; when the values are updated or changed in the component class, the view gets updated.

Let's update the app.component.html file and update it to add the attribute to the element in the template:

```
<button (click)= updateTax() [disabled]="state=='texas'"> Update Tax
  </button>
```

Take a close look, and you will find that we have added the disabled attribute; based on the value of state, the button will either be enabled or disabled.

Now, in the app.component.ts file, let's define a property variable named state and assign a value it:

```
import { Component } from '@angular/core';

@Component({
 templateUrl: './data-binding.component.html',
 styleUrls: ['./data-binding.component.css']
})
export class DataBindingComponent {

 constructor() { }

 title = "Data Binding and Template Syntax";

 tax = 10;
 state = 'texas';

 updateTax() {
  this.tax = 20;
 }
}
```

In the preceding code, we just defined a new variable named `state` and assigned a value to it. Based on the value of `state`--assigned or updated--the button will be either enabled or disabled.

Run the application, and we should see the output shown in the following screenshot:

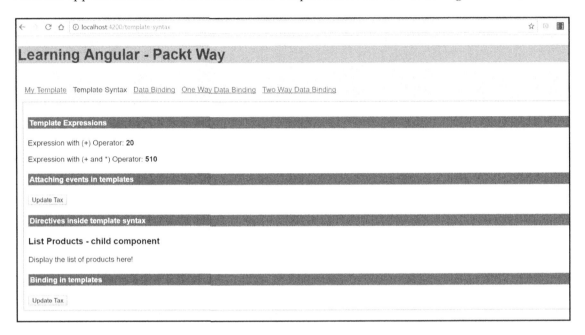

Amazing! You learned all about templates to be used in Angular components.

We discussed how to write Template Syntax, different ways to include Template Syntax, how to attach events, attach properties to the elements, and also how to implement directives in the templates.

In the next section, you will learn about Data Binding--one of the most crucial and striking features of Angular, and one that is most commonly used with Template Syntax.

Angular Data Binding

Angular provides a mechanism to share data between the same view and model easily. We can associate and assign a value in a class component and use it in the view. It provides many kinds of Data Binding. We will start by understanding the various Data Bindings available and then move on to create some examples.

Data Bindings can be grouped into three main categories:

1. One-way Data Binding, that is, from data source to view.
2. One-way Data Binding, that is, from view to data source.
3. Two-way Data Binding, that is, from view target to data source and from data source to view.

One-way Data Binding - Data source to view

In this section, you will learn about One-way Data Binding from data source to view target. In the next section, you will learn about One-way Data Binding from template to data source.

One-way Data Binding in Angular refers to a data flow from data source to view. In other words, we can say that whenever values and data are updated, they reflects in the view target.

One-way Data Binding from data source to view target applies to the following HTML element attributes:

- interpolation
- property
- attribute
- class
- style

Now that we know the attributes and elements that One-way Data Binding from data source to target applies to, let's learn how to use them in our code.

Let's take a look at general syntax to write One-way Data Binding from data source to view template.

```
{{ value_to_display }} // Using Interpolation

[attribute] = "expression" // Attribute binding
```

Let's analyze the previously defined syntax in detail:

- `interpolation` is a value written inside double curly braces as shown in the preceding code.
- The text between the braces `{{  }}` is often the name of a component property. Angular replaces that name with the string value of the corresponding component property.
- We can define One-way Data Binding for `attributes` and `properties` and by writing inside the square brackets `[]`.
- The `value_to_display` and `expression` properties are defined in the component class.

Some developers also prefer to use canonical form by appending prefix to the attribute.

```
<a bind-href = "value"> Link 1</a>
```

Use the prefix bind with the property or attribute along with the element's definition.

Now that we know the syntax for writing a One-way Data Binding, it's time to write examples for this:

```
<h4>{{ title }}</h4>

<div [style.color]="colorVal">Updating element Style CSS
    Attributes</div>
<p>
  <div [className]="'special'" >I am Div with className directive</div>
<p>
  <div [ngClass]="{'specialClass': true, 'specialClass2': true}" >I am
      Div with ngClass directive</div>
<p>
<img [src]="imageUrl" width="100" height="100">
```

Let's quickly analyze some of the key points in the preceding code snippet:

1. We are using interpolation--the value inside the double curly braces {{ }}--to display the value from the data source to the template. The property `title` will be set in the component model.
2. We are defining the `style` attribute `color` by binding the value dynamically to the variable defined in the component class `colorVal`.
3. We are defining the `ngClass` attribute and, based on the condition, whichever property, `specialClass` or `specialClass2`, is set to true, the corresponding class will be assigned.
4. We are providing the image's `src` attribute value dynamically by binding the property `imageUrl` in the component class.

Let's quickly define our variables in the component class `one-way.component.ts` file:

```
import { Component } from '@angular/core';

@Component({
  selector: 'app-one-way',
  templateUrl: './one-way.component.html',
  styleUrls: ['./one-way.component.css']
})
export class OneWayComponent {
 constructor() { }

 title = 'One way data bindings';

 state = 'california';
 colorVal = 'red';
 specialClass : true;
 imageUrl = './././/assets/images/angular.jpeg';
 tax = 20;
}
```

In the preceding code snippet, we have defined our `colorVal`, `isStyleVisible`, and `imageUrl` variables.

Now, let's run the preceding code, and you should see the output shown in the following screenshot:

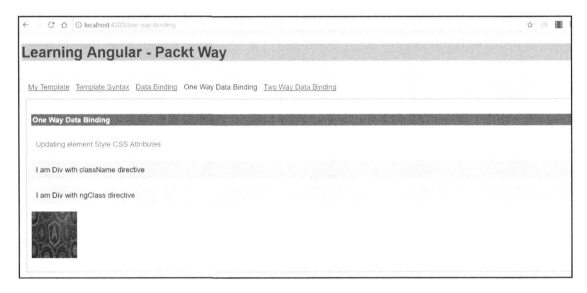

If you note carefully, in all the preceding code snippets, we are binding the data only one-way, that is, from data source to view target only.

So, essentially, it's read-only data for your end user. In next section we will learn about One-way Data Binding from view template to the data source.

Consider the following hands-on exercise: Try creating more variables and mapping them into the views.

One-way Data Binding - View template to data source

In preceding section, we learnt about One-way Data Binding from data source to view template.

In this section we will learn about One-way Data Binding from view template to data source.

One-way Data Binding from view template to data source is implemented mainly for events.

The general syntax for creating a binding is given below:

```
(target)="statement"
```

The binding from view to data source is mainly used for invoking methods or capturing event interactions.

Example of a one way binding from view template to data source is given below

```
<button (click)="updateTax()"></button>
```

We are attaching the `click` event and when the button is clicked, `updateTax` method will be called.

We learned about One-way Data Binding from data source to template as well as view template to data source.

In the next section, you will learn about Two-way Data Binding, displaying the data properties as well as updating those properties when changes are made to the element's property.

Angular Two-way Data Binding

Two-way Data Binding has to be one of the most important features in Angular. Two-way Data Binding helps express the input and output binding into a single notation using the `ngModel` directive.

Two-way Data Binding is a mechanism to map the data directly from model to view and vice versa. This mechanism allows us to keep data in sync between view and model, that is, from data source to view using `[]` and from view to data source using `()`.

In Angular, we achieve Two-way Data Binding using `ngModel`.

The general syntax of a Two-way Data Binding is as follows:

```
<input [(ngModel)]="sample_value" />
```

In the preceding syntax, note the following:

- We are binding the element using `ngModel` written inside `[()]`
- We have associated Two-way Data Binding for the `input` element

> Don't forget to import `FormsModule` from `@angular/forms` or else you will get errors. `ngModel` creates a `FormControl` instance from a domain model and binds it to a form control element.

Now, let's create an example using `ngModel`:

```
<div> {{sample_value}}</div>

<input [(ngModel)]="sample_value" />
```

We added a `div` element and, using Data Binding, we mapped the value of the input element using `ngModel`. Using `ngModel` helps track the value, user interaction, and validation status of the control and keeps the view synced with the model.

Now, when we start typing in the `input` element of type text, we see that what we type is copied to our `div` element as a `value`:

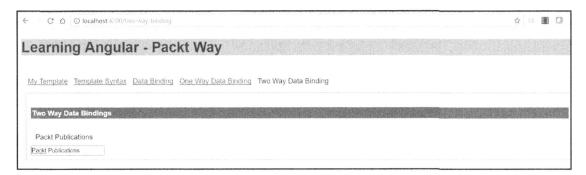

Great! We have made quite a bit of progress with respect to Data Binding and templates. With the all knowledge we have gained throughout this chapter, we can create beautifully elegant, yet fully powerful application interfaces.

Summary

Template Syntax and Data Binding are the skeleton and soul of Angular applications. We covered templates: how to include them in different ways and use expressions inside view templates. We then walked through templates by attaching events and attributes to them.

We explored aspects of Data Binding in Angular applications and focused on how to implement Data Binding for values inside the template.

In Data Binding, we delved into its broad categories. We explored available ways of Data Bindings: One-way Data Binding and Two-way Data Binding.

Using Data Binding and templates together, we can almost create mock functional screens for our Angular applications: that's the power of Data Binding and Template Syntax.

So, go ahead and let your creativity fly! Good luck.

In the next chapter, you will learn about advanced forms in Angular, learn how to use and master reactive forms. We tackle the reactive part of reactive forms by emphasizing the relationship between your html models and your `NgModel` so every change on a given form is propagated to the model

9
Advanced Forms in Angular

In Chapter 7, *Asynchronous Programming Using Observables*, we used Observables to build a simple, yet easily extendable JSON API to query the Marvel Cinematic Universe. In this chapter, we will build the forms that will allow us to query our API in a more user-friendly way. These forms will help us to not only retrieve movies from the Marvel Cinematic Universe, but also to add movies. In addition to the forms themselves, we will obviously need to build on our API, so it supports the addition and modification of movies.

In this chapter, we will see the following topics covered in detail:

- Reactive forms
- Control and ControlGroup
- Form directive
- Using FormBuilder
- Adding validations
- Custom validation

Getting started

As stated in the introduction of this chapter, we will build upon our JSON API for the Marvel Cinematic Universe of Chapter 7, *Asynchronous Programming Using Observables*. To be a bit more precise, we will improve the Promise-based version. Why Promises instead of pure observers? Well, Promises are an extremely powerful tool, and they are used in the majority of Angular/Typescript projects I have seen so far. Consequently, a bit more practice with Promises won't hurt much.

You can find the code of the Promises part here
`http://bit.ly/mastering-angular2-chap7-part3`.

To clone this code into a new repo called `advanced-forms`, use the following command:

```
$ git clone --depth one https://github.com/MathieuNls/mastering-
  angular2 advanced-forms
$ cd advanced-forms
$ git filter-branch --prune-empty --subdirectory-filter chap7/angular-
  promise HEAD
$ npm install
```

These commands pull the latest version of the GitHub repository containing the code for this book to a folder named `advanced-forms`. Then, we go into the `advanced-forms` folder and prune everything that is not inside the `chap7/angular-promise` subdirectory. Magically enough, Git rewrites the history of the repository to keep only the files that were inside the `chap7/angular-promise` subdirectory. Finally, `npm install` will have all our dependencies ready to fire.

As a result, you will have the behavior we achieved in Chapter 7, *Asynchronous Programming Using Observables* (for example querying movies from the Marvel Cinematic Universe) inside a new project named advanced-forms. Now, it won't be much fun if we use forms to create, read, update and delete movies from the Marvel Cinematic Universe, and these changes are not reflected in the querying part. As a reminder, the querying API we built in Chapter 7, *Asynchronous Programming Using Observables* is a static JSON file as a backend mock. To save the changes coming from our forms, we will have to modify the JSON file. While this is possible, it means that we will build a whole new functionality (that is editing a file) only for the purpose of our mock. This new functionality won't help us at all, when we go ahead with a real backend. Consequently, we will use an in-memory reference for our movies from the Marvel Cinematic Universe.

The `app.component.ts` file looks like this:

```
import { Component } from '@angular/core';
import { IMDBAPIService } from './services/imdbapi.service';
import { Movie, MovieFields } from './models/movie';

@Component({
  selector: 'app-root',
  templateUrl: './app.component.html',
  styleUrls: ['./app.component.css']
})
export class AppComponent {
  title = 'app works!';
```

```
private movies:Movie[] = [];
private error:boolean = false;
private finished:boolean = false;

constructor(private IMDBAPI:IMDBAPIService){

    this.IMDBAPI.fecthOneById(1).then(
      value => {
          this.movies.push(value);
          console.log("Component", value)
      },
      error => this.error = true
    );

    this.IMDBAPI.fetchByField(MovieFields.release_year, 2015).then(
      value => {
          this.movies = value;
          console.log("Component", value)
      },
      error => this.error = true
    )

    this.IMDBAPI.byField(MovieFields.release_year, 2015)
      .or(MovieFields.release_year, 2014)
      .or(MovieFields.phase, "Phase Two")
      .fetch()
      .then(
        value => {
            this.movies = value;
            console.log("Component", value)
        },
        error => this.error = true
      );
    }
}
```

And the related HTML template is as follows:

```
<h1>
  {{title}}
</h1>

<ul>
    <li *ngFor="let movie of movies">{{movie}}</li>
</ul>
```

The `IMDBAPIService` didn't change from Chapter 7, *Asynchronous Programming Using Observables* and an `ng start` will have the following result:

app works!

- Movie (movie_id: 1, title: Iron Man, phase: Phase One: Avengers Assembled, category_name: Action, release_year: 2015, running_time: 126, rating_name: PG-13, disc_format_name: Blu-ray, number_discs: 1, viewing_format_name: Widescreen, aspect_ratio_name: 2.35:1, status: 1, release_date: May 2, 2008, budget: 140,000,000, gross: 318,298,180, time_stamp: 2015-05-03)
- Movie (movie_id: 3, title: Iron Man 2, phase: Phase One: Avengers Assembled, category_name: Action, release_year: 2015, running_time: 124, rating_name: PG-13, disc_format_name: Blu-ray, number_discs: 1, viewing_format_name: Widescreen, aspect_ratio_name: 2.35:1, status: 1, release_date: May 7, 2010, budget: 200,000,000, gross: 312,057,433, time_stamp: 2015-05-03)
- Movie (movie_id: 7, title: Iron Man 3, phase: Phase Two, category_name: Action, release_year: 2015, running_time: 130, rating_name: PG-13, disc_format_name: Blu-ray + DVD, number_discs: 2, viewing_format_name: Widescreen, aspect_ratio_name: 2.35:1, status: 1, release_date: May 3, 2013, budget: 200,000,000, gross: 408,992,272, time_stamp: 2015-05-03)
- Movie (movie_id: 11, title: Avengers: Age of Ultron, phase: Phase Two, category_name: Science Fiction, release_year: 2015, running_time: 141, rating_name: PG-13, disc_format_name: Blu-ray, number_discs: 1, viewing_format_name: Widescreen, aspect_ratio_name: 2.35:1, status: 1, release_date: May 1, 2015, budget: 250,000,000, gross: 458,991,599, time_stamp: 2015-12-07)
- Movie (movie_id: 12, title: Ant-Man, phase: Phase Two, category_name: Science Fiction, release_year: 2015, running_time: 132, rating_name: PG-13, disc_format_name: Blu-ray, number_discs: 1, viewing_format_name: Widescreen, aspect_ratio_name: 1.85:1, status: 1, release_date: July 17, 2015, budget: 130,000,000, gross: 179,017,481, time_stamp: 2015-12-07)
- Movie (movie_id: 9, title: Captain America: The Winter Soldier, phase: Phase Two, category_name: Action, release_year: 2014, running_time: 136, rating_name: PG-13, disc_format_name: Blu-ray, number_discs: 1, viewing_format_name: Widescreen, aspect_ratio_name: 2.35:1, status: 1, release_date: April 4, 2014, budget: 170,000,000, gross: 259,746,958, time_stamp: 2014-09-19)
- Movie (movie_id: 10, title: Guardians of the Galaxy, phase: Phase Two, category_name: Science Fiction, release_year: 2014, running_time: 121,

State at the end of chapter 7, *Asynchronous Programming Using Observables.*

Reactive forms

In Chapter 8, *Template and Data Binding Syntax*, we learned how to leverage Data Binding and templating in Angular. Here, we'll combine these new notions with forms. Anyone with two hours, of HTML experience knows what `<form>` means and how to use them. With a couple of hours of HTML behind you, you know how to identify the different information in your forms and choose a method (that is `GET`, `POST`, `PUT`, and `DELETE`) to send everything to the backend of your choice.

In this recipe, however, we will build forms using imperative TypeScript code instead of good old HTML. Why, you ask? Well, this allows us to test our forms without relying on end-to-end tests that need the DOM to be generated. With reactive forms, we can test our form with classical unit tests as described in Chapter 16, *Testing Angular Apps Using Jasmine and Protractor Frameworks*.

Let's start by building the underlying HTML structure for a form, aiming at adding a new movie to the Marvel Cinematic Universe as follows:

```
<form [formGroup]="movieForm">
        <label>movie_id</label>
        <input type="text" formControlName="movie_id"><br/>
```

```
<label>title</label>
<input type="text" formControlName="title"><br/>
<label>phase</label>
<input type="text" formControlName="phase"><br/>
<label>category_name</label>
<input type="text" formControlName="category_name"><br/>
<label>release_year</label>
<input type="text" formControlName="release_year"><br/>
<label>running_time</label>
<input type="text" formControlName="running_time"><br/>
<label>rating_name</label>
<input type="text" formControlName="rating_name"><br/>
<label>disc_format_name</label>
<input type="text" formControlName="disc_format_name"><br/>
<label>number_discs</label>
<input type="text" formControlName="number_discs"><br/>
<label>viewing_format_name</label>
<input type="text" formControlName="viewing_format_name"><br/>
<label>aspect_ratio_name</label>
<input type="text" formControlName="aspect_ratio_name"><br/>
<label>status</label>
<input type="text" formControlName="status"><br/>
<label>release_date</label>
<input type="text" formControlName="release_date"><br/>
<label>budget</label>
<input type="text" formControlName="budget"><br/>
<label>gross</label>
<input type="text" formControlName="gross"><br/>
<label>time_stamp</label>
<input type="text" formControlName="time_stamp"><br/>
</form>
```

In the preceding form, we have one couple label-input for each attribute of the `Movie` model. Now, there are some directives that are definitely not pure HTML in this form. Namely, `[formGroup]="movieForm"` and `formControlName=""`. The first directive (`[formGroup]="movieForm"`) is used to bind this particular form with an instance of `FormGroup`. Then, `formControlName` refers to instances of the `FormControl` class that comprises the `FormGroup`. In other words, `movieForm` is a `FormGroup` comprised of `FormControl`, `FormGroup`, and `FormControl` are in the `@angular/forms` package both. Consequently, we'll have to import this package in our `app.component.ts` file: `import { FormGroup, FormControl }` from `@angular/forms`; after updating the `app.component.html` file with our form. In addition, we need to import the `ReactiveFormsModule` and add it to our application module.

If you were to serve your application right now, it would transpile without a hitch. At runtime, however, it'll complain, as the `movieForm` form group does not exist in your component yet. Let's create it:

```
private movieForm:FormGroup =  new FormGroup({
   movie_id: new FormControl(),
   title: new FormControl(),
   phase: new FormControl(),
   category_name: new FormControl(),
   release_year: new FormControl(),
   running_time: new FormControl(),
   rating_name: new FormControl(),
   disc_format_name: new FormControl(),
   number_discs: new FormControl(),
   viewing_format_name: new FormControl(),
   aspect_ratio_name: new FormControl(),
   status: new FormControl(),
   release_date: new FormControl(),
   budget: new FormControl(),
   gross: new FormControl(),
   time_stamp: new FormControl()
});
```

As you can see, we have a private member of the `AppComponent` component that is an instance of `FormGroup`. This `FormGroup` instance is composed of many `FormControl` instances, one per field to be precise.

Also, the value of each field can be accessed via `this.movieForm.value.my_field`. Consequently, if we add a submit button to our form:

```
<button (click)="submit()" type="submit">SUBMIT</button>
```

And the corresponding `submit()` function in the `AppComponent` component, then we can display the values of each one of our fields.

```
private submit(){
  console.log(
    "Form Values",
    this.movieForm.value.movie_id,
    this.movieForm.value.title,
    this.movieForm.value.phase,
    this.movieForm.value.category_name,
    this.movieForm.value.release_year,
    this.movieForm.value.running_time,
    this.movieForm.value.rating_name,
    this.movieForm.value.disc_format_name,
    this.movieForm.value.number_discs,
```

```
            this.movieForm.value.viewing_format_name,
            this.movieForm.value.aspect_ratio_name,
            this.movieForm.value.status,
            this.movieForm.value.release_date,
            this.movieForm.value.budget,
            this.movieForm.value.gross,
            this.movieForm.value.time_stamp
        );
    }
```

It's as simple as that; we got a communication between our HTML template and our component:

Displaying the rather crude HTML form and the console output of the submit function.

Then, we can create an instance of the `Movie` model and send it to the `IMDBAPI` for persistence. The only thing missing is a working backend.

```
private submit(){
    console.log(
      "Form Values",
      this.movieForm.value.movie_id,
      this.movieForm.value.title,
      this.movieForm.value.phase,
      this.movieForm.value.category_name,
      this.movieForm.value.release_year,
      this.movieForm.value.running_time,
      this.movieForm.value.rating_name,
      this.movieForm.value.disc_format_name,
      this.movieForm.value.number_discs,
      this.movieForm.value.viewing_format_name,
      this.movieForm.value.aspect_ratio_name,
      this.movieForm.value.status,
      this.movieForm.value.release_date,
      this.movieForm.value.budget,
      this.movieForm.value.gross,
      this.movieForm.value.time_stamp
    );

    let movie:Movie = new Movie(
      this.movieForm.value.movie_id,
      this.movieForm.value.title,
      this.movieForm.value.phase,
      this.movieForm.value.category_name,
      this.movieForm.value.release_year,
      this.movieForm.value.running_time,
      this.movieForm.value.rating_name,
      this.movieForm.value.disc_format_name,
      this.movieForm.value.number_discs,
      this.movieForm.value.viewing_format_name,
      this.movieForm.value.aspect_ratio_name,
      this.movieForm.value.status,
      this.movieForm.value.release_date,
      this.movieForm.value.budget,
      this.movieForm.value.gross,
      this.movieForm.value.time_stamp
    );

    console.log(movie);

    //Persist movie

}
```

In the following screenshot, we can see the displayed HTML form and the console output for the improved `submit` function:

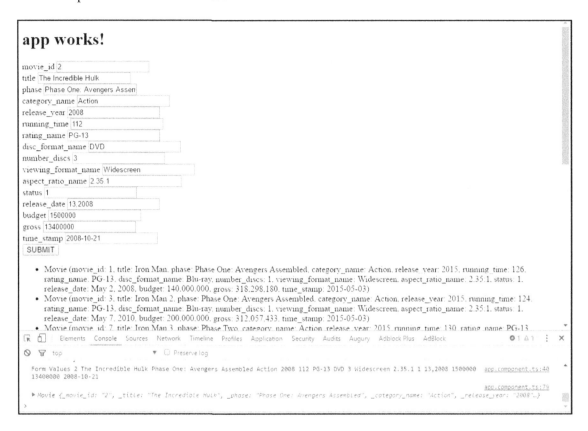

Now that's great; we have retrieved the values from the HTML form into the component side of our application, and we have created a `Movie` object that can be moved around and persisted. There are at least two different things to improve in this form:

- The wordiness of the form creation (`new FormControl() much ?`)
- The verifications on the different input

Using FormBuilder

FormBuilder is an injectable helper class of the @angular/forms package of Angular. This class helps to reduce the wordiness of form creation as demonstrated in the following code:

```
this.movieForm = this.formBuilder.group({
    movie_id: '',
    title: '',
    phase: '',
    category_name: '',
    release_year: '',
    running_time: '',
    rating_name: '',
    disc_format_name: '',
    number_discs: '',
    viewing_format_name: '',
    aspect_ratio_name: '',
    status: '',
    release_date: '',
    budget: '',
    gross: '',
    time_stamp: ''
});
```

As you can see, using the group method of the FormBuilder class, the declaration of FormGroup and FormControl is now implicit. We only need to have the field name followed by its default value. Here, all the default values are blank.

To use the FormBuilder class, we first have to import it:

```
Import { FormGroup, FormControl, FormBuilder } from '@angular/forms';
```

We then inject it using the constructor of our AppComponent component:

```
constructor(private IMDBAPI:IMDBAPIService, private formBuilder:
FormBuilder)
```

Note that we still have the injection of IMDBAPIService from Chapter 7, *Asynchronous Programming Using Observables*.

Consequently, AppComponent now looks like the following:

```
import { Component } from '@angular/core';
import { IMDBAPIService } from './services/imdbapi.service';
import { Movie, MovieFields } from './models/movie';

import { FormGroup, FormControl, FormBuilder } from '@angular/forms';

@Component({
  selector: 'app-root',
  templateUrl: './app.component.html',
  styleUrls: ['./app.component.css']
})
export class AppComponent {
  title = 'app works!';

  private movies:Movie[] = [];
  private error:boolean = false;
  private finished:boolean = false;
  private movieForm:FormGroup;


  constructor(private IMDBAPI:IMDBAPIService, private formBuilder:
    FormBuilder){


    this.movieForm =  this.formBuilder.group({
      movie_id: '',
      title: '',
      phase: '',
      category_name: '',
      release_year: '',
      running_time: '',
      rating_name: '',
      disc_format_name: '',
      number_discs: '',
      viewing_format_name: '',
      aspect_ratio_name: '',
      status: '',
      release_date: '',
      budget: '',
      gross: '',
      time_stamp: ''
    });
```

```
        // IMDB queries have been removed for simplicity
    }

    private submit(){
        // submit body has been removed for simplicity
    }
```

We've solved the first one of our two problems: the wordiness of the form creation. In the next section, we'll tackle the validation part of this chapter where we learn how to validate incoming inputs.

Adding validations

Dealing with forms is often a pain for developers because you obviously can't trust the inputs provided by the user. It is either because they are just not paying attention to what you expect in your forms or because they want to break things. Validating inputs incoming from a form is painful in every language, both server and client-side.

Now, the Angular team came up with a rather simple way to validate inputs by defining what is expected from each field right at the form's creation using `Validators`. Angular contains the following built-in `Validators` that we can use:

- `required`: Requires a non-empty value
- `minLength(minLength: number)`: Requires the control value to have a minimum length of `minLength`
- `maxLength(maxLength: number)`: Requires the control value to have a maximum length of `maxLength`
- `pattern(pattern: string)`: Requires that the control value matches the provided pattern

Adding these built-in `validators` to our form is straightforward:

```
//In AppComponent

import { FormGroup, FormControl, FormBuilder, Validators } from
'@angular/forms';

//[...]

constructor(private IMDBAPI:IMDBAPIService, private formBuilder:
FormBuilder){
```

```
this.movieForm = this.formBuilder.group({
  movie_id: ['', Validators.required],
  title: ['', Validators.required],
  phase: ['', Validators.required],
  category_name: ['', Validators.required],
  release_year: ['', Validators.required],
  running_time: ['', Validators.required],
  rating_name: ['', Validators.required],
  disc_format_name: ['', Validators.required],
  number_discs: ['', Validators.required],
  viewing_format_name: ['', Validators.required],
  aspect_ratio_name: ['', Validators.required],
  status: ['', Validators.required],
  release_date: ['', Validators.required],
  budget: ['', Validators.required],
  gross: ['', Validators.required],
  time_stamp: ['', Validators.required]
});
  }

//[...]
```

In addition to a blank default value for each field, we add the required `validator`, which is a static of the `Validators` class contained in the `@angular/forms` package. We can read the validity of the form (that is, if all the validators are OK'd) using the valid property of our `FormGroup`:

```
private submit(){
    console.log(
      "Form Values",
      this.movieForm.value.movie_id,
      this.movieForm.value.title,
      this.movieForm.value.phase,
      this.movieForm.value.category_name,
      this.movieForm.value.release_year,
      this.movieForm.value.running_time,
      this.movieForm.value.rating_name,
      this.movieForm.value.disc_format_name,
      this.movieForm.value.number_discs,
      this.movieForm.value.viewing_format_name,
      this.movieForm.value.aspect_ratio_name,
      this.movieForm.value.status,
      this.movieForm.value.release_date,
      this.movieForm.value.budget,
      this.movieForm.value.gross,
      this.movieForm.value.time_stamp
    );
```

```
        if(this.movieForm.valid){
          let movie:Movie = new Movie(
            this.movieForm.value.movie_id,
            this.movieForm.value.title,
            this.movieForm.value.phase,
            this.movieForm.value.category_name,
            this.movieForm.value.release_year,
            this.movieForm.value.running_time,
            this.movieForm.value.rating_name,
            this.movieForm.value.disc_format_name,
            this.movieForm.value.number_discs,
            this.movieForm.value.viewing_format_name,
            this.movieForm.value.aspect_ratio_name,
            this.movieForm.value.status,
            this.movieForm.value.release_date,
            this.movieForm.value.budget,
            this.movieForm.value.gross,
            this.movieForm.value.time_stamp
          );

        console.log(movie);
        //Persist movie
      }else{
        console.error("Form not valid");
      }
  }
```

In the previous modification of the `submit` method, if the user does not fill in one of the fields, then the `Movie` object won't be created. Also, we'll display a `console.error("Form not valid");` and, if we add a conditional `<p></p>` block accompanied by some rudimentary CSS, we can provide some feedback to the user.

```
<p class='error' *ngIf=!movieForm.valid>Error</p>
/*app.component.css*/
.error{
    color:red;
}
```

In the following screenshot, we can see the displayed HTML form with feedback on the form's validity:

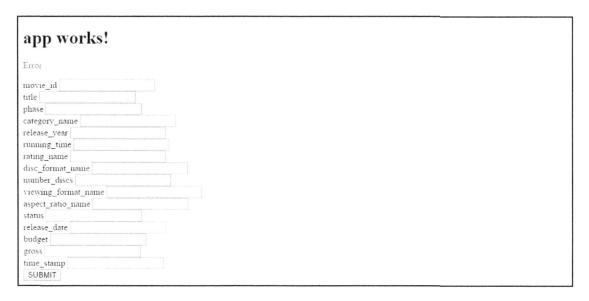

We can go a bit further and provide a visual feedback per field. The status of each field is accessible through the `valid` property of each sub `FormControl`.

```
<form [formGroup]="movieForm">

        <p class='error' *ngIf=!movieForm.valid>Error</p>
        <label>movie_id</label>
        <p class='error' *ngIf=!movieForm.controls.movie_id.valid>This
                field is required</p>
        <input type="text" formControlName="movie_id"><br/>
        <label>title</label>
        <p class='error' *ngIf=!movieForm.controls.title.valid>This
                field is required</p>
        <input type="text" formControlName="title"><br/>
        <label>phase</label>
        <p class='error' *ngIf=!movieForm.controls.phase.valid>This
                field is required</p>
        <input type="text" formControlName="phase"><br/>
        <label>category_name</label>
        <p class='error'
                *ngIf=!movieForm.controls.category_name.valid>This field
                is required</p>
        <input type="text" formControlName="category_name"><br/>
        <label>release_year</label>
```

```
<p class='error'
    *ngIf=!movieForm.controls.release_year.valid>This field
    is required</p>
<input type="text" formControlName="release_year"><br/>
<label>running_time</label>
<p class='error'
    *ngIf=!movieForm.controls.running_time.valid>This field
    is required</p>
<input type="text" formControlName="running_time"><br/>
<label>rating_name</label>
<p class='error'
    *ngIf=!movieForm.controls.rating_name.valid>This field
    is required</p>
<input type="text" formControlName="rating_name"><br/>
<label>disc_format_name</label>
<p class='error'
    *ngIf=!movieForm.controls.disc_format_name.valid>This
    field is required</p>
<input type="text" formControlName="disc_format_name"><br/>
<label>number_discs</label>
<p class='error'
    *ngIf=!movieForm.controls.number_discs.valid>This field
    is required</p>
<input type="text" formControlName="number_discs"><br/>
<label>viewing_format_name</label>
<p class='error'
    *ngIf=!movieForm.controls.viewing_format_name.valid>This
    field is required</p>
<input type="text" formControlName="viewing_format_name"><br/>
<label>aspect_ratio_name</label>
<p class='error'
    *ngIf=!movieForm.controls.aspect_ratio_name.valid>This
    field is required</p>
<input type="text" formControlName="aspect_ratio_name"><br/>
<label>status</label>
<p class='error' *ngIf=!movieForm.controls.status.valid>This
    field is required</p>
<input type="text" formControlName="status"><br/>
<label>release_date</label>
<p class='error'
    *ngIf=!movieForm.controls.release_date.valid>This field is
    required</p>
<input type="text" formControlName="release_date"><br/>
<label>budget</label>
<p class='error' *ngIf=!movieForm.controls.budget.valid>This
    field is required</p>
<input type="text" formControlName="budget"><br/>
<label>gross</label>
```

```
        <p class='error' *ngIf=!movieForm.controls.gross.valid>This
            field is required</p>
        <input type="text" formControlName="gross"><br/>
        <label>time_stamp</label>
        <p class='error'
            *ngIf=!movieForm.controls.time_stamp.valid>This field is
            required</p>
        <input type="text" formControlName="time_stamp"><br/>

        <button (click)="submit()" type="submit">SUBMIT</button>
    </form>
```

This produces the following:

Displaying HTML form with feedback on each field's validity.

As you can see, each form except the movid_id one, displays the This field is required error as they are empty. The *ngIf structural directive listens to any changes in the associated variable and will show/hide the paragraph when the field becomes invalid/valid. Another useful property of the form is pristine. It defines whether or not a given field has been modified by a user. In our case, it could be used to avoid displaying errors, even when no editing occurred.

Another handy thing to know about validators is that they can be composed using the compose method of the Validators class. In the following example, We will compose a validator for the movie_id field from four distinct validators: Validators.required, Validators.minLength, Validators.maxLength, and Validators.pattern.

```
this.movieForm =  this.formBuilder.group({
    movie_id: ['',
        Validators.compose(
        [
            Validators.required,
            Validators.minLength(1),
            Validators.maxLength(4),
            Validators.pattern('[0-9]+')
        ]
        )
    ],
    title: ['', Validators.required],
    phase: ['', Validators.required],
    category_name: ['', Validators.required],
    release_year: ['', Validators.required],
    running_time: ['', Validators.required],
    rating_name: ['', Validators.required],
    disc_format_name: ['', Validators.required],
    number_discs: ['', Validators.required],
    viewing_format_name: ['', Validators.required],
    aspect_ratio_name: ['', Validators.required],
    status: ['', Validators.required],
    release_date: ['', Validators.required],
    budget: ['', Validators.required],
    gross: ['', Validators.required],
    time_stamp: ['', Validators.required]
});
```

The resulting composite validator will henceforth ensure that the `movie_id` is a number that is between `1` and `4` digits long. The following screenshot displays an HTML form with feedback on the **movide_id** field. The field is valid because it's composed of four digits:

Custom validation

In the previous section, we saw how to use validators and combine validators together to create more complex validation. The `Validators.required`, `Validators.minLength`, `Validators.maxLength`, and `Validators.pattern` combinations can cover a lot of validation cases that can arise during the development of your Angular application. If the time comes where you can't handle your validation needs with the built-in validator, then you can build your very own validator.

In this section, we'll see how to validate that the **movie_id** field contains a valid entry (that is a number that is between one and four digits long) and that another movie does not already use the id. To do so, we can create the following class:

```
import { FormControl } from '@angular/forms';

interface ValidationResult {
 [key:string]:boolean;
}

export class MovieIDValidator{
    static idNotTaken(control: FormControl): ValidationResult {

        let movies = require('./marvel-cinematic-
                universe.json').movies;
        let found:boolean = false;

        for (var i = 0; i < movies.length; ++i) {

            if(control.value == movies[i].movie_id){
                return { "idNotTaken": true };
            }
        }

        return null;
    }
}
```

Here, we can see that the validation results are, in fact, a simple `[key:string]:boolean` structure. If the Boolean is true, then, it means that the validator failed (that is, the field is not valid). Moving on to the `MovieIDValidator` class itself, we have a static method returning a `ValidationResult` and accepting as a parameter a `FormControl`. Inside this method, we pull all the movies from our JSON file containing the Marvel Cinematic Universe. Then, we iterate over all the movies and check if the current value of the `movie_id` field matches an existing id. If so, we return `{ "idNotTaken": true }`, meaning that there is a problem with the `idNotTaken` validator. Combining this new custom validator with the other four (that is `Validators.required`, `Validators.minLength`, `Validators.maxLength`, and `Validators.pattern`) is a piece of cake:

```
import { MovieIDValidator } from './movie-id.validator'

// [...]

this.movieForm =  this.formBuilder.group({
        movie_id: ['',
```

```
Validators.compose(
  [
   Validators.required,
   Validators.minLength(1),
   Validators.maxLength(4),
   Validators.pattern('[0-9]+'),
   MovieIDValidator.idNotTaken
  ]
)
],
title: ['', Validators.required],
phase: ['', Validators.required],
category_name: ['', Validators.required],
release_year: ['', Validators.required],
running_time: ['', Validators.required],
rating_name: ['', Validators.required],
disc_format_name: ['', Validators.required],
number_discs: ['', Validators.required],
viewing_format_name: ['', Validators.required],
aspect_ratio_name: ['', Validators.required],
status: ['', Validators.required],
release_date: ['', Validators.required],
budget: ['', Validators.required],
gross: ['', Validators.required],
time_stamp: ['', Validators.required]
});
```

We can also add an asynchronous form validator that returns a Promise (for example `Promise<ValidationResult>` instead of `ValidationResult`). This is very handy when you have to do your validation using a remote API.

```
import { FormControl } from '@angular/forms';

interface ValidationResult {
 [key:string]:boolean;
}

export class MovieIDValidator{
    static idNotTaken(control: FormControl): ValidationResult {

        let movies = require('./marvel-cinematic-
            universe.json').movies;
        let found:boolean = false;

        for (var i = 0; i < movies.length; ++i) {

            if(control.value == movies[i].movie_id){
                return { "idNotTaken": true };
```

```
                }
            }

        return null;
    }

    static idTakenAsync(control: FormControl):
     Promise<ValidationResult> {

        let p = new Promise((resolve, reject) => {
         setTimeout(() => {

            let movies = require('./marvel-cinematic-
                universe.json').movies;
            let found:boolean = false;

            for (var i = 0; i < movies.length; ++i) {

                if(control.value == movies[i].movie_id){
                    resolve({ "idNotTaken": true });
                }
            }

            resolve(null);

         }, 1000)
        });

        return p;

    }
}
```

Here, we build a Promise that simulates a remote API call with a 1-second timeout. What the Promise does is the same thing as idNotTaken, where we check if an id for a movie is already taken. After the Promise creation, we return it so it can be used in the related component.

Two-way Data Binding with ngModel

A very convenient process when creating or updating the model of your Angular application through forms is Two-way Data Binding with ngModel. In the previous application, we had the following submit() method:

```
private submit(){
  console.log(
    "Form Values",
    this.movieForm.value.movie_id,
    this.movieForm.value.title,
    this.movieForm.value.phase,
    this.movieForm.value.category_name,
    this.movieForm.value.release_year,
    this.movieForm.value.running_time,
    this.movieForm.value.rating_name,
    this.movieForm.value.disc_format_name,
    this.movieForm.value.number_discs,
    this.movieForm.value.viewing_format_name,
    this.movieForm.value.aspect_ratio_name,
    this.movieForm.value.status,
    this.movieForm.value.release_date,
    this.movieForm.value.budget,
    this.movieForm.value.gross,
    this.movieForm.value.time_stamp
  );

  if(this.movieForm.valid){
    let movie:Movie = new Movie(
      this.movieForm.value.movie_id,
      this.movieForm.value.title,
      this.movieForm.value.phase,
      this.movieForm.value.category_name,
      this.movieForm.value.release_year,
      this.movieForm.value.running_time,
      this.movieForm.value.rating_name,
      this.movieForm.value.disc_format_name,
      this.movieForm.value.number_discs,
      this.movieForm.value.viewing_format_name,
      this.movieForm.value.aspect_ratio_name,
      this.movieForm.value.status,
      this.movieForm.value.release_date,
      this.movieForm.value.budget,
      this.movieForm.value.gross,
      this.movieForm.value.time_stamp
    );
```

```
        console.log(movie);
    }
  else{
      console.error("Form not valid");
    }
  }
```

To the experimented eye, this looks clumsy. Indeed, we knew that we'd ask the user for a new movie. Hence, all the fields will be displayed and their value used to create the aforementioned movie. Using Two-way Data Binding, you can specify a binding between each HTML input and an attribute of your model. In our case, this is an attribute of the `Movie` object.

```html
<form [formGroup]="movieForm">

        <p class='error' *ngIf=!movieForm.valid>Error</p>
        <label>movie_id</label>
        <p class='error' *ngIf=!movieForm.controls.movie_id.valid>This
            field is required</p>
        <input type="text" formControlName="movie_id"
            [(ngModel)]="movie.movie_id" name="movie_id" ><br/>
        <label>title</label>
        <p class='error' *ngIf=!movieForm.controls.title.valid>This
            field is required</p>
        <input type="text" formControlName="title"
            [(ngModel)]="movie.title" name="movie_title"><br/>
        <label>phase</label>
        <p class='error' *ngIf=!movieForm.controls.phase.valid>This
            field is required</p>
        <input type="text" formControlName="phase"
            [(ngModel)]="movie.phase" name="movie_phase"><br/>
        <label>category_name</label>
        <p class='error' *ngIf=!movieForm.controls.
            category_name.valid>This field is required</p>
        <input type="text" formControlName="category_name"
            [(ngModel)]="movie.category_name"  name="movie_cat"><br/>
        <label>release_year</label>
        <p class='error' *ngIf=!movieForm.controls.release_year
            .valid>This field is required</p>
        <input type="text" formControlName="release_year"
            [(ngModel)]="movie.release_year" name="movie_year"><br/>
        <label>running_time</label>
        <p class='error'*ngIf=!movieForm.controls.
            running_time.valid>This field is required</p>
        <input type="text" formControlName="running_time"
            [(ngModel)]="movie.running_time" name="movie_time"><br/>
        <label>rating_name</label>
```

```
<p class='error' *ngIf=!movieForm.controls.rating_name.
valid>This field is required</p>
<input type="text" formControlName="rating_name"
    [(ngModel)]="movie.rating_name" name="movie_rating"><br/>
<label>disc_format_name</label>
<p class='error' *ngIf=!movieForm.controls.
    disc_format_name.valid>This field is required</p>
<input type="text" formControlName="disc_format_name"
    [(ngModel)]="movie.disc_format_name" name="movie_disc"><br/>
<label>number_discs</label>
<p class='error' *ngIf=!movieForm.controls.number_discs.valid>
    This field is required</p>
<input type="text" formControlName="number_discs"
    [(ngModel)]="movie.number_discs" name="movie_discs_nb"><br/>
<label>viewing_format_name</label>
<p class='error' *ngIf=!movieForm.controls.viewing_format_name.
    valid>This field is required</p>
<input type="text" formControlName="viewing_format_name"
    [(ngModel)]="movie.viewing_format_name"
    name="movie_format"><br/>
<label>aspect_ratio_name</label>
<p class='error' *ngIf=!movieForm.controls.aspect_ratio_name.
    valid>This field is required</p>
<input type="text" formControlName="aspect_ratio_name"
    [(ngModel)]="movie.aspect_ratio_name"
    name="movie_ratio"><br/>
<label>status</label>
<p class='error' *ngIf=!movieForm.
    controls.status.valid>This field is required</p>
<input type="text" formControlName="status"
    [(ngModel)]="movie.status" name="movie_status"><br/>
<label>release_date</label>
<p class='error' *ngIf=!movieForm.controls.release_date.
    valid>This field is required</p>
<input type="text" formControlName="release_date"
    [(ngModel)]="movie.release_date" name="movie_release"><br/>
<label>budget</label>
<p class='error' *ngIf=!movieForm.controls.budget.valid>This
    field is required</p>
<input type="text" formControlName="budget"
    [(ngModel)]="movie.budget" name="movie_budget"><br/>
<label>gross</label>
<p class='error' *ngIf=!movieForm.controls.gross.valid>This
    field is required</p>
<input type="text" formControlName="gross"
    [(ngModel)]="movie.gross" name="movie_gross"><br/>
<label>time_stamp</label>
<p class='error' *ngIf=!movieForm.controls.time_stamp.
```

```
                    valid>This field is required</p>
         <input type="text" formControlName="time_stamp"
           [(ngModel)]="movie.time_stamp" name="movie_timestamp"><br/>

         <button (click)="submit()" type="submit">SUBMIT</button>
</form>
```

Have a look at the `[(ngModel)]` directive. Here, we bind one way using `[]` and the other way using `()`. One way is the model of the form and the other way is from the form to the model. It means that any modification made to the form will impact the model and any modification made to the model will be reflected on the form.

Now, our submit method can be reduced to the following:

```
private submit(){ if(this.movieForm.valid){
  console.log(this.movie);

  //persist
}else{
  console.error("Form not valid");
}
}
```

One important thing to keep in mind is that the values of the form will be transferred to the model even if the validators are not valid. For example, if you were to enter `ABC` into the `movie_id` field, then the `validators` will not be valid but `console.log(this.movie.movie_id)` will display `ABC`.

Keeping things neat (extra credit)

I have always found that forms are the bane of clean, neat, organized HTML templates. Even small forms, well indented and separated by comments, look cluttered to my eyes. To solve this problem in an Angular way, we can create directives that keep forms input organized. Here's an example of what I use when creating a form for `Toolwatch.io`:

```
<toolwatch-input
     [id]            = "'email'"
     [control]       = "loginForm.controls.email"
     [errorLabel]    = "'email-required'"
     [submitAttempt] = "submitAttempt"
     [autoCapitalize] = false
     [autoCorrect]   = false
     [spellCheck]    = false
 >
```

As you can see, the directive accepts a different @Input parameter that controls how the input will look and behave.

Here's the related component:

```
import { Component, Input, EventEmitter, Output  } from '@angular/core';
import {
  FormControl
} from '@angular/forms';



@Component({
    templateUrl: './toowatch-input.html',
    pipes: [TranslatePipe],
    selector: 'toolwatch-input',
})
export class ToolwatchInput {

    @Input()
     id             : string;
    @Input()
     control        : FormControl;
    @Input()
     model          : any = null;
    @Input()
     type           : string = "text";
    @Input()
     label          : string;
    @Input()
     errorLabel     : string;
    @Input()
     formControlName: string;
    @Input()
     submitAttempt  : boolean = true;
    @Input()
     autoCapitalize : boolean = true;
    @Input()
     autoCorrect    : boolean = true;
    @Input()
     autoComplete   : boolean = true;
    @Input()
     spellCheck     : boolean = true;

    @Output()
     update         = new EventEmitter();

    constructor() {
```

```
    }

    ngAfterViewInit() {

        if(this.control == null || this.id == null){
            throw "[Control] and [id] must be set";
        }

        //initialize other variables to the value of id
        //if they are null
        let variablesToInitialize = [
            "label",
            "errorLabel",
            "formControlName"
        ];

        for (var i = variablesToInitialize.length - 1; i >= 0; i--) {
            if(this[variablesToInitialize[i]] == null){
                this[variablesToInitialize[i]] = this.id;
            }
        }
    }

}
```

This component accepts, as inputs, the following attributes:

- `id`: The `id` for the input
- `control`: `FormControl` controlling this input
- `model`: Bound model field
- `type`: Input type
- `label`: Label to display
- `errorLabel`: Error label to display
- `formControlName`: Name of the form control
- `submitAttempt`: If the form has been submitted once
- `autoCapitalize`: HTML attribute for `autoCapitalize` on/off
- `autoCorrect`: HTML attribute for `autoCorrect` on/off
- `autoComplete`: HTML attribute for `autoComplete` on/off
- `spellCheck`: HTML attribute for `spellCheck` on/off

Also, it initializes the value of `label,errorLabel`, and `formControlName` with the value of `id` if they are not provided. Finally, the component also has a `@Output` attribute named `update` that emits an event when the `value` changes, so you can register for it.

On the HTML side, we have something like the following:

```
<div  class="group"
  [ngClass]="{ 'has-error' : !control.valid && submitAttempt }"

    >
    <em *ngIf="!control.valid && submitAttempt">
      {{ errorLabel | translate:{value: param} }}
    </em>

    <input #input_field
      [attr.autocapitalize] = "autoCapitalize ? 'on' : 'off'"
      [attr.autocorrect]    = "autoCorrect ? 'on' : 'off'"
      [attr.autocomplete]   = "autoComplete ? 'on' : 'off'"
      [attr.spellcheck]     = "spellCheck ? 'on' : 'off'"
      class                 = "form-control"
      id                    = "{{id}}"
      type                  = "{{type}}"
      [formControl]         = "control"
      (keyup) = "update.emit(input_field.value)"
    >
    <span class="highlight"></span>
    <span class="bar"></span>
    <label htmlFor="{{id}}">
      {{ label | translate:{value: param} }}
    </label>
</div>
```

The main advantage is that HTML and CSS class managements are encapsulated away and I don't have to copy and paste them every time I want an input.

Summary

In this chapter, we learned how to take advantages of reactive forms. Reactive forms can be created manually or programmatically using `FormBuilder`. Moreover, we tackled the reactive part of reactive forms by emphasizing the relationship between your HTML models and your `ngModel`, so every change on a given form is propagated to the model. We also saw how to customize validations and embed our newly acquired knowledge about forms in clean, reusable directives.

In the next chapter, we will learn how to integrate material design with Angular in order to create dashing and responsive applications.

10
Material Design in Angular

Material Design is the new, much-hyped, design style. It replaced flat design as the new must use design. Material Design was introduced by Google in 2014 and it expanded the card motifs of Google Now. The following is an image of a Google Now card:

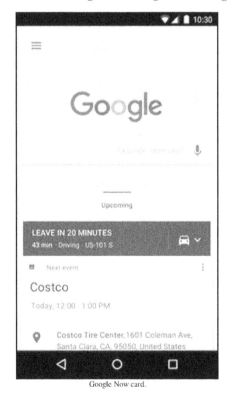

Google Now card.

The whole idea behind Material Design is to build upon the grid based system, the responsiveness of animations and transitions, while adding depth to the design. Matias Duarte, the lead designer behind Material Design, put it this way:

> *"Unlike real paper, our digital material can expand and reform intelligently. Material has physical surfaces and edges. Seams and shadows provide meaning about what you can touch."*

Material Design is a set of very precise and complete specifications that can be found here: `https://material.google.com/`.

Anyone with solid knowledge of CSS3 and HTML5 could take the written documentation and implement each and every component. This will, however, require a tremendous amount of time and effort. Luckily, we will not have to wait that long. Indeed, a team of talented developers assembled and created a Material Design component for Angular. At the time of writing, this is still in beta, meaning that some components are not yet implemented or not fully implemented. However, I rarely found myself stuck to the point where I had to change my whole design because of a component that was not there or not working.

In this chapter, we will learn how to install the Angular component for Material Design and then use some of the most popular components. We will also have a look at material icons. In more detail, we will see:

- How to install Material Design for Angular
- How responsive layout is handled
- Material icons
- Buttons
- Menu
- Toolbars
- Dialogs
- Creating your own themes

Installing the package

First of all, we need to install the Angular Material Design package. That is relatively simple using the Angular CLI:

```
ng new chap10
cd chap10
npm install --save @angular/material
```

```
npm install --save @angular/animations
npm install --save hammerjs
```

We install two packages here, `@angular/material` and the `hammerjs` packages. The first one includes in our app, the Material Design modules, which we will use in the next section. The second package, however, is a JavaScript implementation of touch movements. Some Material Design components such as `slider` depend on `hammerjs`.

Then, as per the `NgModule` specification, we can import `MaterialModule` as follows:

```
//src/app/app.module.ts

import { MaterialModule } from '@angular/material';
import { BrowserModule } from '@angular/platform-browser';
import { NgModule } from '@angular/core';
import { FormsModule, ReactiveFormsModule } from '@angular/forms';
import { HttpModule } from '@angular/http';

import { AppComponent } from './app.component';

@NgModule({
 declarations: [
   AppComponent
 ],
 imports: [
   BrowserModule,
   FormsModule,
   HttpModule,
   ReactiveFormsModule,
   NgbModule.forRoot(),
   MaterialModule.forRoot()
 ],
 providers: [],
 bootstrap: [AppComponent]
})
export class AppModule { }
```

Next, we need to choose a theme. Themes are sets of colors that will be applied to the Angular Material components. In a theme, you have the following colors:

- A primary palette consists of colors most widely used across all screens and components
- An accent palette consists of colors utilized for the floating action button and interactive elements

- A warn palette consists of colors used to convey error state
- A foreground palette consists of colors for text and icons
- A background palette consists of colors used for element backgrounds

Luckily, there are default themes (the ones used by Google on most of their services) that we can use directly. To do so, add the following line to your `/src/styles.css` file:

```
@import '~@angular/material/core/theming/prebuilt/deeppurple-
    amber.css';
```

Here, we use the deep purple theme, which is one of the available default themes. You can see all default themes here:
`node_modules/@angular/material/core/theming/prebuilt`.

Moreover, that is it! You can run `ng serve` to transpile your project again and confirm that everything went according to plan. As expected, there is not much to show for now. Here's a screenshot that was taken after running `ng serve`:

App works!

Responsive layout

An important part of Material Designs are responsive layouts that adapt to any possible screen size. To achieve this, we use breakpoint widths: 480, 600, 840, 960, 1280, 1440, and 1600 dp as defined by the following table from
`https://material.io/guidelines/layout/responsive-ui.html#responsive-ui-breakpoints`:

Breakpoint (dp)	Handset/ Tablet Portrait	Handset/ Tablet Landscape	Window	Columns	Gutter
0	Small handset	xsmall	4	16	
360	Medium handset	xsmall	4	16	
400	Large handset	xsmall	4	16	

480	Large handset	Small handset	xsmall	4	16
600	Small tablet	Medium handset	small	8	16/24
720	Large tablet	Large handset	small	8	16/24
840	Large tablet	Large handset	small	12	16/24
960	Small tablet	small	12	24	
1024	Large tablet	medium	12	24	
1280	Large tablet	medium	12	24	
1440	large	12	24		
1600	large	12	24		
1920	xlarge	12	24		

Note that all the Material Design directive we will use in this chapter already implement these breakpoints. However, you have to keep them in mind if you start theming (see the last section of the chapter) or implementing custom directives. CSS breakpoints are fairly easy to define but can be tedious work:

```
@media (min-width: 600dp) {
  .class {
    content: 'Whoa.';
  }
}
```

Now, the first four columns of the previous table are fairly self-explanatory, we have the breakpoints in dp, the Handset/Tablet Portrait, the Handset/Tablet Landscape, and Window. The last two, however, require some explanation. The Columns column indicates the number of columns equally dividing the screen for each dp size.

The gutters are the space between each of this column. Here's a 12 column grid layout:

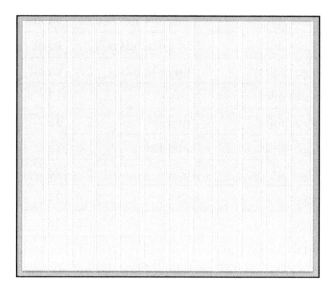

Columns (pink) and gutters (blue).

To use the grid system you can append the `md-columns` to the classes of any given tag. For example, `<button class="md-2">` creates a button which is two columns wide.

To see your website in different sizes, you can use the Google Chrome developer's tools (*F12* then *CTRL + Shift + M*) or `http://material.io/resizer/`. Note that `http://material.io` will fail silently if the website you try to analyze sets *X-Frame-Options* to *DENY*.

Material icons

Let's begin our journey through Material Design with the material icons. Material icons are icon fonts that have been created to work on any resolution and device (web, Android, and iOS are officially supported).

Icons convey a special meaning and developers tend to use the same icons to communicate the same thing. Consequently, users find their way more easily in your apps.

There are hundreds of icons available for you to use and new ones are added on a daily basis.

Here are some examples:

Fold icons.

You can see all the icons at `https://material.io/icons/`.

As material icons are an optional part of Material Design (that is, you could have Material Designed an app with, for example, font awesome icons or even custom ones), there's another one liner to add to your code. In your `src/index.html` file, add the following in the `head` section:

```
<link href="https://fonts.googleapis.com/icon?family=Material+Icons"
    rel="stylesheet">
```

The final `src/index.html` would look like this:

```
<!doctype html>
<html>
<head>
 <meta charset="utf-8">
 <title>Chap10</title>
 <base href="/">

 <meta name="viewport" content="width=device-width, initial-scale=1">
 <link rel="icon" type="image/x-icon" href="favicon.ico">
 <link href="https://fonts.googleapis.com/icon?family=Material+Icons"
    rel="stylesheet">
</head>
<body>
 <app-root>Loading...</app-root>
</body>
</html>
```

Now, to see if the importation was successful, we will add an icon into the autogenerated app component. In `src/app/app.component.html`, add the following `<i class="material-icons">cast_connected</i>` so it looks like this:

```
<h1>
 {{title}}

 <i class="material-icons">cast_connected</i>
</h1>
```

Your browser should refresh the `http://localhost:4200/` page and display the `cast_connected` icon:

Cast connected icon.

As you can see, using material icons is fairly simple. The first step is to identify the name of one icon you want to use on `https://material.io/icons/`, then, create a `<i></i>` tag that has a `class="material-icons"` attribute and, finally, contains the name of the icon you want. Here are some examples:

- `<i class="material-icons">cast_connected</i>`
- `<i class="material-icons">gamepad</i>`
- `<i class="material-icons">dock</i>`
- `<i class="material-icons">mouse</i>`

Buttons

One of the simplest directives to use with Material Design, besides icons, is the button directive. We can have a button that is flat, raised, round, and has three different preset colors: primary, accent, and warn. Here's a component with a template trying out some of the possible combinations:

```
@Component({
 selector: 'buttons',
 template: `
   <button md-button>FLAT</button>
   <button md-raised-button>RAISED</button>
   <button md-fab>
       <md-icon>add</md-icon>
   </button>
   <button md-mini-fab>
       <md-icon>add</md-icon>
   </button>
   <button md-raised-button color="primary">PRIMARY</button>
   <button md-raised-button color="accent">ACCENT</button>
   <button md-raised-button color="warn">WARN</button>
   `
})
export class ButtonsComponent {
 constructor() { }
}
```

And the result is shown here:

It is followed by:

The **Primary**, **Accent**, and **Warn** colors are either defined in your `style.scss` as SCCS variables or in the default Material Design theme if you did not override them.

Menu

In this section, we will interest ourselves in the `menu` directive. The following component creates a menu with four elements in it. The fourth element is disabled (that is, we cannot click it):

```
@Component({
  selector: 'menu',
  template: `
<md-menu>
    <button md-menu-item> Refresh </button>
    <button md-menu-item> Settings </button>
    <button md-menu-item> Help </button>
    <button md-menu-item disabled> Sign Out </button>
</md-menu>
  `
})
export class MenuComponent {
  constructor() { }
}
```

Here's what the menu looks like when it is closed:

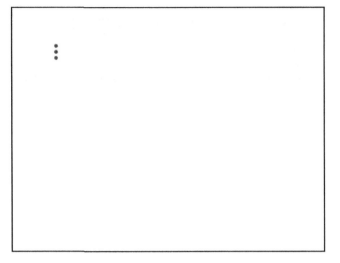

Menu closed.

And the open (after the user clicks it) version is shown in the following screenshot:

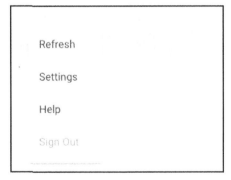

Menu opened.

Toolbars

The toolbar component of Angular Material Design is to be used as followed:

```
<md-toolbar>
 One good looking toolbar
</md-toolbar>
```

This will produce the following:

```
One good looking toolbar
```

Bare-bones toolbar.

In addition, you can use the Angular `[color]="primary"` | `"accent"` | `"warn"` attribute. Also, the toolbar can contain rows by using the `<md-toolbar-row>` markup:

```
<md-toolbar [color]="accent">
  One good looking toolbar
</md-toolbar>
<md-toolbar [color]="warn">
  <span>First Row</span>

  <md-toolbar-row>
    <span>Second Row</span>
  </md-toolbar-row>

  <md-toolbar-row>
    <span>Third Row</span>
  </md-toolbar-row>
</md-toolbar>
<md-toolbar [color]="primary">
  Another good looking toolbar
</md-toolbar>
```

The following will produce three different toolbars, on top of each other. The second toolbar will be composed of three rows.

Dialogs

As per the Google definition: *Dialogs inform users about a specific task and may contain critical information, require decisions, or involve multiple tasks.* Dialogs when used in Angular have the following methods:

- `open(component: ComponentType<T>, config: MdDialogConfig):` `MdDialogRef<T>` that creates and opens a new dialog for the user to interact with
- `closeAll()`: void that closes the dialog

Then, the dialog itself can use four different directives:

- `md-dialog-title` will contain the title of the dialog like so: `<md-dialog-title>My Dialog Title</md-dialog-title>`.
- `md-dialog-content` contains the content of the dialog.
  For example: `<md-dialog-content>My Dialog Content</md-dialog-title>`.
- `md-dialog-close` is to be added to a button (`<button md-dialog-close>Close</button>`). It makes the button close the dialog itself.
- `md-dialog-actions` is used to set the different actions of the dialog, that is, close, discard, agree, and so on.

In the following example, we have a first a draft component. The draft component has a simple template that only contains one button. The `click` event of the button invokes the `openDialog` method. For the definition of the component itself, we have a constructor that receives an `MdDialog` named dialog. The method `openDialog` has two callbacks--one for actually opening the dialog and the second one for printing out the `result` variable contained with the `result`: string when the dialog is closed:

```
@Component({
  selector: 'draft-component',
  template: `
  <button type="button" (click)="openDialog()">Open dialog</button>
  `
})
export class DraftComponent {

  dialogRef: MdDialogRef<DraftDialog>;

  constructor(public dialog: MdDialog) { }

  openDialog() {
```

```
      this.dialogRef = this.dialog.open(DraftDialog, {
        disableClose: false
      });

      this.dialogRef.afterClosed().subscribe(result => {
        console.log('result: ' + result);
        this.dialogRef = null;
      });
  }
}
```

As you can see, the dialogRef attribute of the DraftComponent component is generic.
More specifically, it is a generic instance of the DraftDialog class. Let's define it:

```
@Component({
  selector: 'draft-dialog',
  template: `
  <md-dialog-content>
    Discard Draft?
  </md-dialog-content>
  <md-dialog-actions>
    <button (click)="dialogRef.close('can
cel')">Cancel</button>
    <button md-dialog-close>Discard</button>
  </md-dialog-actions>
  `
})
export class DraftDialog {
  constructor(public dialogRef: MdDialogRef<DraftDialog>) { }
}
```

Once again, this is a simple class. Here, we can see that the template contains three out of
the four possible directives. Indeed, I used <md-dialog-content> to define the content of
the dialog to be displayed, <md-dialog-actions> to have a dedicated space for the
actions button of the dialog, and, finally, md-dialog-close to make the Discard button
close my dialog. The component itself only has a construct that defines the public
property: MdDialogRef<DraftDialog>.

The last thing to do to be able to use this dialog is to reference it in our NgModule like so:

```
@NgModule({
  declarations: [
    ...,
    DraftDialog
  ],
  entryComponents: [
    ...,
```

```
    DraftDialog
  ],
  ...
})
export class AppModule { }
```

Here's an image of the dialog when we press the button:

Draft dialog.

Side navigation drawers

Side navigation drawers are extremely popular on mobile devices. They do, however, start to appear in full-fledged version of websites; hence their coverage in this chapter.

Here's what a side navigation drawer can look like:

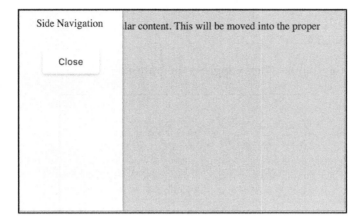

Side navigation drawer.

In light gray, on the left side, we have the navigation drawer that pops over our content when invoked. In a darker gray, we have the content of our page.

With the following component, we reproduce the side navigation shown at the beginning of this section:

```
@Component({
  selector: 'sidenav',
  template: `
    <md-sidenav-container>
    <md-sidenav #side (open)="closeButton.focus()">
      Side Navigation.
      <br>
      <button md-button #closeButton
          (click)="side.close()">Close</button>
    </md-sidenav>

    My regular content. This will be moved into the proper DOM at
        runtime.
    <button md-button (click)="side.open()">Open side sidenav</button>

  </md-sidenav-container>
  `
})
export class SideNavComponent {
  constructor() { }
}
```

The only interesting thing here is the template. Let's break it down. First, we have the enclosing `<md-sidenav-container>` tag that allows us to define two separate areas for our content. These two areas are the `md-sidenav` and the actual content of our page. While the `sidenav` part of the content is clearly defined by the `md-sidenav` tag, the rest of our content (that is, the actual page) isn't enclosed in any special tag. The page content only has to be outside the `md-sidenav` definition. We have a reference to the `md-sidenav` block with the `#side` attribute. As a reminder, adding `#myName` to any Angular directive gives you a reference to access it inside the rest of your template. The `md-sidenav` has an open method that puts the focus on the `#closeButton` defined inside it. This button has a `click` method that invokes the `close` method of `#side`. Finally, in the page content we have a button that invokes `#side.open` when clicked. In addition to these two methods (`open` and `close`), the `md-sidenav` directive also has a `toggle` method that toggles the `sidenav` (that is, `opened = !opened`).

Theming

Now, we could describe each and every available component available in Angular Material Design. However, there are a lot of them and their uses are all but complicated. Here's a list of the supported directives available at the time I am writing this chapter:

- buttons
- cards
- checkbox
- radio
- input
- sidenav
- toolbars
- list
- grid
- icon
- progress
- tabs
- slide
- slider
- menu
- tooltip

- ripples
- dialogs
- snackbar

In the coming months, more directives will be added to the mix. You can find them all here: `https://github.com/angular/material2`.

Needless to say, we are covered in terms of directives. Despite this wide range of possibilities, we can further customize Material Design for Angular by creating a custom theme. In Angular Material, a theme is created by composing multiple palettes. In particular, a theme consists of:

- A primary palette consists of colors most widely used across all screens and components
- An accent palette consists of colors utilized for the floating action button and interactive elements
- A warn palette consists of colors used to convey error state
- A foreground palette consists of colors for text and icons
- A background palette consists of colors used for element backgrounds

Here's an example of a custom theme:

```scss
//src/styles.scss

@import '~https://fonts.googleapis.com/icon?family=Material+Icons';
@import '~@angular/material/core/theming/all-theme';
// Plus imports for other components in your app.

// Include the base styles for Angular Material core. We include this here
so that you only
// have to load a single css file for Angular Material in your app.
@include md-core();

// Define the palettes for your theme using the Material Design
   palettes available in palette.scss
// (imported above). For each palette, you can optionally specify a
   default, lighter, and darker
// hue.
   $candy-app-primary: md-palette($md-indigo);
   $candy-app-accent:  md-palette($md-pink, A200, A100, A400);

// The warn palette is optional (defaults to red).
   $candy-app-warn:    md-palette($md-red);
```

```
// Create the theme object (a Sass map containing all of the palettes).
  $candy-app-theme: md-light-theme($candy-app-primary, $candy-app-
    accent, $candy-app-warn);

// Include theme styles for core and each component used in your app.
// Alternatively, you can import and @include the theme mixins for each
    component
// that you are using.
@include angular-material-theme($candy-app-theme);
```

Hence we have learned to create custom themes for Material Designing.

Summary

In this chapter, we learned about Material Design and responsive design for Angular by using Angular/Material2 module. We saw some of the most used directives such as `buttons`, `icons`, `dialogs`, or `sidenav`. In addition, we tackled Material Design customization using the theming capabilities of Angular/Material2.

In `Chapter 15`, *Integrating Bootstrap with Angular Application*, we'll see how to drive the design of our Angular2 application by using Bootstrap (by Twitter) instead of Material Design (by Google).

11

Implementing Angular Pipes

In this chapter, you will learn about Angular pipes. Think of Angular pipes as a modernized version of filters, comprising functions that help us to format the values within the template. Pipes in Angular are basically an extension of what filters were in Angular v1. There are many useful built-in pipes we can use easily in our templates. You will learn about built-in pipes and we will also create our own custom user-defined pipes.

At the end of this chapter, you will learn and implement the following:

- Introduction to Angular pipes
- Defining and implementing a pipe
- Understand the various built-in pipes
    - DatePipe
    - DecimalPipe
    - CurrencyPipe
    - LowerCasePipe and UpperCasePipe
    - JSON Pipe
    - SlicePipe
    - async Pipe
- Learn to implement custom user-defined pipes
- Parameterizing the pipes
- Chaining the pipes
- Learn about pure and impure pipes

Angular Pipes - An overview

Pipes allow us to format the values within the view of the templates before it's displayed. For example, in most modern applications, we want to display terms, such as today, tomorrow, and so on, and not system date formats, such as April 13 2017 08:00. Let's take a look at more real-world scenarios.

Do you want the hint text in the application to always be lowercase? No problem; define and use `LowercasePipe`. In a weather app, if you want to show the month name as MAR or APR instead of its full name, use `DatePipe`.

Cool, right? You get the point. Pipes help you to add your business rules, so you can transform the data before it's actually displayed in the templates.
A good way to relate to Angular pipes is through Angular 1.x filters, but pipes do a lot more than just filtering.

 We have used the Angular router to define the route path, so we have all the functionalities of pipes in one page; you can create it in the same or different apps. Feel free to use your creativity.

In Angular 1.x, we had filters--pipes are a replacement of filters.

In the next section, you will learn how to define and use an Angular pipe.

Defining a pipe

The pipe operator is defined with a pipe symbol, (|), followed by the name of the pipe:

```
{{ appvalue | pipename }}
```

The following is an example of a simple `lowercase` pipe:

```
{{"Sridhar Rao" | lowercase}}
```

In the preceding code, we are transforming the text to lowercase using the `lowercase` pipe.

Now, let's write an example `Component` using the `lowercase` pipe example:

```
@Component({
  selector: 'demo-pipe',
  template: `
  Author name is {{authorName | lowercase}}
  `
```

```
})
export class DemoPipeComponent {
 authorName = 'Sridhar Rao';
}
```

Let's analyze the preceding code in detail:

- We defined a `DemoPipeComponent` component class
- We created a string variable, `authorName`, and assigned the value, `'Sridhar Rao'`
- In the template view, we displayed `authorName`; however, before we printed it in the UI, we transformed it using the `lowercase` pipe

Run the preceding code, and you should see the following output:

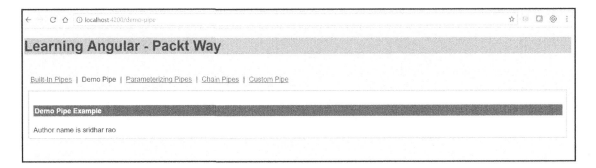

Well done! In the preceding example, we have used a built-in pipe. In the subsequent sections, you will learn more about the built-in pipes and also create a few custom pipes.

Note that the pipe operator only works in your templates and not inside controllers.

Built-in Pipes

Angular pipes are a modernized version of Angular 1.x filters. Angular comes with a lot of predefined built-in pipes. We can use them directly in our views and transform the data on the fly.

The following is the list of all the pipes that Angular has built-in support for:

- DatePipe
- DecimalPipe
- CurrencyPipe
- LowercasePipe and UppercasePipe
- JSON Pipe
- SlicePipe
- async Pipe

In the following sections, let's implement and learn more about the various pipes and see them in action.

DatePipe

DatePipe, as the name itself suggest, allows us to format or transform the values that are related to a date. DatePipe can also be used to transform values in different formats based on parameters passed at runtime.

The general syntax is shown in the following code snippet:

```
{{today | date}} // prints today's date and time
{{ today | date:'MM-dd-yyyy' }} //prints only Month days and year
{{ today | date:'medium' }}
{{ today | date:'shortTime' }} // prints short format
```

Let's analyze the preceding code snippet in detail:

- As explained in the preceding section, the general syntax is a variable followed by a (|) pipe operator, which is then followed by the name of the pipe operator
- We used DatePipe to transform the `today` variable
- Also, in the preceding example, you will note that we passed a few parameters to the pipe operator; we will cover passing parameters to the pipe in the following section

Now, let's create a complete example of the `DatePipe` component; the following is the code snippet for implementing the `DatePipe` component:

```
import { Component } from '@angular/core';

@Component({
  template: `
```

```
<h5>Built-In Pipes</h5>
<ol>
<li>
<strong class="packtHeading">DatePipe example 1</strong>
<p>Today is {{today | date}}
</li>
<li>
<strong class="packtHeading">DatePipe example 2</strong>
<p>{{ today | date:'MM-dd-yyyy' }}
<p>{{ today | date:'medium' }}
<p>{{ today | date:'shortTime' }}
</li>
</ol>
`,
})
export class PipeComponent {
 today = new Date();
}
```

Let's analyze the preceding code snippet in detail:

1. We created a `PipeComponent` component class.
2. We defined a `today` variable.
3. In the view, we transformed the value of the variable into various expressions based on different parameters.

Now, run the application, and we should see the following output:

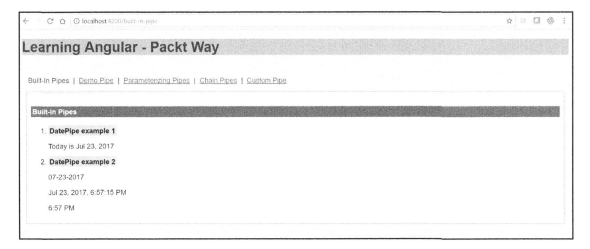

You learned about `DatePipe` in this section. In the following sections, you will continue to learn and implement other built-in pipes and also create some custom user-defined pipes.

DecimalPipe

In this section, you will learn about yet another built-in pipe--DecimalPipe.

DecimalPipe allows us to format a number according to locale rules. DecimalPipe can also be used to transform a number in different formats.

The general syntax is as follows:

```
appExpression | number [:digitInfo]
```

In the preceding code snippet, we use the number pipe, and optionally, we can pass the parameters.

Let's take a look at how to create a `DatePipe` that implements decimal points; the following is an example code of the same:

```
import { Component } from '@angular/core';
@Component({
 template: `
  <h5>Built-In Pipes</h5>
  <ol>
<li>
<strong class="packtHeading">DecimalPipe example</strong>
  <p>state_tax (.5-5): {{state_tax | number:'.5-5'}}</p>
  <p>state_tax (2.10-10): {{state_tax | number:'2.3-3'}}</p>
  </li>
  </ol>
  `
})
export class PipeComponent {
 state_tax: number = 5.1445;
}
```

Let's analyze the preceding code snippet in detail:

1. We defined a component class, that is, `PipeComponent`.
2. We defined a `state_tax` variable.
3. We then transformed `state_tax` in the view.
4. The first pipe operator tells the expression to print the decimals up to five decimal places.

5. The second pipe operator tells the expression to print the value up to three decimal places.

The output of the preceding pipe component example is as follows:

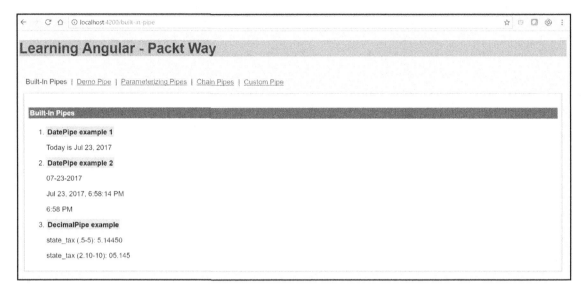

Undoubtedly, the number pipe is one of the most useful and commonly used pipes across various applications. We can transform the number values especially dealing with decimals and floating points.

CurrencyPipe

For applications that want to cater to multinational geographies, we need to show country-specific codes and their respective currency values--that's where `CurrencyPipe` comes to our rescue.

The `CurrencyPipe` operator is used to append the `country` codes or `currency` symbol in front of the number values.

Take a look at the code snippet implementing the `CurrencyPipe` operator:

```
{{ value | currency:'USD' }}

Expenses in INR: {{ expenses | currency:'INR' }}
```

Let's analyze the preceding code snippet in detail:

1. The first line of code shows the general syntax of writing `CurrencyPipe`.
2. The second line shows the currency syntax, and we used it to transform the `expenses` value and append the Indian currency symbol to it.

So now that we know how to use a `CurrencyPipe` operator, let's put together an example to display multiple `currency` and `country` formats; the following is the complete component class, which implements a `CurrencyPipe` operator:

```
import { Component } from '@angular/core';

@Component({
 selector: 'currency-pipe',
 template: `
<h5>CurrencyPipe Example</h5>
<ol>
<li>
<p>Salary in USD: {{ salary | currency:'USD':true }}</p>
<p>Expenses in INR: {{ expenses | currency:'INR':false }}</p>
</li>
</ol>
`
})
export class CurrencyPipeComponent {
 salary: number = 2500;
 expenses: number = 1500;
}
```

Let's analyze the preceding code in detail:

1. We created a component class, `CurrencyPipeComponent`, and declared few variables, namely `salary` and `expenses`.
2. In the component template, we transformed the display of the variables by adding the `country` and `currency` details.
3. In the first pipe operator, we used `'currency : USD'`, which will append the ($) dollar symbol before the variable.
4. In the second pipe operator, we used `'currency : 'INR':false'`, which will add the currency code, and `false` will tell it not to print the symbol.

Now, launch the app, and we should see the following output:

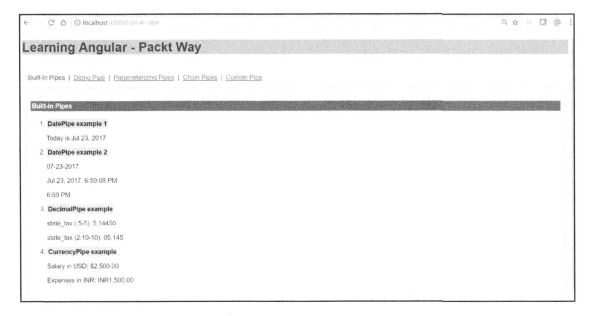

In this section, we discussed and implemented `CurrencyPipe`. In the following sections, we will keep exploring and learning about other Built-in pipes and much more.

LowerCasePipe and UpperCasePipe

The LowerCasePipe and UpperCasePipe, as the names suggest, help in transforming the text into lowercase and uppercase, respectively.

Take a look at the following code snippet:

```
Author is Lowercase {{authorName | lowercase }}
Author in Uppercase is {{authorName | uppercase }}
```

Let's analyze the preceding code in detail:

1. The first line of code transformed the value of `authorName` to lowercase using the `lowercase` pipe.
2. The second line of code transformed the value of `authorName` to uppercase using the `uppercase` pipe.

Now that we have seen how to define lowercase and uppercase pipes, it's time to create a complete component example, which implements the pipes to show the author name in both lowercase and uppercase.

Take a look at the following code snippet:

```
import { Component } from '@angular/core';

@Component ({
  selector: 'textcase-pipe',
  template: `
  <h5>Built-In LowercasPipe and UppercasePipe</h5>
  <ol>
  <li>
  <strong>LowercasePipe example</strong>
  <p>Author in lowercase is {{authorName | lowercase}}
  </li>
  <li>
  <strong>UpperCasePipe example</strong>
  <p>Author in uppercase is {{authorName | uppercase}}
  </li>
  </ol>
  `
})
export class TextCasePipeComponent {
  authorName = "Sridhar Rao";
}
```

Let's analyze the preceding code in detail:

1. We created a component class, `TextCasePipeComponent`, and defined an `authorName` variable.
2. In the component view, we used the `lowercase` and `uppercase` pipes.
3. The first pipe will transform the value of the variable to a lowercase text.
4. The second pipe will transform the value of the variable to an uppercase text.

Run the application, and we should see the following output:

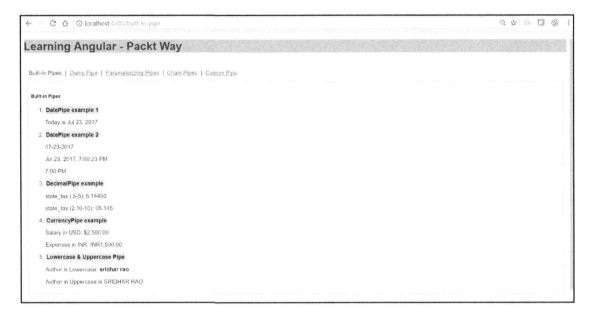

In this section, you learned how to use `lowercase` and `uppercase` pipes to transform the values.

JSON Pipe

Similar to a JSON filter in Angular 1.x, we have the JSON pipe, which helps us to transform the string into a JSON format string.

In a lowercase or an uppercase pipe, we transformed the strings; using a JSON pipe, we can transform and display the string into a JSON format string.

The general syntax is shown in the following code snippet:

```
<pre>{{ myObj | json }}</pre>
```

Now, let's use the preceding syntax and create a complete `Component` example, which uses the JSON Pipe:

```
import { Component } from '@angular/core';

@Component({
  template: `
```

```
<h5>Author Page</h5>
<pre>{{ authorObj | json }}</pre>
`
})
export class JSONPipeComponent {
authorObj: any;
constructor() {
this.authorObj = {
name: 'Sridhar Rao',
website: 'http://packtpub.com',
Books: 'Mastering Angular2'
};
}
}
```

Let's analyze the preceding code in detail:

1. We created a component class, `JSONPipeComponent` and `authorObj`, and assigned the JSON string to the variable.
2. In the component template view, we transformed and displayed the JSON string.

Run the app, and we should see the following output:

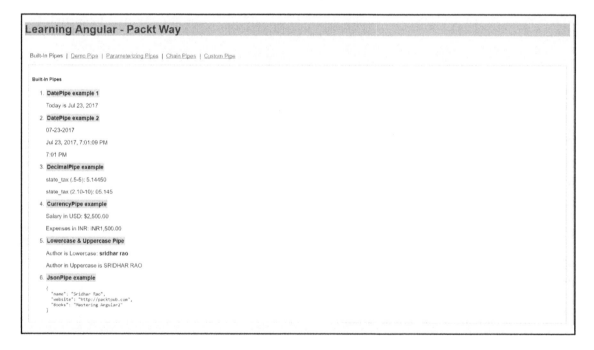

JSON is soon becoming de facto standard of web applications to integrate between services and client technologies. Hence, the JSON pipe comes in handy every time we need to transform our values to a JSON structure in the view.

SlicePipe

SlicePipe is very similar to an array slice JavaScript function. Slice pipe extracts the characters from a string between two specified indices and returns the new sub string.

The general syntax to define a SlicePipe is as follows:

```
{{email_id | slice:0:4 }}
```

In the preceding code snippet, we are slicing the email address to show only the first four characters of the variable value, email_id.

Now that we know how to use a SlicePipe, let's put it together in a component.

The following is the complete code snippet implementing SlicePipe:

```
import { Component } from '@angular/core';

@Component({
 selector: 'slice-pipe',
 template: `
 <h5>Built-In Slice Pipe</h5>
 <ol>
 <li>
 <strong>Original string</strong>
 <p> Email Id is {{ emailAddress }}
 </li>
 <li>
 <strong>SlicePipe example</strong>
 <p>Sliced Email Id is {{emailAddress | slice : 0: 4}}
 </li>
 </ol>
 `
})
export class SlicePipeComponent {
 emailAddress = "test@packtpub.com";
}
```

Let's analyze the preceding code snippet in detail:

1. We created a `SlicePipeComponent` class.
2. We defined a string variable `emailAddress` and assigned it a value, `test@packtpub.com`.
3. Then, we applied SlicePipe to the `{{emailAddress | slice : 0: 4}}` variable.
4. We get the substring starting from the 0 position and get 4 characters from the variable value of `emailAddress`.

Run the app, and we should see the following output:

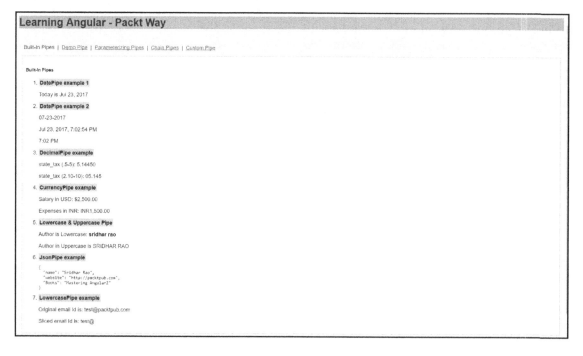

SlicePipe is certainly a very helpful built-in pipe, especially dealing with strings or substrings.

async Pipe

An async pipe allows us to directly map promises or observables into our template view. To understand the async Pipe better, let me throw some light on an observable first.

Observables are Angular-injectable services, which can be used to stream data to multiple sections in the application. In the following code snippet, we use an `async` pipe as a promise to resolve the list of authors being returned:

```
<ul id="author-list">
 <li *ngFor="let author of authors | async" >
 <!-- loop the object here -->
 </li>
</ul>
```

The `async` pipe now subscribes to `Observable` (authors) and retrieves the last value.

Let's look at examples of how we can use the `async` pipe as both a `Promise` and an `Observable`.

Add the following lines of code in our `app.component.ts` file:

```
getAuthorDetails(): Observable<Author[]> {
 return this.http.get(this.url).map((res: Response) => res.json());
}

getAuthorList(): Promise<Author[]> {
 return this.http.get(this.url).toPromise().then((res: Response) =>
 res.json());
}
```

Let's analyze the preceding code snippet in detail:

1. We created a `getAuthorDetails` method and attached an observable with the same. The method will return the response from the `url`, which is a JSON output.
2. In the `getAuthorList` method, we bound a promise, which needs to be resolved or rejected in the output returned by the `url` called through a `http` request.

In this section, we have seen how the `async` pipe works. You will find it very similar to dealing with services. We can either map a promise or an observable and map the result to the template.

Parameterizing pipes

A pipe can take parameters as well. We can pass parameters along with the pipe. A parameter is separated with a colon symbol (`:`) after the pipe:

```
{{appValue | Pipe1: parameter1: parameter2 }}
```

Let's quickly build a simple example of a pipe to see it in action. Here's an example of `DatePipe` with the `MM-dd-yyyy` parameters:

```
{{today | date:'MM-dd-yyyy' }}
```

One more example of a pipe with parameters is given as follows:

```
{{salary | currency:'USD':true}}
```

Let's analyze the preceding code snippet in detail:

1. We passed USD as a parameter to `CurrencyPipe`, which will tell the pipe to display the currency code, such as *USD* for the US dollar and *EUR* for the euro.
2. The `true` parameter stands for displaying the symbol of the currency ($). By default, it's set to false.

Let's see them in action with complete code for the component:

```
import { Component } from '@angular/core';

@Component({
 template: `
 <h5>Parametrizing pipes</h5>

 <p>Date with parameters {{ today | date:'MM-dd-yyyy' }}
 <p>Salary in USD: {{salary | currency:'USD':true}}</p>
 `,
})
export class ParamPipeComponent {
 today = new Date();
 salary: number = 1200;
}
```

In the preceding code snippet, we created a `ParamPipeComponent` class and defined the `today` and `salary` variables.

In the `Component` template view, we pass the `date:'MM-dd-yyyy'` parameters for `DatePipe` and the `currency:'USD' :true` parameters for `CurrencyPipe`.

Here's the output of the preceding code:

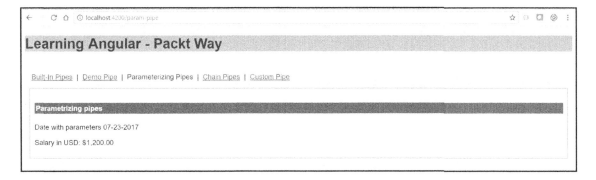

In the preceding example, we passed custom parameters, such as currency and date formats, to the pipes and viewed the output accordingly.

In most application use cases, we will need to pass parameters to pipes to transform values based on business logic. In this section, we focused on paramterizing the pipes by passing values.

So far, we have been using the built-in pipes and passing parameters to the pipes.

In the following sections, you will learn about chaining pipes, creating custom pipes, and also passing parameters to the custom user-defined pipes.

Chaining pipes

We can chain multiple pipes together. This particularly helps in scenarios where we need to associate more than one pipe that needs to be applied, and the final output will be transformed with all the pipes applied.

The workflow or chains will be triggered and apply the pipes one after another. An example of the chain pipe syntax is given as follows:

```
{{today | date | uppercase | slice:0:4}}
```

We applied two chain pipes in the preceding code. First, DatePipe is applied to the today variable, and just after that, the uppercase pipe is applied. The following is the entire code snippet for ChainPipeComponent:

```
import {Component } from '@angular/core';

@Component({
  template: `
  <h5>Chain Pipes</h5>
```

```
    <p>Month is {{today | date | uppercase | slice:0:4}}
     `,
    })
    export class ChainPipeComponent {
     today = new Date();
    }
```

We have used the slice to show only the first four characters of the month. The following screenshot shows the output of the preceding component:

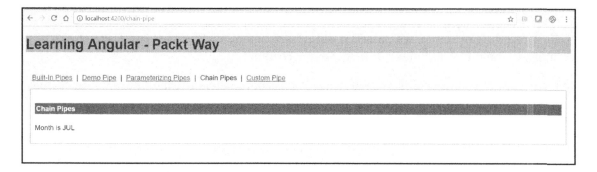

Some of the key things to remember when applying chain pipes are as follows:

- The order of execution is from left to right
- The pipes are applied one after another

In this section, you learned about how to chain multiple pipes together in our applications. In the next section, you will learn how to create your own custom pipes in detail.

Creating custom pipes

So far, so good. Pipes have really impressed us, but wait, there's more awesome things we can do with pipes. Built-in pipes, as you see, are very limited and few. We certainly need to create our own custom pipes, which cater to our app's functionality.

In this section, you will learn how to create a custom pipe for our application.

In this example, we will build a pipe, which will be a tax calculator. We pass the price of the product and use a pipe functionality to automatically calculate and display the sales tax. Magic, right?

To create a custom pipe, we need to perform the following steps:

1. Create a template to apply it to the pipe (in our example, it's `updateTaxPipe`).
2. Create a pipe file, that is, `update-tax.pipe.ts`.
   1. Every pipe file will have to import the pipe from the Angular core.
   2. Define the pipe metadata.
   3. Create the `Component` class. It should have the `transform` function, which holds the business logic of what the pipe should do.

In the following code snippet, we are defining a custom pipe called `UpdateTaxPipe`, which will take a `percentage` parameter and does the sales tax calculation and displays it in our template:

```
{{ productPrice | UpdateTaxPipe: percentage }}
```

Let's create our `update-tax.pipe.ts` file:

```
import { Pipe, PipeTransform } from '@angular/core';

@Pipe({
 name : "UpdateTaxPipe"
})

export class UpdateTaxPipe implements PipeTransform{
 transform(value:number, taxVal: number) :number{
 return (value*taxVal)/100;
 }
}
```

Let's analyze the preceding code snippet in detail:

1. To tell Angular that this is a pipe, we applied the `@Pipe` decorator, which you import from the core Angular library.
2. We created a custom pipe named `UpdateTaxPipe`, using the `name` pipe metadata.
3. We created a `transform` method, which is mandatory for the pipe and defined our business logic and rule inside the method.
4. We passed two parameters to the `transform` method, and it returned the updated value.

Angular looks for and executes the `transform` method, regardless of whether we include the interface PipeTransform or not.

Run the app, and we should see the output as shown in the following screenshot:

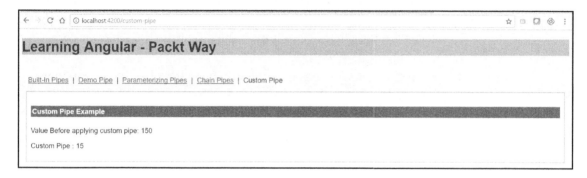

In this section, you learned how to create a custom pipe. Creating user-defined pipes is very simple and easy. Custom pipes definitely help us to easily integrate the business logic of our application.

 Try and create custom pipes, which can fit the write once and use logic many times and also in many component views; for example, validating a phone number, address, and so on.

Pure and Impure Pipes

Pipe also accepts a metadata called Pure. Pipes are of two states:

- Pure Pipe
- Impure Pipe

Pure Pipes

A Pure Pipe will execute only when the value of the input parameter is changed. It will not remember or trace any of the previous values or states. Angular built-in pipes are all `pure` pipes.

All the pipes we have seen so far as examples are Pure Pipes.

Impure Pipes

An impure pipe is called for every change detection cycle, regardless of whether the value or parameters change. In order to use impure pipes, we should use the pipe decorator `pure` as `false`.

 By default, all pipe decorators have `pure` set as `true`.

Setting the pipe decorator value as `pure` will check for the pipe's output irrespective of whether it's value changed or not and will keep updating the value provided by the pipe.

Defining an impure pipe is same as creating any custom user-defined pipe, the only difference being that in the `@Pipe` decorator we will explicitly mention the pipe to be impure by setting the value to `false`.

Below is the syntax to define a impure pipe by setting the value of pipe to false:

```
import { Pipe, PipeTransform } from '@angular/core';

@Pipe({
  name: 'authorName'
  pure: false
})
```

In this section, you learned about the different types of Angular pipes, namely pure and impure pipes. Pure pipes are called only when the value of the input component changes. Impure pipes are called on every change detection, irrespective of whether the values change or not.

Summary

In this chapter, you learned all about Angular pipes. Angular pipes are very useful in transforming the data in the view template. Angular pipes are the modernized version of filters available in Angular 1.x.

There are many useful built-in pipe operators we can use easily in our templates. You learned about built-in pipes as well as created custom user-defined pipes in this chapter.

When working with numbers, we can make use of DatePipe, DecimalPipe, and CurrencyPipe. When working with strings exclusively, we can always use SlicePipe, LowercasePipe, and UppercasePipe.

We can use JSONPipe and asyncPipe when we are mostly dealing with server-side responses or making an async call and processing the response. We also covered passing parameters to the pipes and customizing according to the need of our apps.

We explored how to create and implement custom user-defined pipes, which can also take parameters to customize them better based on our application needs.

So go ahead, and transform your views with pipes.

In next chapter you will learn about implementing Angular services. You will learn about service and factory, creating Angular service, accessing data from components using service and creating asynchronous service.

12
Implementing Angular Services

Services play a vital role in any Angular application. We may design our own Angular services by taking full advantage of the many built-in services in Angular. In this chapter, we will discuss how to do both, so that you have an idea of how to create as well as manage Angular services.

In this chapter, we will cover the following topics:

- Why use a service or factory?
- Creating a service
- Accessing data from components using service
- Creating an asynchronous service

Why use a service or factory?

We have discussed One-way Data Binding, Two-way Data Binding, and data sharing between components. We may have very clear views defined and uncluttered components implemented, but the business logic and data fetching/storing logic has got to be there somewhere. Building great Angular apps comes from making the most out of the built-in services. The Angular framework includes services to help you with networking, caching, logging, promises, and so on.

Writing our own services or factories helps to achieve reusability in code and enables us to share the application-specific logic across the application blocks, such as components, directives, and so on. Organizing the application-specific logic into services or factories leads to cleaner, better-defined components, and helps you to organize your project with more maintainable code.

In AngularJS, we implement services or factories for this purpose. The services are invoked using a new keyword at runtime such as a constructor function. The following code snippet shows the AngularJS code of a service implementation:

```
function MovieService($http) {
  this.getMovieList = function   getMovieList() {
    return $http.get('/api/movies');
  };
}
angular.module('moviedb').service('MovieService',   MovieService);
```

The MovieService function can be injected into any controller that needs to fetch the list of movies from the API.

The same feature can be implemented using a factory in Angular with additional capabilities. A factory is one type of design pattern that deals with creating objects. We can return new classes, functions, or closures from a factory. Similar to a service, a factory can also be injected into a controller. The following code snippet shows the AngularJS code of a factory implementation:

```
function MovieService($http) {
  return {
    getMovieList: function() {
        return $http.get('/api/movies');
    }
  };
}
angular.module('moviedb').factory('MovieService',   MovieService);
```

Both a service and a factory can be injected into a controller, and the getMovieList function can be called as follows:

```
function MovieController(MovieService   service) {
  service.getMovieList().then(function   (response) {
      // manage response
    });
}
angular.module('moviedb').controller('MovieController',
      MovieController);
```

Though a factory is flexible, a service is the best choice to make the migration to ES6 easier. When using a service, a constructor function in ES5 can be smoothly replaced with ES6 classes during the migration process to ES6. We can rewrite the `MovieService` service in ES6 as follows:

```
class MovieService {
 getMovieList() {
   return $http.get('/api/movies');
  }
}
app.service('MovieService', MovieService);
```

Services are user-defined classes that solve specific purposes, and can be injected into the component. Angular recommends that you have only view-specific codes in components that enrich the UI/UX in your Angular application. Components are the consumers of services where they serve as the source of application data and the library of business logic. Keeping the components clean and injecting the service enables us to test the components against a mock service:

Creating a service

Application-specific or business logic functions, such as persisting application data, logging the errors, file storage, and so on, should be delegated to services, and the components should consume the respective services to deal with the appropriate business or application-specific logics:

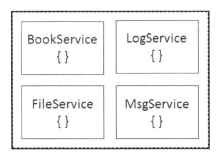

Let us create a simple service called `BookService` that deals with fetching the collection of books available in the source. The source may be data returned from a web API service or a JSON file.

First, let us create a `Book` model to persist the domain object value. The code snippet of a `Book` class is shown here:

```
export class Book {
  id: number;
  title: string;
  author: string;
  publisher: string;
}
```

The preceding code snippet shows a TypeScript class for `Book`, with properties such as `id`, `title`, `author`, and `publisher`. Now let us create a service named `BookService` that handles operations related to `Book`:

```
import { Injectable } from '@angular/core';
import {Book} from './book';
@Injectable()
export class BookService {
  getBooks() {
  var books: Book[] = [
    { "id": 1, "title": "ASP.NET Web API Security Essentials", author:
        "Rajesh Gunasundaram", publisher: "Packt Publishing" },
    { "id": 2, "title": "Learning Angular for .Net Developers", author:
        "Rajesh Gunasundaram", publisher: "Packt Publishing" },
    { "id": 3, "title": "Mastering Angular", author: "Rajesh
        Gunasundaram", publisher: "Packt Publishing" },
  ];
  return books;
  }
}
```

Here, we first imported the `Book` model class. Then, we defined the `BookService` class with a `getBooks` method that returns the collection of books.

Now we need a component to inject the `BookService` and consume. Let us create a `BookListComponent` that retrieves the list of books by calling a method, `getBooks`, from `BookService`. The following code snippet shows the `BookListComponent` class:

```
import { Component, OnInit } from '@angular/core';
import { Book } from './book';
import { BookService } from './book.service';
@Component({
```

```
selector: 'book-list',
template: `
<div *ngFor="let book of books">
{{book.id}} - {{book.title}}<br/>
Author: {{book.author}}<br/>
Publication: {{book.publisher}}
</div>
`,
providers: [BookService]
})
export class BookListComponent implements OnInit {
  books: Array<Book>;
  constructor(private bookService: BookService) { }
  ngOnInit() {
      this.books = this.bookService.getBooks();
    }
  }
```

Here, we started with importing `Component` and `OnInit` from `@angular/core` and then we imported the `Book` model class and the `BookService` class. Then we annotated the `BookListComponent` class with the `@Component` attribute, along with the metadata information, such as the selector and template. The `BookListComponent` class is defined with a `books` variable of `Book` array and a constructor that is injected with `BookService`. Note that the `BookListComponent` implements the `OnInit` life cycle hook, and it calls the `getBooks` method from the `BookService` class by using the instance of the `BookService` that is injected into the constructor. The list of books returned by `getBooks` is assigned to the `books` variable of the `BookListComponent` class.

Now let us create a root component, `AppComponent`. Pass the `BookListComponent` as a directive and `BookService` as a provider. The following is the code snippet of `AppComponent`:

```
import { Component } from '@angular/core';
import { BookService } from './book.service';
@Component({
  selector: 'my-books',
  template: '
    <h2>Book Library</h2>
  <book-list></book-list>
  '
})
export class AppComponent { }
```

Here, we started with importing `Component` from `@angular/core`, `BookListComponent` and `BookService`. Then we annotated the `AppComponent` with the `@Component` attribute, along with metadata such as the selector and template. Note that we have a special HTML tag `<book-list/>` in the template. Somewhere, we need to instruct Angular to initialize `BooklistComponent` and render the view accordingly. We also need to inform Angular that `AppComponent` is the root component by bootstrapping it. We can achieve this by creating an `entrypoint` for our Angular application.

Create a class named `AppModule` and annotate it with `NgModule` (`app.module.ts`). This instructs the Angular module that this class is the `entrypoint` of the application. A code snippet of `AppModule` is given here:

```
import { NgModule }         from '@angular/core';
import { BrowserModule }  from '@angular/platform-browser';
import { AppComponent }   from './app.component';
import { BookListComponent }  from './book-list.component';
@NgModule({
  imports:       [ BrowserModule ],
  declarations: [ AppComponent,  BooklistComponent ],
  bootstrap:    [ AppComponent ]
})
export class AppModule { }
```

Here, we started by importing `NgModule` from the Angular core. Then we imported the `BrowserModule` from the Angular platform browser, as our application runs on a web browser. Then we imported the application components, such as `AppComponent` which is a bootstrapped root component, and the `BooklistComponent`, imported and added in declarations. Not that the `AppModule` is decorated with `NgModule`, along with the metadata, such as imports, declarations, and bootstrap, respectively.

Now let us create an `index.html` page with the following code snippet:

```
<!DOCTYPE html>
<html>
  <head>
    <base href="/">
    <title>Book   Library</title>
    <meta charset="UTF-8">
    <meta name="viewport"   content="width=device-width, initial-
          scale=1">
  </head>
  <body>
    <h1>TodoList Angular app for   Packt Publishing...</h1>
```

```
        <my-books>Loading...</my-books>
    </body>
</html>
```

Here, we have not referred any necessary libraries from `node_modules` as they will be loaded by Webpack. Webpack is a tool used to bundle resources and serve them from a server to a browser. Webpack is a recommended alternative to systemJS.

Accessing data from components using services

As the Angular application evolves, we keep introducing more components, and these components will be dealing with the core data of the application. As a result, we may end up writing repetitive code to access the data. However, we can avoid writing redundant code by introducing reusable data services. The component that is in need of the data can be injected with the data service, and that can be used to access the data. In this way, we can reuse logic, write less code, and have more separation in designing our components.

We will use the Angular `HttpModule`, which is shipped as an `npm` package. In order to use `HttpModule` in our application, we need to import `HttpModule` from `@Angular/http` and the HTTP service should be injected into the constructor of the controller or the application service.

Implementing services

An application may share data between components. Consider a movie database application, where a `Movies` list or a single `Movie` object will be shared across the components. We need a service to serve the `Movies` list or a single `Movie` object as and when requested by any components.

First, let us create a movie service using Angular CLI. Execute the following command in the command prompt to generate boilerplate code for `movie.service`:

```
e:\Explore\packt\MovieDB>ng generate    service Movie
installing service
  create src\app\movie.service.spec.ts
  create src\app\movie.service.ts
e:\Explore\packt\MovieDB>
```

Here, the Angular CLI has created two files, namely `movie.service.ts` and `movie.service.spec.ts`. The boilerplate code of the `movie.service.ts` generated is shown here:

```
import { Injectable } from '@angular/core';
@Injectable()
export class MovieService {
  constructor() { }
}
```

Note that the `MovieService` class is decorated with the `@Injectable` attribute to facilitate a Dependency Injection to instantiate and inject this service into any component that is in need of it. We made this `Injectable` function available by importing it from the Angular core.

Moving on, we need to add the `getMovies` function to the `MovieService` generated. Introduce the `getMovies()` function to the `MovieService` class as follows:

```
import { Injectable } from '@angular/core';
@Injectable()
export class MovieService {
  constructor() { }
  getMovies(): void {}
}
```

Note that we have given the return type as void for now, but we need to change it when we move on to further implementation.

We need to introduce a domain model, `Movie`, to represent a movie across the application. Let us generate a boilerplate code for the `Movie` class using Angular CLI as follows:

```
e:\Explore\packt\MovieDB>ng generate    class Movie
installing class
  create src\app\movie.spec.ts
  create src\app\movie.ts
e:\Explore\packt\MovieDB>
```

Here, this command has created two files, namely `movie.ts` and `movie.spec.ts`. Actually, while in domain mode, we may not write any test methods to assert it, so you can safely delete `movie.spec.ts`. The code snippet of the `movie.ts` generated is shown here:

```
export class Movie {
}
```

Let us add a few properties to make it represent the characteristics of a movie. The code for that is given here:

```
export class Movie {
    public constructor(
            private _movie_id:number,
            private _title: string,
            private _phase: string,
            private _category_name: string,
            private _release_year: number,
            private _running_time: number,
            private _rating_name: string,
            private _disc_format_name:   string,
            private _number_discs: number,
            private _viewing_format_name:   string,
            private _aspect_ratio_name:   string,
            private _status: string,
            private _release_date: string,
            private _budget: number,
            private _gross: number,
            private _time_stamp:Date){
    }
    public toString = () : string => {
            return `Movie (movie_id:   ${this._movie_id},
            title: ${this._title},
            phase: ${this._phase},
            category_name:   ${this._category_name},
            release_year:   ${this._release_year},
            running_time: ${this._running_time},
            rating_name:   ${this._rating_name},
            disc_format_name:   ${this._disc_format_name},
             number_discs:   ${this._number_discs},
            viewing_format_name:   ${this._viewing_format_name},
            aspect_ratio_name: ${this._aspect_ratio_name},
            status: ${this._status},
            release_date:   ${this._release_date},
            budget: ${this._budget},
            gross: ${this._gross},
            time_stamp:   ${this._time_stamp})`;
    }
}
```

We have the domain model in place. Now let us update the return type of the `getMovies()` function in `MovieService` as follows:

```
getMovies(): Movie[] {
    let movies: Movie[] = [
        {
```

```
                "movie_id" : 1,
                "title" : "Iron    Man",
                "phase" : "Phase    One: Avengers Assembled",
                "category_name"    : "Action",
                "release_year" :    2015,
                "running_time" :    126,
                "rating_name" : "PG-13",
                "disc_format_name"    : "Blu-ray",
                "number_discs" :    1,
                "viewing_format_name"    : "Widescreen",
                "aspect_ratio_name"    : " 2.35:1",
                "status" : 1,
                "release_date" :    "May 2, 2008",
                "budget" : "140,000,000",
                "gross" : "318,298,180",
                "time_stamp" : "2015-05-03"
        },
          {
                "movie_id" : 2,
                "title" : "Spiderman",
                "phase" : "Phase    One",
                "category_name"    : "Action",
                "release_year" :    2014,
                "running_time" :    126,
                "rating_name" : "PG-13",
                "disc_format_name"    : "Blu-ray",
                "number_discs" :    1,
                "viewing_format_name"    : "Widescreen",
                "aspect_ratio_name"    : " 2.35:1",
                "status" : 1,
                "release_date" :    "May 2, 2008",
                "budget" : "140,000,000",
                "gross" : "318,298,180",
                "time_stamp" : "2015-05-03"
        }
        ];
        return movies;
    }
```

The complete code snippet of `MovieService` is given here:

```
import { Injectable } from '@angular/core';
import { Movie} from './movie';
@Injectable()
export class MovieService {
  getMovies(): Movie[] {
    let movies: Movie[] = [
            {
```

```
        "movie_id" : 1,
        "title" : "Iron    Man",
        "phase" : "Phase   One: Avengers Assembled",
        "category_name"    : "Action",
        "release_year" :    2015,
        "running_time" :    126,
        "rating_name" : "PG-13",
        "disc_format_name"    : "Blu-ray",
        "number_discs" :    1,
        "viewing_format_name"    : "Widescreen",
        "aspect_ratio_name"    : " 2.35:1",
        "status" : 1,
        "release_date" :    "May 2, 2008",
        "budget" : "140,000,000",
        "gross" : "318,298,180",
        "time_stamp" : "2015-05-03"
    },
      {
        "movie_id" : 2,
        "title" : "Spiderman",
        "phase" : "Phase   One",
        "category_name"    : "Action",
        "release_year" :    2014,
        "running_time" :    126,
        "rating_name" : "PG-13",
        "disc_format_name"    : "Blu-ray",
        "number_discs" :    1,
        "viewing_format_name"    : "Widescreen",
        "aspect_ratio_name"    : " 2.35:1",
        "status" : 1,
        "release_date" :    "May 2, 2008",
        "budget" : "140,000,000",
        "gross" : "318,298,180",
        "time_stamp" : "2015-05-03"
      }
    ];
    return movies;
  }
 }
```

Here, the `getMovies()` function returns the collection of movies of type `Movie[]`.

Consuming the service

We have `MovieService` ready to be consumed. Let us consume it in a component. Using Angular CLI, we will create a component by executing the following command:

```
e:\Explore\packt\MovieDB>ng generate   component movie
installing component
  create src\app\movie\movie.component.css
  create   src\app\movie\movie.component.html
  create   src\app\movie\movie.component.spec.ts
  create src\app\movie\movie.component.ts
e:\Explore\packt\MovieDB>
```

This creates four files, namely `movie.component.ts`, `movie.component.html`, `movie.component.css`, and `movie.component.spec.ts`. The code snippet of the `movie.component.ts` file is shown here:

```
import { Component, OnInit } from '@angular/core';
@Component({
  selector: 'app-movie',
  templateUrl: './movie.component.html',
  styleUrls: ['./movie.component.css']
})
export class MovieComponent implements   OnInit {
  constructor() { }
  ngOnInit() {
  }
}
```

The `MovieComponent` is decorated with the `@Component` decorator, along with the metadata, such as selector, `templateUrl`, and `styleUrls`. The `MovieService` will be hooked under the `ngOnInit` method. Let us proceed with modifying `MovieComponent` to consume `MovieService`.

First things first; we need to import `MovieService` to our component `MovieComponent`. This import statement provides a reference to `MovieService` in `MovieComponent`. But to consume `MovieService`, we need to create the instance of `MovieService`. How do we do it? In a standard way, we can instantiate `MovieService` as follows:

```
let movieService = new MovieService();
```

The code snippet of `MovieComponent` after importing `MovieService` and instantiating `MovieService` in the `OnInit` life cycle hook method is shown here:

```
import { Component, OnInit } from '@angular/core';
import { MovieService } from './movie.service';
import { Movie } from './movie';
@Component({
  selector: 'app-movie',
  templateUrl: './movie.component.html',
  styleUrls: ['./movie.component.css']
})
export class MovieComponent implements  OnInit {
  movies : Movie[];
  constructor() { }
  ngOnInit() {
    let movieService = new  MovieService();
    this.movies =  movieService.getMovies();
  }
}
```

Here, when the `OnInit` event is fired, `MovieService` gets instantiated, and the collection of movies will be retrieved by calling the `getMovies()` function. The movies list will be assigned to the `movies` properties of `MovieComponent` for further consumption in the template.

Creating an asynchronous service

We just created a service called `MovieService` that synchronously calls the `getMovies()` method to retrieve the collection of movies. As we are consuming an external source, such as a web API, to retrieve the collection of movies, our application has to wait until the server responds with the list of movies, as the `getMovies` function is synchronous.

So we need to implement an asynchronous mechanism to retrieve the collection of movies. In such way, we can avoid making our application wait until the web API responds with the collection of movies. We can achieve this by using promises.

What is a Promise?

A **Promise** is a sincere assurance that an action will be performed. It calls back a function when the server responds with the result. We request an asynchronous service with a callback function to perform some operation and the service calls our callback function with either the result or with the error. You can read more about promises in `Chapter 7, Asynchronous Programming Using Observables`.

Using a Promise in a service

Let us update the `getMovies` function in `MovieService` to return a resolved `Promise` as follows:

```
getMovies(): Promise<Movie[]> {
    let movies: Movie[] = [
        {
            "movie_id" : 1,
            "title" : "Iron    Man",
            "phase" : "Phase   One: Avengers Assembled",
            "category_name"    : "Action",
            "release_year" :    2015,
            "running_time" :    126,
            "rating_name" : "PG-13",
            "disc_format_name"    : "Blu-ray",
            "number_discs" :    1,
            "viewing_format_name"    : "Widescreen",
            "aspect_ratio_name"    : " 2.35:1",
            "status" : 1,
            "release_date" :    "May 2, 2008",
            "budget" : "140,000,000",
            "gross" : "318,298,180",
            "time_stamp" : "2015-05-03"
        },
        {
            "movie_id" : 2,
            "title" : "Spiderman",
            "phase" : "Phase   One",
            "category_name"    : "Action",
            "release_year" :    2014,
            "running_time" :    126,
            "rating_name" : "PG-13",
            "disc_format_name"    : "Blu-ray",
            "number_discs" :    1,
            "viewing_format_name"    : "Widescreen",
            "aspect_ratio_name"    : " 2.35:1",
```

```
            "status" : 1,
            "release_date" :    "May 2, 2008",
            "budget" : "140,000,000",
            "gross" : "318,298,180",
            "time_stamp" : "2015-05-03"
        }
    ];
  return Promise.resolve(movies);
}
```

Note that we return the collection of movies as a resolved `Promise` from the `getMovies` function. Now we need to modify the code that assigns the collection of movies to the `movies` property in `MovieComponent`.

The existing code in `MovieComponent` assigns `Promise` to the `movies` property instead of the collection of movies, as the `getMovies` in `MovieService` returns the resolved `Promise` now. So let us modify the code of the `ngOnInit` event as follows:

```
ngOnInit() {
    let movieService = new   MovieService();
    movieService.getMovies().then(movies   => this.movies = movies);
}
```

We provide our callback function to the `then` method of `Promise`, so the chain function `then` in `getMovies` has the command to assign the collection of movies returned from the web API to the property of `MovieComponent`, `this.movies`.

Here, the application will not wait until the `MovieService` returns the collection of movies. The `movies` property gets the list of movies assigned from the callback function.

Summary

Cool! This brings us to the end of the chapter. We learned about the importance and advantages of implementing services in our application. We also learned about how to consume services in components.

However, instantiating `MovieService` directly is a bad approach. Components need not know how to instantiate the services; their only purpose is to know how to consume the services. Services also enable the components to tightly couple with the type of `MovieServices` and their way of instantiating. This is unacceptable; the components should be loosely coupled as far as possible.

In the next chapter, we will discuss injecting services into components using Dependency Injections, which enable us to have loosely coupled components.

13
Applying Dependency Injection

In this chapter, you will learn about Angular Dependency Injection. Dependency Injection is one of the most striking features in Angular; it allows us to create injectables that can be used as shared resources between various components.

In this chapter, we will discuss the following:

- Exploring Dependency Injection
- Learning about provider classes in detail
- Understanding hierarchical Dependency Injection
- Creating an Injectable
- Learning to inject providers into services
- Learning to inject providers inside the components
- Learning to resolve dependencies for a provider class
- Creating examples using the `@Inject,` `provide,` and `useValue` decorators

Applications without Dependency Injection

Without the Dependency Injection framework, the life of a developer would be very tough. Take a look at the following drawbacks of not using Dependency Injection:

- Every time a constructor parameter needs to be passed, we will need to edit the constructor definition of the class in all instances

- We will need to create constructors and inject each of the required dependency classes individually

Let's take a look at an application without Dependency Injection to understand the challenges and shortfalls:

```
class products {
 available;
 category;

 constructor() {
  this.available = new warehouse();
  this.category = new category();
 }
}
```

Let's analyze the preceding code snippet to understand better:

1. We created a `class` named `products`.
2. In the `constructor` method, we instantiated the dependent classes, `warehouse` and `category`.
3. Note that, if the `warehouse` or `category` class constructor definition changes, we will need to update manually all the instances of the classes.

The preceding code is not fully testable and maintainable since as a developer our task would be to manually define all the dependencies. That's where Angular Dependency Injection comes for our rescue.

Dependency Injection - Introduction

Dependency Injection(DI) is a coding pattern in which a class receives dependencies rather than creating them itself. Some developers and technology mavericks also refer to this as a design pattern.

It's widely used and is often called DI. We will refer to the Dependency Injection system as DI in all our sections.

Here's why we absolutely need DI:

- DI is a software design pattern in which a class receives its dependencies rather than creating the object itself
- DI creates and delivers objects, which are required dynamically just-in-time
- We can consider the injectables as our application's reusable repository
- DI allows independent development of dependency modules for remote development teams.

 No Angular apps can be completely written without using DI.

Now, let's revisit the preceding code we wrote without DI and write it with Angular DI:

```
class products {

constructor(private _warehouse: warehouse, private _category: category) {

  // use _warehouse and _category now as reference
  }
}
```

Here's what is happening in the preceding code:

1. We have created a `products` class.
2. In the `constructor`, we passed the dependent classes--`warehouse` and `category`--as parameters.
3. We can now use the instances, `_warehouse` and `_category` throughout the class.
4. Note that we have not created the objects of the dependent classes; instead we just receive them through the DI system.
5. We don't have to worry about the dependencies required by `warehouse` or `category`; that will be internally resolved by Angular DI.

Now that we know what Angular DI is, let's focus on how it's implemented and used in our Angular applications. Before we jump into learning about provider classes and more, we should know some of the basic things about the Angular DI framework.

urse, cover these in detail in the next few sections. It's good to have a basic *g:*

njectable: This decorator marks a class as available to an injector for instantiation.

2. `@Inject`: Using the `@Inject` decorator, we can inject the configuration object into any constructor that needs it.

3. `Provider`: A Provider is a way by which we register our dependencies that need to be injected.

Now let's jump into learning about provider classes.

Understanding provider classes

To start using DI in our applications, we will need to understand the concept of Providers. Providers configuration in the component decorator tells Angular which classes need to be provided to the component.

In the provider configuration, DI takes an array of all the classes i.e injection tokens, we want to provide to the component. We can also specify the `class` using `useClass` to instantiate for the registered token.

Take a quick look at the syntax for using the providers configuration:

```
@Component({
  templateUrl: './calculate-tax.component.html',
  styleUrls: ['./calculate-tax.component.css'],
  providers: [MyTax]
})
```

In the preceding code, we are telling Angular that the preceding component needs to be provided by the `MyTax` class.

The following are the advantages of using the provider classes:

- Providers are maintained per injector
- Each `provider` provides a single instance of an Injectable
- The provider class provides the return value of the method invoked

We can also explicitly mention the class that should be used from the service.

Here's the general syntax:

```
@Component({
 templateUrl: './calculate-tax.component.html',
 styleUrls: ['./calculate-tax.component.css'],
 providers: [
    { provide: MyTax, useClass: MyTax }
  ]
})
```

In the preceding code snippet, we are explicitly telling Angular to inject the MyTax provider and use the MyTax class using the useClass configuration.

Let's learn more about how the provider classes can be registered and used; let's take a look at the following diagram:

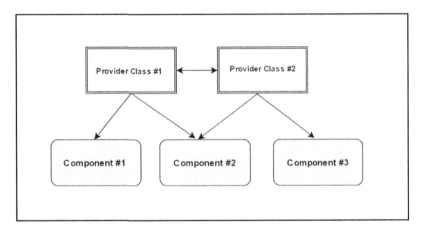

Let's analyze the preceding diagram in detail to learn the key take-away:

- Components shared resources are provided via the provider class
- Provider classes can be registered into multiple components(one or more)
- We can also register a provider class into other provider classes
- In the preceding diagram, Component #1 has a dependency on Provider Class #1

- In the preceding diagram, Component #2 has a dependency on Provider Class #1 and Provider Class #2
- In the preceding diagram, Component #3 has a dependency on Provider Class #2 and Provider Class #3

By now, we understand how critical DI is for our applications. DI really helps in organizing data and is the most suitable design pattern for implementing individual independent modules or components.

The idea is to keep components developed independently and write more generic shared or commonly used functionality in providers or injectables.

Let's create a quick example of a provider class, which can be injected in a component. We create a provider class--the MyTax.ts file--and add the following code snippet to it:

```
export class MyTax {
 public taxValue: string;
 constructor () {
     }

 getTaxes() {
  this.taxValue=Math.round(Math.random()*100);
  return this.taxValue;
 }

}
```

Let's analyze the preceding code snippet in detail:

1. We created a provider class named MyTax.
2. We defined a taxValue variable as number.
3. We created a getTaxes method, which will return a random number.
4. We assigned a value to the taxValue variable and returned the value via the getTaxes method.

Now, we need to register this provider class in our component's providers array configuration and display the value of taxValue.

We will need to create a `component` class--`calculate-tax.component.ts` and add the following lines of code to it:

```
import { Component } from '@angular/core';
import { MyTax } from './my-tax';

@Component({
 template: `<p>tax option: {{ taxName }}</p>`,
 styleUrls: ['./calculate-tax.component.css'],
 providers: [MyTax]
})
export class CalculateTaxComponent{

 public taxName: string;

 constructor( _myTax : MyTax) {
   this.taxName = _myTax.getTaxes();
 }

}
```

Let's analyze the preceding code in detail :

1. We imported the recently created provider class--`MyTax`.
2. We created and defined the `CalculateTax` component.
3. We defined a `taxName` variable and mapped the variable in the template using data binding.
4. In the constructor, we registered `MyTax` in the providers array of the application module, `MyTax`, and Angular DI will create an instance of the provider class and assign it to _myTax.
5. Using the instance of the provide class, we called the `getTaxes` method.

Run the app, and we should see the output shown in the following screenshot:

In this section, you learned how to create provider classes and register them in components to use them. You can register the same provider class into multiple components; this is certainly ideal in cases where we want to share multiple reusable methods.

In the next section, you will learn about hierarchical DI--when we have multiple nested components.

Understanding hierarchical DI

In the preceding section, we covered DI through provider classes and also sharing the provider classes between various individual components. In this section, you will learn how to use provider classes with DI between hierarchical components.

Angular internally creates an index tree tracing all the components and tree structure being created and also maintaining its dependency matrix, which gets loaded in real time to provide all the necessary modules, services, and components.

The best part about hierarchical components and DI among the various components is that we don't have to worry about how those dependencies are created, or what dependencies they need themselves internally.

Overview - Hierarchical components and DI

It's an open secret that Angular internally maintains the tree structure of components. It also maintains the tree index of dependencies.

In any real-world Angular application, we will work with many components and services. The components will have a tree structure ranging from a root component to child components and inner child components, and so on.

That forms a component tree structure internally. Since our components will also have dependencies and injectables, Angular will internally form a dependency tree matrix to track and resolve all the dependencies required for a service or component.

The following are the key things you need to know about hierarchical DI:

- The Angular framework internally creates a hierarchical tree structure for DI for components
- The provider class needs to be registered into the component
- We can register a provider class to be registered into other provider classes as well

In the next section, you will create injectable services and also use them in your components.

Creating an injectable

We don't have to create an Angular injector, it's injected by default. Angular creates an application-wide injector during the bootstrap process.

We define an injectable using the @Injectable decorator and define the methods in the class. @Injectable makes a class available to an injector for instantiation.

The following is sample code to create an @Injectable service:

```
import { Injectable } from '@angular/core';

@Injectable()
 export class ListService {
  getList() {
   console.log("Demo Injectable Service");
  }
}
```

Let's analyze the code snippet in detail:

1. We have imported Injectable from the Angular core module.
2. We used the @Injectable decorator to tell Angular that the following class can be injected and is available to an injector for instantiation.
3. We have created a class called ListService.
4. We implemented a method called getList, which at this point is just print a message in console.log.

Registering providers

An injector creates dependencies using providers. Providers are required to be registered into the consuming services or components. By registering them, the provider class allows us to create independent reusable features and functionalities by individual team members.

Configuring and registering provider classes also allows to break down functionalities into smaller modules, which are easy to maintain and modify. We can register provider classes into services and components in different ways. Important points to always keep in mind about injectors are as follows:

- We have to create a provider in our NgModule, component constructor, or in a directive
- Register the service in the component's constructor

We have created a ListService service in the preceding section, which has a method and can now be registered and used in multiple components:

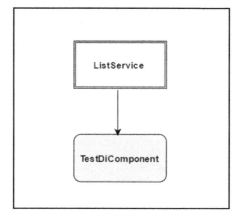

Let's analyze the preceding diagram in detail to understand the use case we are building:

1. We will create an Injectable service class, ListService.
2. We will create a component, TestDiComponent.
3. We will need to register ListService into TestDiComponent.

So, now let's jump right into learning how to register a provider in ngModule. Take a look at the ngModule file:

```
import { ListService } from "./shared/list.service";

@NgModule({
 providers: [
 {
  provide: ListService,
  useClass: ListService
 }
```

```
  ]
})
```

In shorthand, the preceding code is often written as follows:

```
import { ListService } from "./shared/list.service";

@NgModule({
 providers: [
   ListService
 ]
})
```

Let's analyze the preceding code snippet in detail:

1. We have imported the `ListService` service class into the `ngModule`.
2. Note that we registered the `ListService` in providers. Angular will internally resolve and create an injector at runtime.
3. In the shorthand notation, we just mention the name of the provider, and Angular will map the `provide` property to register and use the value of `useClass`.

In the preceding section, you learned how to register services in the provider's configuration array in `ngModule`.

The main difference between registering a provider in AppModule versus registering it in a component is the visibility of the service. Services registered in AppModule are available throughout the application, and services registered inside a specific component will be available only inside the component.

Registering providers inside the component

Now, you will learn how to register a provider in a component and use the injectable service class inside a component.

First, let's quickly generate a component and service using the Angular CLI `ng` command:

```
ng g component ./test-di
```

This will generate the component and the required files. The output of the command is shown in the following screenshot:

```
●  ●  ●                              src — bash — 160×46
E2ML11514s-MacBook-Pro:src Admin$ ng g component ./test-di
installing component
  create src/app/test-di/test-di.component.css
  create src/app/test-di/test-di.component.html
  create src/app/test-di/test-di.component.spec.ts
  create src/app/test-di/test-di.component.ts
  update src/app/app.module.ts
E2ML11514s-MacBook-Pro:src Admin$ ▌
```

Now, we have to generate an Angular service in the same folder:

```
ng g service ./test-di
```

The output of the preceding command is as follows:

```
●  ●  ●                              src — bash — 160×46
E2ML11514s-MacBook-Pro:src Admin$ ng g component ./test-di
installing component
  create src/app/test-di/test-di.component.css
  create src/app/test-di/test-di.component.html
  create src/app/test-di/test-di.component.spec.ts
  create src/app/test-di/test-di.component.ts
  update src/app/app.module.ts
E2ML11514s-MacBook-Pro:src Admin$ ng g service ./test-di
installing service
  create src/app/test-di.service.spec.ts
  create src/app/test-di.service.ts
  WARNING Service is generated but not provided, it must be provided to be used
E2ML11514s-MacBook-Pro:src Admin$ ▌
```

 We see that Angular CLI generates a warning message that the service is generated but not provided.

So far, we have created our component and service separately, but now we need to register the providers in our component so that we can use the service.

Before we proceed to register the providers in our component, let's take a quick look at the service code generated by the CLI tool.

Here's our `test-di.service.ts` file code:

```
import { Injectable } from '@angular/core';

@Injectable()
 export class TestDiService {
  constructor() { }
}
```

That's the default code generated by the scaffolding Angular CLI tool. Let's add a method, which we want to access inside the component:

```
import { Injectable } from '@angular/core';

@Injectable()

 export class TestDiService {
  getAuthors() {
  let Authors =[
   {name :"Sridhar"},
   {name: "Robin"},
   {name: "John"},
   {name: "Aditi"}
  ];
  return Authors;
 }
}
```

Now let's register the service in the providers array in the component `test-di.component.ts` file:

```
import { Component } from '@angular/core';
import { TestDiService } from './test-di.service';

@Component({
 selector: 'app-test-di',
 templateUrl: './test-di.component.html',
 styleUrls: ['./test-di.component.css'],
 providers: [TestDiService]
})

export class TestDiComponent{
 constructor(private _testDiService: TestDiService) {}
 authors = this._testDiService.getAuthors();
}
```

Let's analyze the preceding code in detail:

1. We created a component called `TestDiComponent`.
2. We imported the newly created service `TestDiService` into the component.
3. We registered the `TestDiService` in the providers to tell Angular to create an instance of the service dynamically.
4. Angular DI will create a new `private` instance of the `_testDiService` service class that we passed inside the `constructor`.
5. We used the instance of the `_testDiService` service and called the `getAuthors` method to get a list of authors.

Run the app, and we should see the output as shown in the following screenshot:

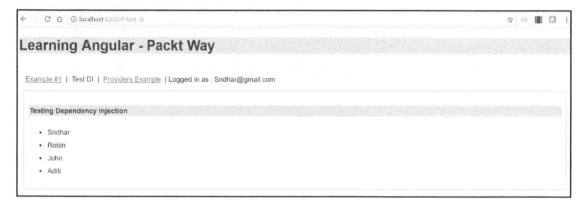

We have made it so far, which is great, as you learned to create an `Injectable` service, register the services in the providers array inside the component decorator, and use the instance of the service to call methods.

In this section, you learned how to create multiple components using the same shared set of provider classes.

Provider classes with dependencies

In our previous sections, we discussed registering a service into components, but what if our service itself requires some dependencies? In this section, you will learn and implement ways to resolve dependencies required for services.

To understand provider classes with dependencies better, let's understand the following use case. We have two services--`CityService` and `TestDiService`, and a component, that is, `TestDiComponent`.

Let's visualize the dependency tree for these services and components:

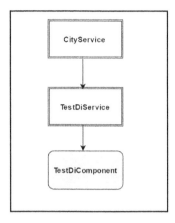

Let's analyze the preceding diagram in detail to understand the use case we are building:

1. We will create an `Injectable` service--`CityService`.
2. We will create an `Injectable` service--`TestDiService`.
3. We will need to register `CityService` into the `TestDiService` class.
4. We will create a `TestDiComponent`
5. We will need to register `TestDiService` into `TestDiComponent`

We will continue to use the previously created service, `TestDiService`, and the component--`TestDiComponent`--in this section as well.

Now, we will create an additional service called `CityService` and save the file as `city.service.ts`.

Add the following code snippet to the service file:

```
import { Injectable } from '@angular/core';

@Injectable()
export class CityService {

  getCities() {
   let cities =[
   { name :"New York" },
   { name: "Dallas" },
   { name: "New Jersey" },
   { name: "Austin" }
   ];

  return cities;
  }
}
```

Let's analyze the preceding code snippet:

1. We created and exported a new service called `CityService`.
2. We implemented a `getCities` method, which returns a list of cities.

After creating a service, we import the file and register the service as a provider in the `app.module.ts` file:

```
import { CityService } from "./test-di/city.service";

@NgModule({
  providers: [
    CityService
  ]
})
```

Since we have registered the service in the providers array in the `app.module.ts` file, it is now available across the application.

To use the service in `TestDiService`, we have to import the service and create an instance of `CityService` in the constructor:

```
import { Injectable } from '@angular/core';
import { CityService } from './city.service';

@Injectable()
export class TestDiService {
  constructor(private _city: CityService) { }
    getAuthors() {
      let Authors =[
          {name :"Sridhar"},
          {name: "Robin"},
          {name: "John"},
          {name: "Aditi"}
        ];
      return Authors;
  }
  getCityList() {
    let cities = this._city.getCities();
    return cities;
  }
}
```

In the example mentioned in the preceding section, we used the service to display a list of authors.

Now, let's analyze the preceding code:

1. We created a service called `CityService` and imported the class inside `TestDiService`.
2. We created an instance of the `CityService` class--`_City` in the constructor method.
3. We defined a method, that is, `getAuthors`.
4. Using the `this` operator, we invoked the `getCities` method of the `CityService` class inside the `getCityList` method.
5. The `getCities` method returns the list of cities.

Run the app, and you will see the output of the preceding code as shown in the following screenshot:

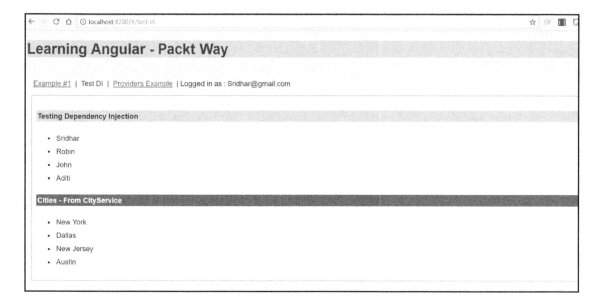

In this section, you learned and implemented how to resolve dependencies of providers classes by registering other provider classes using the @Injectable decorator.

Using @Inject, provide, and useValue

Let's take a quick recap on how things have progressed so far while learning DI. We discussed how to write provider classes and Dependency Injection for hierarchical components and above all how to write reusable providers using the @injectable decorator.

In this section, you will learn how to use @Inject, provide, and useValue to share data across different components.

To declare that a service can be injected in a class, we need an @Injectable decorator. The decorator tells Angular to make the class defined with @Injectable available to an injector for instantiation into other classes, services, or components and that the class should be resolved dynamically through DI. We use them mostly to write generic services and create our own repository.

Like we mentioned earlier, even if a service requires dependencies to be injected in it, we use the @Injectable decorator. We can also register a service into another service or any component.

Whenever we need to inject the type of constructor parameters, we will use the @inject decorator.

Take a look at the following sample code for ngModule in the app.module.ts file:

```
import { ListService } from "./shared/list.service";

@NgModule({
 providers: [
  {
   provide: ListService,
   useClass: ListService
  }
 ]
})
```

Quick points to note about the preceding code:

1. We imported the service we have created earlier, that is, ListService.
2. Now that we have imported the service, we need to add it to the list of providers.
3. We are explicitly mentioning that we need to register the service name ListService.
4. Using useClass we will instruct Angular to instantiate and use the ListService class.

If we note carefully, we will see that we are mainly dealing with service/provider classes. However, what if we need to inject certain variables so that we can share the value across different components and services?

Bingo! That's where we can easily use the @Inject decorator and create a variable or class name, which we can reuse in other components and services.

Take a look at the ngModule file now; we have modified it to accommodate our variable, which we want to share between various services and components:

```
import { ListService } from "./shared/list.service";

@NgModule({
 providers: [
  {
```

```
      provide : 'username',
      useValue: 'Sridhar@gmail.com'
  }
  ]
})
```

Let's analyze the preceding code:

1. Inside the providers, we created a new entry, and for `provide`, we applied a name, `username`. Remember whatever name you mention here, as we will need to use it throughout in other services or components.
2. We provided a value for the `username` variable.
3. Note that this value will not be changed or updated; think of it as a constant value throughout the application.

Now that we have created a value constant provider, let's see how we can use it in our components.

In the `app.component.ts`, add the following code snippet:

```
import { Component, Inject } from '@angular/core';
  @Component({
    selector: 'app-root',
    templateUrl: './app.component.html',
    styleUrls: ['./app.component.css']
  })

export class AppComponent {
  title = 'Learning Angular - Packt Way';
  constructor ( @Inject('username') private username ) {}
}
```

Let's analyze the preceding code snippet in detail:

1. We imported the `component` and `Inject` modules from `@angular/core`.
2. We created our component and defined the respective HTML and style sheet for the component to HTML and CSS files.
3. In the `AppComponent` class, we defined a `title` variable and assigned it a value.
4. We created a constructor of the class and passed an `@inject` decorator to pass the name, `username`, which we defined in the `app.module.ts` file.

5. Now that we have registered the `username` variable in the provider's array configuration, we can use the value of the variable anywhere in the component template.

Awesome, now let's run the app; we should the output shown in the following screenshot:

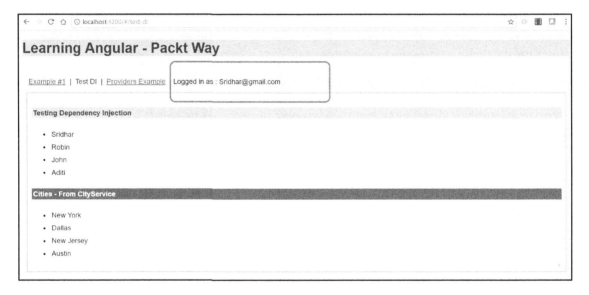

An important thing to note in the following screenshot is the variable value flagged in green, `'Sridhar@gmail.com'` which is getting printed in the template.

In this section, you learned to define and use a constant provider using the `@Inject` decorator.

You learned to use `@Injectable` for our service class; we can register it as a provider and use it in other services or in components.

We can define some constant variables, which can also inject and use the value across different components.

You should be now able to create multiple reusable services, provider classes, and also constant variables, which can be used to create our application repository.

Summary

In this chapter, we discussed Angular DI as we know it now. DI allows us to inject the provider class and injectables into components using providers. We learned and implemented provider classes and hierarchical Dependency Injection. We also learned to register providers in the `NgModule` or inside components directly.

We focused on how to create and configure Injectors and also how to register services in providers inside the component decorator.

This chapter explained that a provider class can also have dependencies, which internally can be injected again into services or components. In the next chapter, you will learn about Angular animations. Angular animations is a core library that provides a better user experience by applying motions and transitions to apps.

We will learn about various transitions and motions, and how to style animations; above all, we will create some cool stuff along the way.

14
Handling Angular Animation

In this chapter, we will learn about Angular animations. Animation; the very word sounds fun and creative, so tighten your seat belt; we will have fun learning Angular animations. Motion in web applications is one of the critical and crucial design factors and is a primary driver for good user experience. Transitions in particular are of great interest, as they enable the elements of the applications move to from one state or another.

The following topics are covered in detail in this chapter:

- Introduction to Angular animations
- Built-in classes in Angular 2 to support animation
- Understanding and learning to use animation modules, `transition`, `states`, `keyframes`, and so on
- Animating page transitions
- Animating toggle/collapse accordion slides

Introduction to Angular animations

Angular comes with solid native support for animations since motion and transition are a major part of any application.

Angular has a built-in animation engine, which also supports and extends the Web animations API that runs on most modern browsers.

We have to install Angular animations separately in your project folder. We will create some examples for animations in the following sections.

Installing the Angular animations library

As we discussed earlier, Angular animations have been forked out as a separate library and need to be installed separately.

In this section, we will discuss how to get the latest Angular animation version and install it; follow these steps:

1. Get the latest Angular animations library.

    You can install it using the following npm command:

    ```
    npm install @angular/animations@latest --save
    ```

    Running the preceding command will save the latest version of the Angular animations library and add it as a dependency in the package.json file.

2. Verify the latest installed Angular animation library.

    To make sure that we have installed the Angular animations library, open the package.json file, and there should be an entry of @animations/animations in the list of dependencies.

    Once Angular animations library has been imported and installed correctly, the package.json file should look the following screenshot:

3. Import the Angular animations library inside the `app.module.ts` file.

    We need to import the Angular animations library in our `app.module.ts` file. For including the library, we will use the following code snippet:

    ```
    import { BrowserAnimationsModule } from '@angular/platform-
        browser/animations';
    ```

4. Include the Angular animations library in imports for `ngModule` decorator:

    ```
    @ngModule({
     imports: [
    BrowserModule,
    BrowserAnimationsModule
     ],
    //other imports
    })
    ```

    In the preceding code snippet, we are just importing `BrowserAnimationsModule` into our `ngModule` to make it available for use across the application.

Great! Now we have the Angular animations library as part of our application, and we can continue building our components as usual with animations and effects.

Before we start writing examples of components using animations, it's important for us to spend some time and explore all the available classes in Angular animations, that we can take advantage of.

Angular animation - Specific functions

As mentioned in the earlier section, Angular comes with a separate animations library of its own, which has a lot of built-in classes and methods to support various animations.

Let's learn about the various built-in classes available in this section:

*   `trigger`
*   `transition`
*   `state`
*   `style`
*   `animate`

We will learn each of the afore mentioned methods in detail but before we do that, let's quickly see the general syntax for using these methods.

An example of general syntax for writing animations is as follows:

```
animations : [
  trigger('slideInOut', [
    state('in', style({
        transform: 'translate3d(0, 0, 0)'
      })),
    state('out', style({
        transform: 'translate3d(100%, 0, 0)'
      })),
    transition('in => out', animate('400ms ease-in-out')),
    transition('out => in', animate('400ms ease-in-out'))
  ])
]
```

Let's quickly analyze the preceding code in detail:

1. We are defining a trigger named `slideInOut`.
2. We are defining two `states`: `in` and `out`.
3. With each of the states, we are assigning a style, that is, the CSS `transform` property for each of the respective states.
4. We are also adding `transition` to mention the `state` and `animation` details.

Looks simple, right? Yep, you bet it is!

Now that we know the syntax of how to write animations, let's learn about each of these methods available in the Angular animation library, in some depth.

Trigger

Trigger defines a name that will trigger the animation. Trigger names help us identify which trigger should be triggered based on events.

The general syntax to define a trigger is as follows:

```
trigger('triggerName', [
   we define states and transitions here
])
```

In the preceding code syntax, we are defining the following:

1. Trigger is defined by passing a mandatory parameter, the name and optional parameters, which can include `state` and `transition`.
2. Trigger name; we define a name to identify the trigger.
3. Optionally we can also define our states and transitions as parameters in the trigger definition.

States

States are the defined animation property of an element at a given point of time.

States are our application's logical states, for example, active and inactive. We define the state name and the respective style properties for the state.

The general syntax for writing syntax to define states is as follows:

```
state('in', style({
 backgroundColor: '#ffffcc'
}))
```

In the preceding code syntax, we are defining the following:

1. We are defining a `state` by the name `'in'`, which is one of the logical states in our application.
2. In style, we define the `CSS` properties of the state that needs to be applied to the element. Regular `CSS` style attributes are defined here.

Transitions

Transitions allow elements to move smoothly from one state to another. In the transition, we define various states (one or more) of animations.

States are part of transitions.

The general syntax for writing a `transition` is as follows:

```
//Duration Example - seconds or milliseconds
transition('in => out', animate('100'))

// Easing Example: refer http://easings.net
transition('in => out', animate('300ms ease-in'))
```

```
// Using Delay in Animation
transition('in => out', animate('10s 50ms'))
```

In the preceding code syntax, we are defining the following

1. We are defining our transition states, that is, from start state to the end state. In our syntax it is from **in** state to **out** state.
2. The animate options are as follows:
   1. Easing: How smoothly the animation takes place
   2. Duration: how long the animation takes to run from start to finish
   3. Delay : The delay controls the length of time between the animation trigger and the beginning of the transition.

With a strong understanding of the concepts and syntax of how to write Angular animations, let's go ahead and create examples using all the preceding functions in the following sections.

Animating page transitions

In the preceding section, we created a few states for animations. In this section, we will learn how to create transitions using states.

`transition` is the most important method in the Angular animations library since it's responsible for all effects and state changes.

Let's create an example of a complete page transition. We will create the component class, `learn-animation.component.ts`:

```
import { Component } from '@angular/core';
import { state, style, animate, trigger, transition, keyframes} from
'@angular/core';

@Component({
 templateUrl: './learn-animation.component.html',
 styleUrls: ['./learn-animation.component.css'],
 animations : [
 trigger('customHover', [
  state('inactive', style({
   transform: 'scale(1)',
    backgroundColor: '#ffffcc'
  })),
  state('active', style({
   transform: 'scale(1.1)',
   backgroundColor: '#c5cae8'
```

```
    })),

   transition('inactive => active', animate('100ms ease-in')),
   transition('active => inactive', animate('100ms ease-out'))
   ]),
   ]
})
export class AppComponent {
 title = 'Animation works!';
 constructor() {}

 state: string = 'inactive';
 toggleBackground() {
  this.state = (this.state === 'inactive' ? 'active' : 'inactive');
 }
}
```

Let's analyze the preceding code in detail to understand Angular animations:

1. We are defining a trigger named `customHover`.
2. We are defining two `states`: `inactive` and `active`.
3. With each of the states, we are assigning a style, that is, CSS; `transform`, and `backgroundColor` properties for each of the respective states.
4. We are also adding transition to mention the state and animation details:
    1. `transition` affects when the state moves from `inactive` to `active`.
    2. `transition` affects when the state moves from `active` to `inactive`.
5. We are defining a `toggleBackground` method that, which when called upon, will toggle states from `inactive` to `active` and vice versa.

Now that we have created the component class, we have called the `toggleBackground` method in our `learn-animation.component.html` template:

```
<div>
 <div id="content" [@customHover]='state'
      (mouseover)="toggleBackground()"
      (mouseout)="toggleBackground()">Watch this fade</div>
</div>
```

Let's analyze the preceding code in detail:

1. In the `learn-animation.component.html`, we are defining a `div` element.
2. We are binding the `mouseover` and `mouseout` events with the `toggleBackground` method.

3. Since we defined our trigger as `@customHover` we will use this for property binding. On any element that we place [`@customHover`], the animation defined will be applied.

4. As we have applied property binding, the value for the property `@customHover` will toggle between `active` and `inactive`.

5. When we take the mouse over of the element, the `toggleBackground` method is called, and we see the background color change along with the `transform` property.

6. On the mouse-out event, again the `toggleBackground` method is called and the style gets reset back to the original.

Run the app, and we should see the output in the following screenshot:

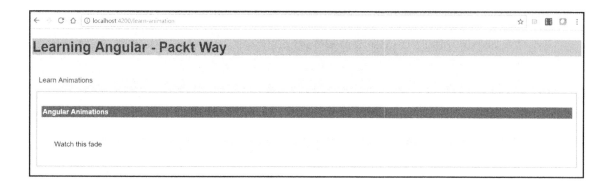

In this section, we discussed how to use basic Angular animation. In the next section, we will explore more examples of animation.

One more example - Angular animations

In the preceding section, we learned about the basics of animation; in this section, we will create one more example using Angular animations.

In this example, we will create a button and a `div` element. When the button is clicked, the `div` element will slide into to the page. Cool, right?

Let's get this started. Add the following code to the component file we created in the preceding section: `learn-animation.component.ts`:

```
trigger('animationToggle', [
  transition('show => hide', [
    style({transform: 'translateX(-100%)'}),
    animate(350) ]),
    transition('hide => show', animate('3000ms'))
])
```

The following are the important things to note in the preceding code:

1. We are creating a trigger with `animationToggle`.
2. We are defining two transitions, that is, from `show => hide` and `hide => show`.
3. We are adding style properties to the `show => hide` transition.
4. We did NOT add style properties to the `hide => show` transition.

> It's not mandatory to define style for transition but more often than not we will need to define custom styling for our elements with animations.

Run the app, and you should see the application and animation as mentioned below after the screenshot:

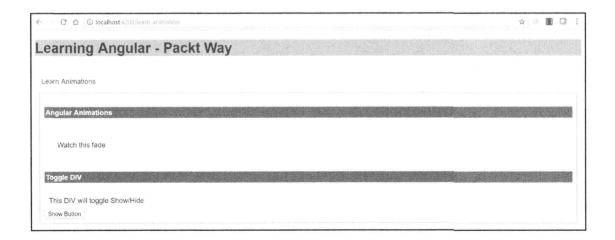

In our application when you click on the **show button,** The DIV element will slide-in to the page from right side to left. Click on the button again it toggle to hide.

It's cool, right? Yep. Angular animation gives us the ability to create beautiful animations and transition effects for elements, which will add up to a great user experience.

We will build a lot of cool examples implementing animations.

Using keyframes - Sequence of styles

So far, we have implemented examples using various methods for Angular animations.

When we design/decide motion and the transitions of elements, we need to iterate through various styles for smooth transitions.

Using keyframes we can define iterations of different styles while transitioning. keyframes essentially are a sequence of styles defined for an element.

To understand this better, let's take a look at the following code snippet:

```
transition('frameTest1 => frameTest2', [
  animate(300, keyframes([
  style({opacity: 1, transform: 'rotate(180deg)', offset: 0.3}),
  style({opacity: 1, transform: 'rotate(-90deg)', offset: 0.7}),
  style({opacity: 0, transform: 'rotate(-180deg)', offset: 1.0})
  ]))
```

Let's analyze the preceding code snippet in detail:

1. We are defining a transition from frameTest1 => frameTest2
2. We are defining the animate property with 300 milliseconds.
3. We are defining the keyframes under which we are defining three different styles; the element will go through each of the transition frames step by step.

Now, let's expand the preceding created example in the preceding section with the subsequent code.

The updated learn-animation.component.ts file will have code as follows:

```
import { Component } from '@angular/core';
import { state, style, animate, trigger, transition, keyframes} from
'@angular/animations';

@Component({
```

```
selector: 'app-learn-animation',
templateUrl: './learn-animation.component.html',
styleUrls: ['./learn-animation.component.css'],
animations: [
trigger('animationState', [
  state('frameTest1', style({ transform: 'translate3d(0, 0, 0)' })),
  state('frameTest2', style({ transform:
              'translate3d(300px, 0, 0)' })),
  transition('frameTest1 => frameTest2',
              animate('300ms ease-in-out')),

  transition('frameTest2 => frameTest1', [
    animate(1000, keyframes([
      style({opacity: 1, transform: 'rotate(180deg)', offset: 0.3}),
      style({opacity: 1, transform: 'rotate(-90deg)', offset: 0.7}),
      style({opacity: 0, transform: 'rotate(-180deg)', offset: 1.0})
    ]))
  ])
 ])
]
})
export class LearnAnimationComponent{
 constructor() {}

 public left : string = 'frameTest1';
 public onClick () : void
 {
  this.left = this.left === 'frameTest1' ? 'frameTest2' : 'frameTest1';
 }
}
```

Let's analyze the preceding code in detail:

1. We are importing the required modules from the Angular animation library: `state`, `style`, `animate`, `keyframes`, and `transition`. These modules help us in creating animations in our applications.

2. We create a `LearnAnimationComponent` component.

3. We specify `animations` for the component.

4. We define a trigger named `animationState`.

5. For the trigger created, we are defining two states--`frameTest1` and `frameTest2`.

6. We define two transitions: `'frameTest2 => frameTest1'` and `'frameTest2 => frameTest1'`.

7. For each of the transitions defined, we have implemented `keyframes`, that is, a sequence of styles attached with the `animate` method to achieve smooth transition with a time delay.

8. In the component class, we define a `left` variable.

9. We are defining an `onClick` method, toggling the values from `frameTest1` and `frameTest2`.

So far, so good. We have implemented the component.

Now it's time to update our `learn-animation.component.html` and add the following code snippet to the file:

```
<h4>Keyframe Effects</h4>

<div class="animateElement" [@animationState]="left"
  (click)="onClick()">
    Click to slide right/ Toggle to move div
</div>
```

Alright, all set. Now, run the app, and you should see the output as shown in the screenshot and animations as mentioned below:

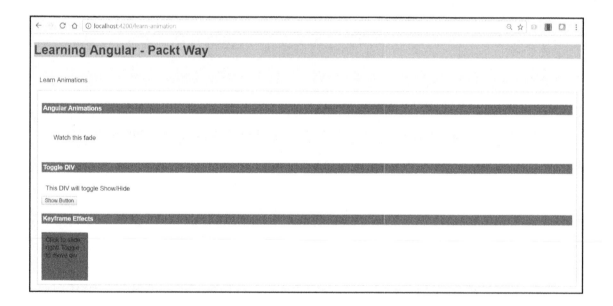

You should the following animations when you run the app

1. When you click on the DIV element --it should slide towards right
2. Click on the DIV element again and the element should move towards right with the DIV element transforming --giving a look-n-feel that the DIV is spinning.

In this section, you learned how to use keyframes and create a sequence of styles for elements for smoother transitions.

Animate collapse menu

In the this section, we will create a very important aspect of any application, that is, a sidebar menu for our application.

With what we have learned so far about Angular animations, we will create an example of a collapsing sidebar in this section.

Let's update the component template learn-animation.component.html and update the file with the following code snippet:

```
<h4>Collapse Menu</h4>

<button (click)="toggleMenu()" class="menuIcon">Toggle Menu</button>
 <div class="menu" [@toggleMenu]="menuState">
 <ul>
    <li>Home</li>
    <li>Angular</li>
    <li>Material Design</li>
    <li>Sridhar Rao</li>
    <li>Packt Publications</li>
 </ul>
</div>
```

An analysis of the preceding code is given here:

1. We are adding a <h4> heading, a Collapse menu.
2. We are defining a button and attaching the click event with the toggleMenu method.
3. We are creating an unordered list <ul> with sample list items <li> in our menu.

Now, we will add some basic CSS styling to the `learn-animation.component.css` file:

```css
.animateElement{
   background:red;
   height:100px;
   width:100px;
}
.menu {
   background: #FFB300;
   color: #fff;
   position: fixed;
   left: auto;
   top: 0;
   right: 0;
   bottom: 0;
   width: 20%;
   min-width: 250px;
   z-index: 9999;
   font-family: Arial, "Helvetica Neue", Helvetica, sans-serif;
}

ul {
   font-size: 18px;
   line-height: 3;
   font-weight: 400;
   padding-top: 50px;
   list-style: none;
}
.menuIcon:hover {
   cursor: pointer;
}
```

So far, we have created our application component template `learn-animation.component.html` and styled the menu component `learn-animation.component.css`.

Now, we will create the menu component class.

Add the following code to the `learn-animation.component.ts` file:

```typescript
import { Component } from '@angular/core';
import { state, style, animate, trigger, transition, keyframes} from '@angular/core';

@Component({
 selector: 'app-learn-animation',
 templateUrl: './learn-animation.component.html',
 styleUrls: ['./learn-animation.component.css'],
```

```
animations: [

  trigger('toggleMenu', [
   state('opened', style({
    transform: 'translate3d(0, 0, 0)'
   })),
   state('closed', style({
    transform: 'translate3d(100%, 0, 0)'
   })),
   transition('opened => closed', animate('400ms ease-in-out')),
   transition('closed => opened', animate('400ms ease-in-out'))
  ])
 ])
 ]
})
export class LearnAnimationComponent{

constructor() {}
 menuState : string = 'opened';
 toggleMenu()
 {
  this.menuState = this.menuState === 'closed' ? 'opened' : 'closed';
 }
}
```

Let's analyze the preceding code in detail:

1. We are importing the required Angular animation library modules, such as `state`, `style`, `animate`, `trigger`, `transition`, and `keyframes`.
2. In the animations, we define a trigger: `toggleMenu`.
3. We are creating two states: `opened` and `closed`.
4. For each of the states, we are defining some style attributes with `transform`.
5. We now define the transition `opened => closed` and `closed => open` with some animate details delay.
6. We have defined a `menuState` variable.
7. In the component class, we define the `toggleMenu`.
8. In the `toggleMenu` method, we are toggling the variable value of `menuState` to `opened` or `closed` and vice versa.

It's demo time. Run the application, and you should see output as follows:

Click on the **Toggle Menu** button again, we should see the menu sliding to the right as shown in the following screenshot:

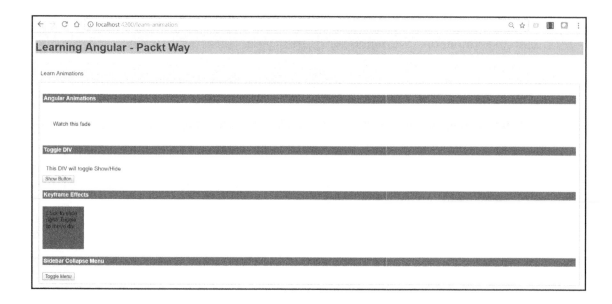

In this section, we created our application's sidebar menu with Angular animations.

Summary

In this chapter, we introduced Angular animations. Animations are key to designing and building beautiful user experiences with smooth transitions and element effects.

We covered how to install and import the Angular animations library and use various modules inside the library.

We discussed important modules, such as `state`, `style`, `animate`, `trigger`, `transition`, and `keyframes`.

We created and implemented some examples using Angular animations.

Finally, we created a web application sidebar menu with some animations. Now, over to you!

In the next chapter, you will learn how to integrate Bootstrap with Angular applications. Bootstrap is arguably the most popular frontend framework out there and, in this chapter, you will learn what it means to have an Angular x Bootstrap application.

15
Integrating Bootstrap with Angular Application

Bootstrap is arguably the most popular frontend framework out there. Isn't Angular itself a frontend framework, you ask? Well, yes. Then why in the world do I need to use two frontend frameworks for the same app? The answer is, you don't. Bootstrap has been created by and for Twitter, and is incredibly popular. It allows you to manage many things, such as the disposition of HTML components on the page, using a system called the grid. This system, which I will explain at length in the following pages, allows you to divide the web page space into zones without explicitly using CSS. Moreover, everything will be responsive out of the box. Also, Bootstrap provides dynamic elements such as a carousel, Progress bar, form reaction to user input, and more. Simply put, Angular allows you to create the application structure and manages data presentation, while Bootstrap deals with the presentation of the graphics.

Bootstrap is based around three elements:

- `bootstrap.css`
- `bootstrap.js`
- `glyphicons`

Here, `bootstrap.css` contains the framework that allows the responsive division of space, while `bootstrap.js` is a JavaScript framework that makes your pages dynamic.

 It is important to note that `bootstrap.js` depends on the jQuery library.

Finally, `glyphicons` is a font containing all the icons you might need when using Bootstrap.

In `Chapter 10`, *Material Design in Angular*, you will learn how to create apps that manage dynamic elements, the carousel, and other Progress bars using the `Material Design` package provided as an official extension of Angular by Google (ng2-material). Bootstrap (by Twitter) and Material Design (by Google for Angular) ultimately tend to achieve the same thing: facilitate your life when it comes to strictly presenting pages to your user. For example, they both ensure cross-browser compatibility, prevent the repetition of code between projects, and add consistency in the code base.

In my opinion, which one you should use is a personal choice, and I can see flame wars along the lines of C# versus Java or the PC versus the Mac ahead in the coming months. On the one hand, if you are already proficient with Bootstrap and use it everywhere, then you can use it here too. On the other hand, if Bootstrap is not part of your skill set, you can use this opportunity to pick it up and then choose the one you prefer.

The third option will be to skip this chapter altogether if you have already picked the Material Design (by Google for Angular) approach. I will not mind, promise. The topics covered in this chapter are:

- Installing Bootstrap
- Understanding Bootstrap's grid system
- Using Bootstrap directives

Installing Bootstrap

Without further ado, let's get started and install Bootstrap for Angular.

When using Bootstrap with a standard web application without a frontend framework such as Angular--you need to use **content delivery network** (**CDN**) to fetch the three parts that comprise the Bootstrap framework (`bootstrap.css`, `bootstrap.js`, and `glyphicons`). These calls, even when downloading minified files, still take time (for example, three HTTP requests, downloading, check summing, and so on) for your clients. With Angular, we could follow the same approach and simply add references to some CDN in `src/index.html`, but it would be a considerable mistake.

First of all, if the user does not own a cached copy of the resource, then we will suffer the same side-effects as a standard web app, as our customers would have to wait for the CDNs to serve the Bootstrap framework, especially considering that our app is minified and served in a single file, thanks to the Angular CLI deployment processes. Secondly, we won't be able to easily control the Bootstrap components in our Angular components.

The better way to integrate Bootstrap with our Angular application is to use the ng-bootstrap package. This package allows us to use an Angular directive for Bootstrap and to manage them in our components. At the time of writing, this is the most comprehensive, well maintained, and well integrated package that allows us to use Bootstrap in Angular.

To explore Bootstrap, we will build upon our JSON API for the Marvel Cinematic Universe used in Chapter 7, *Asynchronous Programming Using Observables* and Chapter 9, *Advanced Forms in Angular*.

You can find the code for Chapter 9, *Advanced Forms in Angular* at https://github.com/MathieuNls/mastering-angular/tree/master/chap9.

To clone this code into a new repository called angular-bootstrap, use the following commands:

```
$ git clone --depth one https://github.com/MathieuNls/mastering-angular
    angular-bootstrap
$ cd angular-bootstrap
$ git filter-branch --prune-empty --subdirectory-filter chap9 HEAD
```

These commands pull the latest version of the GitHub repository containing the code for this book to a folder named angular-bootstrap. Then, we go into the angular-bootstrap folder and prune everything that is not inside the Chapter 9, *Advanced Forms in Angular* directory.

Now let's install the ng-bootstrap package:

```
npm install --save @ng-bootstrap/ng-bootstrap
```

Now, in `src/app/app.module.ts`, import the package `import {NgbModule}` from `@ng-bootstrap/ng-bootstrap` and add `NgbModule.forRoot()` to the list of imports for the `AppModule` class. It should look like this, if you reused the code from Chapter 9, *Advanced Forms in Angular*:

```
import { BrowserModule } from '@angular/platform-browser';
import { NgModule } from '@angular/core';
import { FormsModule, ReactiveFormsModule } from '@angular/forms';
import { HttpModule } from '@angular/http';
import { NgbModule } from '@ng-bootstrap/ng-bootstrap

import { AppComponent } from './app.component';

@NgModule({
  declarations: [
    AppComponent
  ],
  imports: [
    BrowserModule,
    FormsModule,
    HttpModule,
    ReactiveFormsModule,
    NgbModule.forRoot()
  ],
  providers: [],
  bootstrap: [AppComponent]
})
export class AppModule { }
```

This package allows us to get rid of the jQuery and `bootstrap.js` dependencies, but, unfortunately, it does not include the `bootstrap.css`. It contains the required styles for the grid system and the components we are about to use.

Go to `http://getbootstrap.com/` and import the following displayed link in your `src/index.html`:

```
<!doctype html>
<html>
<head>
  <meta charset="utf-8">
  <title>Chap15</title>
  <base href="/">
  <link rel="stylesheet"
      href="https://maxcdn.bootstrapcdn.com/bootstrap/4.0.0-
      alpha.4/css/bootstrap.min.css" integrity="sha384-
      2hfp1SzUoho7/TsGGGDaFdsuuDL0LX2hnUp6VkX3CUQ2K4K+xjboZdsXyp4oUHZj"
      crossorigin="anonymous">
```

```
    <meta name="viewport" content="width=device-width, initial-scale=1">
    <link rel="icon" type="image/x-icon" href="favicon.ico">
  </head>
  <body>
    <app-root>Loading...</app-root>
  </body>
  </html>
```

Upon these small changes, we can already see that Bootstrap is taking over our style. In the following picture, the left side is what our form looked like at the end of Chapter 9, *Advanced Forms in Angular*.

The right side, however, is what our form looks like now. As you can see, there are small differences here and there. For example, the h1 tag, the error field, and the inputs have different styles:

Before and after Bootstrap.

If we use the Google Chrome inspection features, we can clearly see that the applied style for our h1 markup comes from http://maxcdn.bootstrapcdn.com, as shown in the following screenshot:

Chrome inspect style.

That is it: We're done with the initialization of Bootstrap. Let's learn how to use the Angular directives for Bootstrap.

Understanding the grid system

In this chapter, we are more concerned with learning how to use the different Bootstrap directives for Angular than learning about Sass mixins and other presentation skills. In other words, the advanced features of the grid system fall outside the scope of this chapter. However, in this section, I'll quickly introduce what the grid system is and give an overview of how to use it.

If you have used Bootstrap before, and, more particularly, have used the grid system, you can skip this section and go directly to the next one, where we learn how to use the accordion directive.

So, the grid system splits our presentation into twelve columns. The size of the columns can be extra small, small, medium, large, and extra large. The size of the columns can be manually set via the CSS class prefix (col-xs, col-sm, col-md, col-lg, and col-xl respectively) and corresponds to different screen widths (less than 540px, 540px, 720px, 960px, and 1140px, respectively).

To get an idea of how to leverage the grid system to separate our presentation, let's add the following to `src/app/app.component.html` just after our `<h1>{{title}}</h1>` markup:

```
<div class="container">
    <div class="row">
      <div class="col-md-1">col-md-1</div>
      <div class="col-md-1">col-md-1</div>
      <div class="col-md-1">col-md-1</div>
      <div class="col-md-1">col-md-1</div>
      <div class="col-md-1">col-md-1</div>
      <div class="col-md-1">col-md-1</div>
      <div class="col-md-1">col-md-1</div>
      <div class="col-md-1">col-md-1</div>
      <div class="col-md-1">col-md-1</div>
      <div class="col-md-1">col-md-1</div>
      <div class="col-md-1">col-md-1</div>
      <div class="col-md-1">col-md-1</div>
    </div>
    <div class="row">
      <div class="col-md-8">col-md-8</div>
      <div class="col-md-4">col-md-4</div>
    </div>
    <div class="row">
      <div class="col-md-4">col-md-4</div>
      <div class="col-md-4">col-md-4</div>
      <div class="col-md-4">col-md-4</div>
    </div>
    <div class="row">
      <div class="col-md-6">col-md-6</div>
      <div class="col-md-6">col-md-6</div>
    </div>
  </div>
```

As you can see, we have several CSS classes at work here. First, let us look at the container. This one is mandatory and defines the space on which the Bootstrap grid system will be applied. Then, we have rows that contain `col-` `divs`. Each row occupies the full width of the screen and is divided into columns. The actual width of the columns depends on the number you used at the end of the column class declaration (4, 8, 6, and so on). Knowing that the rows are separated into 12 columns, and that we used the `col-md` class prefix, we can extrapolate that the maximum size of a row is 720px. Consequently, each column is 60px wide. Within the first row, we use the `-1` suffix for our declaration; hence, we have 60px-wide column (that is, the size of the screen width divided by 12). On the second row, however, we use the `-8` and the `-4` suffixes.

This means that we will have one column that will be eight times the width of a-1 column (480px) and another column that will be four times the width of a-1 column (240px). In the third row, we use three four columns and, finally, in the fourth row, we have two six columns.

To see what is happening, add the following to app/app.component.css:

```
.row > [class^="col-"]{
  padding-top: .75rem;
    padding-bottom: .75rem;
    background-color: rgba(86, 61, 124, 0.15);
    border: 1px solid rgba(86, 61, 124, 0.2);
}
```

This piece of CSS will add a background and border to any col classes, regardless of the prefix or suffix they might have:

The grid system in action.

As you can see in the preceding picture, the space is nicely divided as planned. Now, that's not the real strength of the grid system. The main strength is that the columns would automatically stack on top of each other if the screen width became smaller than 720px.

On an iPhone 6, for example, whose screen is 375px in width, all the columns will be stacked as shown in the following screenshot:

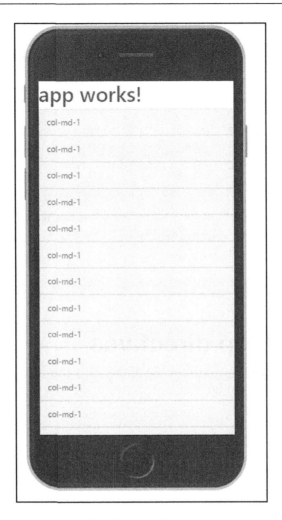

The grid system on an iPhone 6.

Here's another example from the official documentation, found at
`https://v4-alpha.getbootstrap.com/layout/grid/`:

```
<!-- Stack the columns on mobile by making one full-width and the other
half-width -->
 <div class="row">
   <div class="col-xs-12 col-md-8">.col-xs-12 .col-md-8</div>
   <div class="col-xs-6 col-md-4">.col-xs-6 .col-md-4</div>
 </div>

 <!-- Columns start at 50% wide on mobile and bump up to 33.3% wide on
```

```
desktop -->
 <div class="row">
   <div class="col-xs-6 col-md-4">.col-xs-6 .col-md-4</div>
   <div class="col-xs-6 col-md-4">.col-xs-6 .col-md-4</div>
   <div class="col-xs-6 col-md-4">.col-xs-6 .col-md-4</div>
 </div>

 <!-- Columns are always 50% wide, on mobile and desktop -->
 <div class="row">
   <div class="col-xs-6">.col-xs-6</div>
   <div class="col-xs-6">.col-xs-6</div>
 </div>
```

I will not go any further in detailing the grid system, but know that you can find a lot of awesome books about this topic in the Packt Library. Just look up the following:

- *Mastering Bootstrap 4*
- *Bootstrap 4 Blueprints*

Using Bootstrap directives

In this section, we will learn how to use some of the most commonly used Bootstrap directives to build your application.

Accordion

The first directive we will overview is the accordion directive. Accordion allows you to create a different panel of content that can be displayed independently by clicking its respective header.

We will use the form we made back in `Chapter 9`, *Advanced Forms in Angular*, which allows the user to add movies in the Marvel Cinematic Universe, to experiment with accordion. The goal here is to have one panel for the form and another panel for the enumeration of the movies.

Let's start by studying the minimal HTML needed to have a Bootstrap accordion, which is shown as follows:

```
<ngb-accordion>
  <ngb-panel>
    <template ngbPanelTitle>
      <span>Mastering angular X Bootstrap</span>
```

```
      </template>
      <template ngbPanelContent>
        Some deep insights
      </template>
    </ngb-panel>
    <ngb-panel>
      <template ngbPanelTitle>
        <span>Some Title</span>
      </template>
      <template ngbPanelContent>
        Some text
      </template>
    </ngb-panel>
  </ngb-accordion>
```

The previous HTML template will result in the following:

A simple accordion.

Analyzing the preceding code snippet, we can see the following features:

- ngb-accordion : This is the main accordion directive. It defines an accordion that will contain ngb-panel.
- ngb-panel: This represents a single panel of the accordion. Its visibility can be toggled by clicking on the panel title. ngb-panel contains a template that can be used for the title or the content.
- <template ngbPanelContent> : This contains the title or the content of a given panel.
- <template ngbPanelTitle>: This contains the title.

So far, everything is fairly simple. Now, where it becomes powerful is when you manage it from your TypeScript component. First of all, the `ngb-accordion` directive has three different `@Input` properties that we leverage. The first one is `activeIds`, which is `string[]` and contains the IDs of the panel you wish to be opened. Panel IDs are auto-generated from `ngb-panel-0`. The panel IDs are generated with the format `ngb-panel-x`. The second `@Input` is a Boolean: `closeOthers`. This one allows you to specify whether only one panel should be opened at a time. Finally, the `string` type is used to specify the type of the accordion in terms of its style. In Bootstrap, four types are recognized: `success`, `info`, `warning`, and `danger`.

In addition to these three `@Inputs`, the `ngb-accordion` directive provides an `@Output` named `panelChange`. This `@Output` will fire each time a panel's visibility is about to be toggled.

Let's experiment with these `@Input` and `@Output` properties by transforming `app/app.component.html` to the following:

```html
<div class="container">

    <!-- First Row -->
    <div class="row">
        <h1 class="col-md-12">
          {{title}}
        </h1>
    </div>

    <!-- Second Row -->
    <div class="row">

        <!-- Start of the accordion -->
        <ngb-accordion class="col-md-12"
        <!-- Bind to a variable called activeIds -->
        [activeIds]="activeIds"
        <!-- Simply use the string 'success' -->
        type="success"
        <!-- Simply use true -->
        closeOthers="true"
        <!-- Bind to the output -->
        (panelChange)=panelChanged($event)
        >
          <!-- Firt pannel -->
          <ngb-panel>
            <template ngbPanelTitle>
              <span>Add a Movie</span>
            </template>
```

```
<!-- Form content is here -->
<template ngbPanelContent>
  <form [formGroup]="movieForm">
    <!-- Form content omitted for clarity -->
  </form>
</template>
</ngb-panel>
<!-- Second pannel -->
<ngb-panel>
  <template ngbPanelTitle>
    <span>Movies</span>
  </template>
  <!-- Movie enumeration is here -->
  <template ngbPanelContent>

    <ul>
      <li *ngFor="let movie of movies">{{movie}}</li>
    </ul>

  </template>
</ngb-panel>
</ngb-accordion>

</div>
</div>
```

Here, we used [activeIds]="activeIds", type="success", closeOthers="true", and (panelChange)=pannelChanged($event) to bind to a variable named activeIds in our component, set the type of the form to success, and set closeOthers to true. Then, we bound a method named pannelChanged to the panelChange output. In the app.component.ts, we need to add the activeIds variable and the pannelChanged method as follows:

```
private activeIds = ["ngb-panel-1"];

private pannelChanged(event:{panelId:string, nextState:boolean}){
  console.log(event.nextState, event.panelId);
}
```

Here, private activeIds = ["ngb-panel-1"]; allows us to define that the panel-1 (the second one) should be opened by default and the pannelChanged method should receive an event payload composed of a panelId:string and a nextState:boolean. We log both payload attributes.

The app now looks like the one shown in the following screenshot:

- Movie (movie_id: 1, title: Iron Man, phase: Phase One: Avengers Assembled, category_name: Action, release_year: 2015, running_time: 126, rating_name: PG-13, disc_format_name: Blu-ray, number_discs: 1, viewing_format_name: Widescreen, aspect_ratio_name: 2.35:1, status: 1, release_date: May 2, 2008, budget: 140,000,000, gross: 318,298,180, time_stamp: 2015-05-03)
- Movie (movie_id: 3, title: Iron Man 2, phase: Phase One: Avengers Assembled, category_name: Action, release_year: 2015, running_time: 124, rating_name: PG-13, disc_format_name: Blu-ray, number_discs: 1, viewing_format_name: Widescreen, aspect_ratio_name: 2.35:1, status: 1, release_date: May 7, 2010, budget: 200,000,000, gross: 312,057,433, time_stamp: 2015-05-03)
- Movie (movie_id: 7, title: Iron Man 3, phase: Phase Two, category_name: Action, release_year: 2015, running_time: 130, rating_name: PG-13, disc_format_name: Blu-ray, number_discs: 2, viewing_format_name: Widescreen, aspect_ratio_name: 2.35:1, status: 1, release_date: May 3, 2013, budget: 200,000,000, gross: 408,992,272, time_stamp: 2015-05-03)
- Movie (movie_id: 11, title: Avengers: Age of Ultron, phase: Phase Two, category_name: Science Fiction, release_year: 2015, running_time: 141, rating_name: PG-13, disc_format_name: Blu-ray, number_discs: 1, viewing_format_name: Widescreen, aspect_ratio_name: 2.35:1, status: 1, release_date: May 1, 2015, budget: 250,000,000, gross: 458,991,599, time_stamp: 2015-12-07)
- Movie (movie_id: 12, title: Ant-Man, phase: Phase Two, category_name: Science Fiction, release_year: 2015, running_time: 132, rating_name: PG-13, disc_format_name: Blu-ray, number_discs: 1, viewing_format_name: Widescreen, aspect_ratio_name: 1.85:1, status: 1, release_date: July 17, 2015, budget: 130,000,000, gross: 179,017,481, time_stamp: 2015-12-07)
- Movie (movie_id: 9, title: Captain America: The Winter Soldier, phase: Phase Two, category_name: Action, release_year: 2014, running_time: 136, rating_name: PG-13, disc_format_name: Blu-ray, number_discs: 1, viewing_format_name: Widescreen, aspect_ratio_name: 2.35:1, status: 1, release_date: April 4, 2014, budget: 170,000,000, gross: 259,746,958, time_stamp: 2014-09-19)
- Movie (movie_id: 10, title: Guardians of the Galaxy, phase: Phase Two, category_name: Science Fiction, release_year: 2014, running_time: 121, rating_name: PG-13, disc_format_name: Blu-ray, number_discs: 1, viewing_format_name: Widescreen, aspect_ratio_name: 2.35:1, status: 1, release_date: August 1, 2014, budget: 170,000,000, gross: 333,130,696 , time_stamp: 2014-12-07)
- Movie (movie_id: 7, title: Iron Man 3, phase: Phase Two, category_name: Action, release_year: 2015, running_time: 130, rating_name: PG-13, disc_format_name: Blu-ray + DVD, number_discs: 2, viewing_format_name: Widescreen, aspect_ratio_name: 2.35:1, status: 1, release_date: May 3, 2013, budget: 200,000,000, gross: 408,992,272, time_stamp: 2015-05-03)

A TypeScript--managed accordion.

When you toggle the panels, it logs the following in the console:

```
true "ngb-panel-0"
false "ngb-panel-0"
```

Alert

The next directive we will explore in this chapter is the `ng-alert`. In the Bootstrap vocabulary, alerts are important information that is displayed to the user in a colored `div`. There exist four types of alert: `success`, `info`, `warning`, and `danger`.

To create a Bootstrap alert, the minimum viable HTML template is as follows:

```
<ngb-alert>
  Something important
</ngb-alert>
```

The result of this code is shown in the following screenshot:

A basic alert.

Similar to the accordion, the alert directive provides some `@Input` and `@Output`. We can use as `@Input` the `dismissible:boolean`, which manages the dismissibility of the alert, and `type:string`, which accepts `success`, `info`, `warning`, and `danger`.

To make our form a bit more Bootstrappy, we can replace our error messages with alerts. For now, in the forms the error messages look like this:

```
<p class='error' *ngIf=!movieForm.controls.movie_id.valid>This field is required</p>
```

Now the objective is to have the following:

```
<ngb-alert
 [dismissible]="false"
 *ngIf=!movieForm.controls.movie_id.valid
 type="danger"
 >
   This field is required
</ngb-alert>
```

For each of the fields in the preceding snippet, the aforementioned code will produce the following:

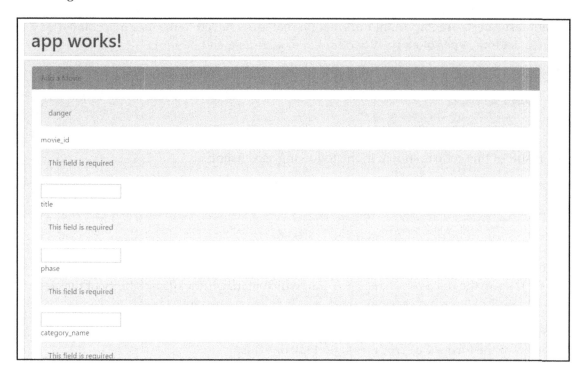

Danger alert as form errors.

Datepicker

The next directive in this chapter is the datepicker. Regardless of the technology you use, dates are always somewhat finicky as every vendor proposes many formats. Also, date internationalization makes things even harder.

Luckily, Bootstrap comes with a simple enough datepicker that allows the user to pick a date in a pop-up calendar graphically. The code for this is given as follows:

```
<div class="input-group">
    <input class="form-control" placeholder="yyyy-mm-dd"
       ngbDatepicker #dp="ngbDatepicker">
    <div class="input-group-addon" (click)="dp.toggle()" >
       <img src="https://ng-bootstrap.github.io/img/calendar-icon.svg"
          style="width: 1.2rem; height:
```

```
                    1rem; cursor: pointer;"/>
        </div>
    </div>
```

Many things are going on here. First, we have a `formControl` input that has a placeholder set to `yyyy-mm-dd`. The placeholder you define is important as it will act as a mandatory formatter for the data your users pick. For the syntax of the formatter, you can use every classical symbol for dates (for example, d, D, j, l, N, S, w, z, and so on). In other words, the dates we enter will automatically match this pattern. Then, we have `ngbDatepicker` `#d="ngbDatepicker"`. The `ngbDatepicker` defines that our input is a `ngbDatepicker` and the `#dp="ngbDatepicker"` allows us to create a local reference to our input. This local reference, named `dp`, is used on the `(click)` event of the following `div`: `(click)="dp.toggle()"`. This `div` contains the image of the calendar. On clicking it, a dynamic calendar will pop up and we will be able to choose a date.

This HTML will give us the following:

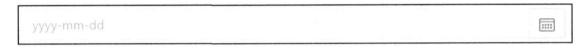

datepicker.

Then, once the `click` event is triggered, the following will be displayed :

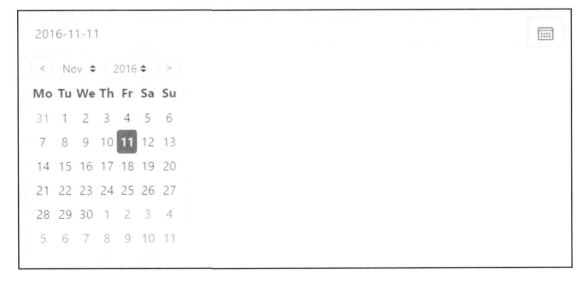

datepicker clicked.

To improve our management of the Marvel Cinematic Universe, we can change the `release_date` field to a datepicker. For now, the `release_date` field looks like the following:

```
<label>release_date</label>
 <ngb-alert [dismissible]="false" type="danger"
        *ngIf=!movieForm.controls.release_date.valid>This field is
required</ngb-alert>
 <input type="text" formControlName="release_date"
[(ngModel)]="movie.release_date"><br/>
```

We have the input and the Bootstrap alert if the field is not valid. The Bootstrap alert is active by default (that is, when the field is empty). Let's transform our input to the following:

```
<label>release_date</label>
 <ngb-alert [dismissible]="false" type="danger"
    *ngIf=!movieForm.controls.release_date.valid>This
    field is required</ngb-alert>
<div class="input-group">
  <input
  formControlName="release_date"
  placeholder="yyyy-mm-dd"
  ngbDatepicker #dp="ngbDatepicker"
  [(ngModel)]="movie.release_date">
  <div class="input-group-addon" (click)="dp.toggle()" >
    <img src="https://ng-bootstrap.github.io/img/calendar-icon.svg"
        style="width: 1.2rem;
        height: 1rem; cursor: pointer;"/>
  </div>
</div>
```

What's different here is that we link the input to our `formControl`. Indeed, in `Chapter 9`, *Advanced Forms in Angular*, we defined the form as follows:

```
this.movieForm =  this.formBuilder.group({
        movie_id: ['',
          Validators.compose(
            [
            Validators.required,
            Validators.minLength(1),
            Validators.maxLength(4),
            Validators.pattern('[0-9]+'),
            MovieIDValidator.idNotTaken
            ]
          )
        ],
```

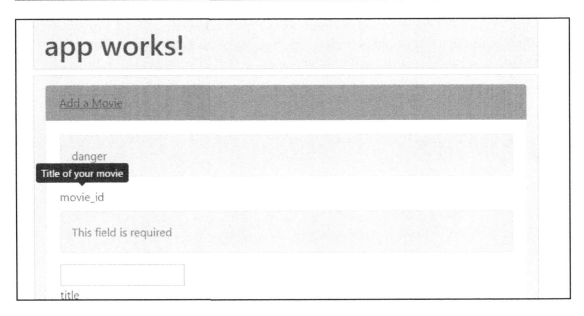

A tooltip on **movie_id**.

Progress bar

There exist some other Bootstrap components that we could use to enhance our form; however, too many will quickly become a case of overkill in terms of usability. For example, it will be tricky to integrate a Progress bar in to our form. What we can do, however, is add a panel to our accordion for each new Bootstrap directive we want to test.

Let's add a panel for the Progress bar:

```
<ngb-panel>
    <template ngbPanelTitle>
        <span>Progress Bar</span>
    </template>

    <template ngbPanelContent>

        <ngb-progressbar type="success" [value]="25"></ngb-progressbar>

    </template>
</ngb-panel>
```

The `progressbar` directive is another simple directive. It takes two `@Input` attributes: type and value. As usual, the type can be a `success`, `danger`, `warning`, or `info`. The value attribute can be bound to a TypeScript variable instead of hardcoding 25, as I did.

Here's the result:

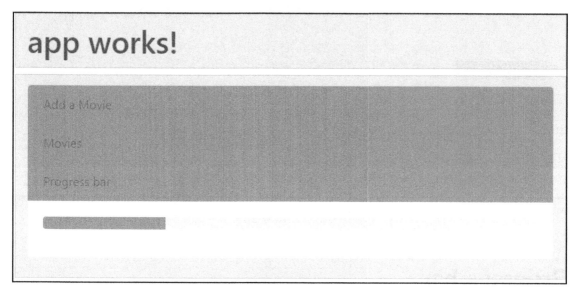

Progress bar on **movie_id.**

Rating

The rating directive is also fairly well known. It allows users to rate something, or to display a given rate.

As expected, this directive is simple to understand. It has a rate input that you can hardcode (for example, `"rate"=25`), bind (`[rate]="someVariable"`), or apply Two-way Data Binding (`[(rate)]="someVariable"`). In addition to the rate input, you can use `[readonly]="read-only"` to make your rate bar non-modifiable.

By default, the rating bar consists of 10 stars. The rate value can range from 0 to 10, including decimal numbers.

Here's an example of a default rate bar inside a new panel:

```
<ngb-panel>
      <template ngbPanelTitle>
        <span>Rating bar</span>
      </template>
      <template ngbPanelContent>

          <ngb-rating rate="5"></ngb-rating>

      </template>
  </ngb-panel>
```

This will produce the following result:

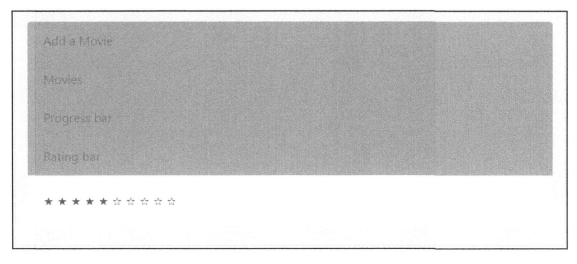

Rate bar.

Summary

In this chapter, we saw some of the most popular Bootstrap components out there. We learned how to use them with native Angular directives provided by the ng2-Bootstrap package. We did not, however, explore every single Bootstrap component there is. You can have a look at the official documentation hosted at `https://ng-bootstrap.github.io/`.

In the next chapter, you will learn how to test your Angular application with unit testing.

16
Testing Angular Apps Using Jasmine and Protractor Frameworks

Testing is one of the most important aspects in the modern application development process. We even have dedicated software development methodologies, primarily driven by a test-first approach.

Along with the testing utilities provided by Angular, there are a few recommended frameworks, such as Jasmine, Karma, and Protractor, using which it's easy to create, maintain, and write test scripts. Test scripts written in Jasmine and Protractor save time and effort, and above all yield good returns by finding defects much earlier in the development process.

In this chapter, you will learn all about testing Angular applications using Jasmine and Protractor. In this chapter, we will discuss the following:

- Learn about important concepts in testing
- Understanding Angular CLI for unit-testing specific environments
- Introducing the Jasmine framework
- Writing tests scripts using Jasmine
- Writing test scripts to test Angular components
- Testing Angular components: an advanced example
- Testing Angular services using Jasmine test scripts
- Learning about Protractor
- Writing E2E test scripts using Protractor

Concepts in testing

Before we start testing our Angular applications, it's important that we quickly brush up on and understand some of the most commonly used terms in testing:

- **Unit test**: One can view a unit test as the smallest testable part of an application.
- **Test case**: This is a set of test inputs, execution conditions, and expected results for achieving an objective. In the Jasmine framework, these are referred to as specs.
- **TestBed**: TestBed is a method of testing a particular module in an isolated fashion by passing all the required data and objects.
- **Test suite**: This is a collection of test cases that are intended to be used to test a module end to end.
- **System test**: The tests conducted on a complete and integrated system to evaluate the system functionality.
- **E2E test**: It is a testing method, which determines whether the behavior of the application is as required. We pass the data, required objects, and dependencies and is performed from start to finish under mocking the real-time use cases and scenarios.

Now that we know the preceding terms, let's learn about testing Angular applications.

Understanding and setting up Angular CLI for testing

So far, we have used Angular CLI for setting up our project, creating new components, services, and more. We will now discuss how to use the command-line tool to set and execute test suites to test our Angular applications.

First things first, a quick recap on how to create a project quickly using Angular CLI:

```
npm install -g angular-cli
```

Using the preceding code snippet, we installed the Angular command-line tool. Now, let's create a new directory named `test-app` and navigate inside the project directory:

```
ng new test-app
cd test-app
```

It's time to quickly create a new component called `test-app`:

```
ng g component ./test-app
```

Now, we will see the output as follows:

```
E2ML11514s-MacBook-Pro:dashboard Admin$ ng g component ./test-app
installing component
  create src/app/test-app/test-app.component.css
  create src/app/test-app/test-app.component.html
  create src/app/test-app/test-app.component.spec.ts
  create src/app/test-app/test-app.component.ts
  update src/app/app.module.ts
E2ML11514s-MacBook-Pro:dashboard Admin$
```

We should see the new directory and the corresponding files created in the directory. The command-line tool has created four files related to the component, including the `test-app.component.spec.ts` test script placeholder file.

Now, let's get our application up-and-running:

```
ng serve
```

At this point, we have our application up-and-running. Now it's time to get started with testing our Angular applications.

Introduction to Jasmine framework

Jasmine is a behavior-driven development framework for testing JavaScript code. This is how the official site explains Jasmine:

> *Jasmine is a behavior-driven development framework for testing JavaScript code. It does not depend on any other JavaScript frameworks. It does not require a DOM. And it has a clean, obvious syntax so that you can easily write tests.*

The general syntax of a Jasmine test suite is given as follows:

```
describe("Sample Test Suite", function() {
  it("This is a spec that defines test", function() {
    expect statement // asserts the logic etc
  });
});
```

Let's analyze the preceding code snippet to understand the test suite syntax. The following steps have been followed:

1. Every Jasmine test suite will have a `describe` statement, where we can give a name.
2. Inside the test suite, we create smaller tests cases using the `it` statement; each test case will have two parameters, a name and a function, which will have our application logic that needs be tested.
3. We use the `expect` statements to verify the data to make sure that our application and the data are working as expected.

In the next section, you will learn about the Jasmine framework and the available methods and functions that we can use in our test scripts in detail.

The Jasmine framework - Global methods we can use

The Jasmine framework supports and provides a lot of predefined methods for us to use and write our test suites. Jasmine has vast support for testing environments, spying on elements, and much more. Refer to the official website for complete help and documentation on available methods.

For writing test scripts, we will need a basic understanding and knowledge of some of the most commonly and frequently used methods in the Jasmine framework.

Commonly used methods in Jasmine

Here's a list of the most commonly used Jasmine global methods available to write test suites:

Global Methods	Description
describe	The describe function is a block of code that implements the test suite
it	Specs are defined by calling the global Jasmine function `it`, which as described takes a string and a function
beforeEach	This method is called once before each spec in the describe in which it is called
afterEach	This method is called once after each spec

beforeAll	This method is called once before all specs in the describe
afterAll	This method is called only once after all the specs are called
xdescribe	This temporarily disables tests that you don't want to execute
pending	Pending specs do not run; they are added to the pending results list
xit	Any spec declared with xit is marked as pending
spyOn	A spy can stub any function and tracks calls to it and all arguments; this is used inside the describe or it statements
spyOnProperty	Every call to a spy is tracked and exposed on the calls property

For more details and complete documentation, refer to Jasmine framework documentation on GitHub.

Angular CLI and Jasmine framework - First test

When we install Angular CLI, the Jasmine framework is automatically shipped with the tool.

In the preceding section, we saw the general syntax of writing a test in Jasmine. Now, let's write a quick test script using the Jasmine framework:

```
describe('JavaScript addition operator', function () {
  it('adds two numbers together', function () {
  expect(1 + 2).toEqual(3); });
});
```

The following are the important things to note about the preceding test script:

1. We write a `describe` statement to describe the test script.
2. We then define a test script using an `it` statement and a corresponding method.
3. In the `expect` statement, we assert two numbers, and using `toEqual` we test whether the addition of two numbers matches to 3.

Testing Angular components with Jasmine

It's time to create our test suite using the Jasmine framework. In the first section, *Understanding and setting up Angular CLI for testing*, we created the component `TestAppComponent` and the `test-app.component.ts` file using the `ng` command. We will continue to use the same in this section.

To get started, add all the contents of the file with the following code:

```
import { async, ComponentFixture, TestBed } from '@angular/core/testing';

import { TestAppComponent } from './test-app.component';

describe('Testing App Component', () => {
   it('Test learning component', () => {
    let component = new TestAppComponent();
    expect(component).toBeTruthy();
   });
});
```

Let's analyze the preceding test suite step by step. The steps that have been followed in the code block are as follows:

1. In the first step, we imported all the required modules for testing from `@angular/core/testing`.
2. We imported the newly created component, `TestAppComponent`.
3. We created a test suite by writing a `describe` statement with a name, `Testing App Component`.
4. We wrote a test script using `it` and the corresponding method: `() =>`.
5. We created a `component` object of the `TestAppComponent` class.
6. We then asserted whether the value returned is true or not. A value is `toBeTruthy` if the coercion of this value to a `boolean` yields the value true.

 All test suites written will end with a `.spec.ts` extension, for example, `test-app.component.spec.ts`.

We are good so far! That's great, and now we will run our test suite and see its output.

We are still using the Angular CLI tool; let's run the tests using the `ng` command in the project directory, and run the following command in the terminal:

ng test

The command-line tool will build the entire application, open a new Chrome window, run the tests using Karma test runner, and run the Jasmine test suite.

Karma test runner spawns a web server that executes all the tests in the browser and watches all the configurations specified in `karma.conf.js`. We can use the test runner to run work with various frameworks, including Jasmine and Mocha. The web server collects the results from all of the captured browsers and displays them to the developers.

We should see the output as shown in the following screenshot:

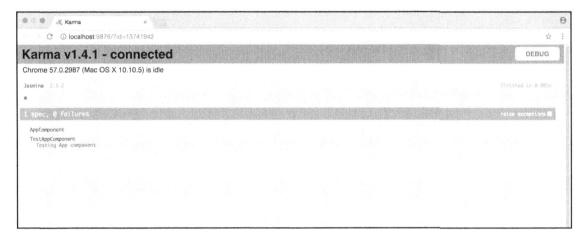

If you see the preceding screenshot, congrats. You have successfully executed the test suite, and note that the test script has passed.

Congrats! Now, let's dig deep and create more complex test scripts for testing components and services.

Testing Angular components with Jasmine

In our preceding example, we have seen a basic example of writing a test script and testing Angular components.

In this section, we will explore writing best practices for testing Angular components. We will use the same component we created in the preceding section--`TestAppComponent`--and expand the test suite more by adding variables and methods.

In the `test-app.component.ts` file, let's create a few variables and map them into the view:

```
import { Component, OnInit } from '@angular/core';

@Component({
  selector: 'app-test-app',
  templateUrl: './test-app.component.html',
  styleUrls: ['./test-app.component.css']
})
export class TestAppComponent implements OnInit {
  public authorName = 'Sridhar';
}
```

Let's analyze the preceding code we have written in our `test-app.component.ts` file:

1. We created a component--`TestAppComponent`.
2. We mapped the respective HTML and CSS files in `templateUrl` and `styleUrls`.
3. We declared a public `variable` called `authorName` and assigned the value `'Sridhar'`.

Now, let's move over to `test-app.component.spec.ts`. We will write our test suite and define a test case to verify that `authorName` matches the string passed:

```
import { async, ComponentFixture, TestBed } from '@angular/core/testing';
import { TestAppComponent } from './test-app.component';

  describe('TestAppComponent', () => {
    it('Testing App component', () => {
      let component = new TestAppComponent();
      expect(component.authorName).toMatch('Sridhar');
    });
  });
```

Let's analyze the preceding code snippet in the `test-app.component.spec.ts` file. The subsequent steps have been followed for the code block:

1. We imported all the required modules `async`, `componentFixture`, and `TestBed` for running the tests.
2. We created a test suite by writing the `describe` statement and assigned the `Testing App Component` name.
3. We created a test case and created a new instance of the component `TestAppComponent` class.

4. In the `expect` statement, we asserted whether the `authorName` variable matches the string. The result will return true or false.

Great! So far, so good. Now, read on.

Time to take it to the next level. We will add new methods to the `component` class and test them in the `specs` file.

In the `test-app.component.ts` file, let's add a variable and a method:

```
import { Component, OnInit } from '@angular/core';

@Component({
  selector: 'app-test-app',
  templateUrl: './test-app.component.html',
  styleUrls: ['./test-app.component.css']
})
export class TestAppComponent {
 public authorName = 'Sridhar';
 public publisherName = 'Packt'

 public hiPackt() {
 return 'Hello '+ this.publisherName;
 }
}
```

Let's create the `test-app.component.spec.ts` file and test the variable and the method we defined in the `component` class.

In the `test-app.component.spec.ts` file, add the following lines of code:

```
it('Testing Component Method', () => {
 let component = new TestAppComponent();
 expect(component.hiPackt()).toBe("Hello Packt");
});
```

Let's analyze the preceding code snippet in detail. The following steps have been adhered to:

1. We created a test case and created a `component` instance of the `TestAppComponent` class.
2. In the `expect` statement, we asserted and verified that the string passed matches the return value of the `hiPackt` method.

Before we run the preceding test script, let's also quickly take a look at one more test case:

```
describe('TestAppComponent', () => {
  beforeEach(function() {
    this.app = new TestAppComponent();
  });

  it('Component should have matching publisher name', function() {
    expect(this.app.publisherName).toBe('Packt');
  });
});
```

Let's analyze the preceding code snippet:

1. We implemented the `beforeEach` Jasmine method. We are creating an instance of `AppComponent` before each test script.
2. We wrote a test script and used the instance of the component, that is, `this.app`, we get the value of the `publisherName` variable, and assert whether the value of the `publisherName` variable matches `toBe('Packt')`.

Now, the tests should autobuild or else invoke `ng test` to run the tests.

We should see the following screenshot:

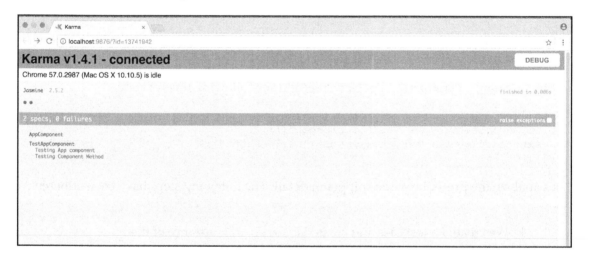

Great! You learned to write test scripts to test our Angular components, both variables and methods.

You learned to use some of the Jasmine framework's built-in methods, such as `beforeEach`, `expect`, `toBeTruthy`, and `toBe`.

In the next section, we will continue to learn advanced techniques and write more test scripts to test Angular components in even more detail.

Testing Angular components - Advanced

In this section, we will delve more deeply and learn some more important and advanced aspects of testing Angular components.

If you observe, you can note the following in the example mentioned in the preceding section:

1. We create an instance of the object individually each time in each test case.
2. We have to inject all the providers individually for each test case.

Instead, it will be great if we can define an instance of the component before each test script. We can achieve this by using `TestBed`--one of the most important utilities provided by Angular for testing.

TestBed

`TestBed` is the most important testing utility provided by Angular. It creates an Angular testing module--an `@NgModule` class, which we can use for our testing purposes.

Since it creates an `@NgModule`, we can define providers, imports, and exports--similar to our regular `@NgModule` configuration.

We can configure `TestBed` in either `async` or `sync` mode.

- For configuring `TestBed` asynchronously, we will use `configureTestingModule` to define the metadata of the object
- For configuring `TestBed` synchronously, we will define object instances of the component as discussed in our preceding section

Now, let's take a look at the code snippet as follows:

```
beforeEach(() => {
 fixture = TestBed.createComponent(AppComponent);
 comp = fixture.componentInstance;
 de = fixture.debugElement.query(By.css('h1'));
 });
```

The important things to note in the preceding code snippet:

1. We defined `beforeEach`, which means that this piece of code will run before each test case.
2. We created a component instance using `TestBed`.
3. Using `TestBed` sync way, we defined a `fixture` variable, which creates the component, `AppComponent`.
4. Using `componentInstance`, we created a `comp` variable, which is a test instance of `AppComponent`.
5. Using the `debugElement` function, we can define and target a specific element in the view.
6. Using `debugElement`, we can target an individual element by the CSS element selector.

Now, using the preceding `beforeEach` method, which has the component instance, we will create our test scripts for testing Angular components.

Example - Writing test scripts with change detection

In this section, we will continue to write some more test scripts unit tests with a twist. We will implement change detection and element tracking as well.

Let's get started by creating a simple `app.component.ts` component:

```
import { Component } from '@angular/core';

@Component({
 selector: 'test-root',
 templateUrl: './app.component.html',
 styleUrls: ['./app.component.css']
})

export class AppComponent {
 title = 'Packt Testing works';
}
```

Let's analyze the preceding code snippet:

1. We created a `AppComponent` component class.
2. We declared a `title` variable with a value.
3. We mapped the component's template and style files to their respective `templateUrl` and `styleUrls`.

In `app.component.html`, add the following code:

```
<h1> {{ title }} </h1>
```

In the preceding code, we are adding a `<h1>` tag and mapping the `title` variable.

Now, it's time to create our test script with multiple assertions. However, before we write our test script, let's understand the use cases:

1. We will write the script to check whether `ChangeDetectTestComponent` is created.
2. We will write the assertion to check whether `title` is equal to `Packt Testing works`.
3. Finally, we will check for a change detection and verify that the h1 tag should be rendered and contains the value `Packt Testing works`.
4. We will also make use of `querySelector` to target a specific element and match the value.

Now, let's take a look at the test scripts for the preceding use cases:

```
import { async, ComponentFixture, TestBed } from '@angular/core/testing';
import { ChangeDetectTestComponent } from './change-detect-test.component';
import { By } from '@angular/platform-browser';
import { DebugElement } from '@angular/core';

describe('ChangeDetectTestComponent', () => {

 let comp:ChangeDetectTestComponent;
   let fixture: ComponentFixture<ChangeDetectTestComponent>;
   let de:DebugElement;
   let el:HTMLElement;

 beforeEach(() => {
    TestBed.configureTestingModule({
      declarations: [ ChangeDetectTestComponent ]
    });
    fixture = TestBed.createComponent(ChangeDetectTestComponent);
```

```
      comp = fixture.componentInstance;
      de = fixture.debugElement.query(By.css('h1'));
      el = de.nativeElement;
   });

  it('should have as title 'Packt Testing works!'', async(() => {
     const fixture = TestBed.createComponent(ChangeDetectTestComponent);
     const app = fixture.debugElement.componentInstance;
     expect(app.title).toEqual('Packt Testing works');
   }));

  it('should render title in a h1 tag', async(() => {
    const fixture = TestBed.createComponent(ChangeDetectTestComponent);
    fixture.detectChanges();
    const compiled = fixture.debugElement.nativeElement;
    expect(compiled.querySelector('h1').textContent).toContain('Packt
      Testing works');
  }));
});
```

Let's analyze the preceding code snippet in detail:

1. We import the required modules, namely `TestBed`, `ComponentFixture`, and `async`, from `angular/core/testing`.
2. We define `beforeEach` and initiate the variables fixture, `comp` and `de`.
3. In the first test script, we write a simple expect statement for the component, `tobeTruthy`.
4. In the second test script, we create an instance of the component via `TestBed.createComponent`.
5. Using `debugElement`, we create the instance of the created component, that is, `app`.
6. Using the instance of the `app` component, we are able get the `title` of the component and assert `toEqual`.
7. In the last test script, we make use of the `async` method. We make use of the `debugElement nativeElement` method and target an element--<h1>, in our case--and check whether the title contain `Packt Testing Works`.
8. The difference between the second and third test script is that we are making use of the `async` method and waiting for changes to be detected--`detectChanges`--in the third test script.

Run the tests, and we should see the output as shown in the following screenshot:

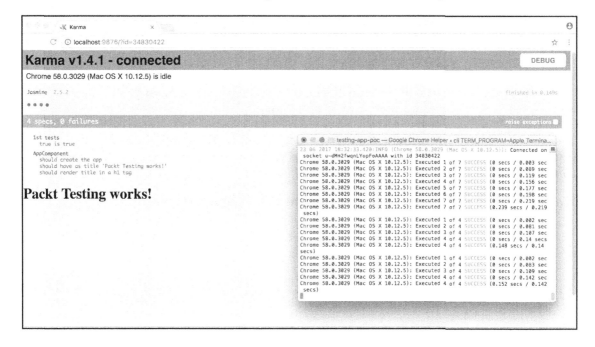

In this section, you learned how to create a component instance using `beforeEach` for all the test scripts and how to use `nativeElement` to target any element.

We used the `detectChanges` method to identify the changes happening in the element.

In the subsequent sections, we will continue to learn more about the Jasmine framework for testing Angular services.

Testing Angular services

In this section, we will learn about testing Angular services.

In most Angular applications, writing services is an important and core aspect as it performs the interactions with backend services; creating and sharing data between components and are easy to maintain in the long run. Hence, it's equally important to make sure that we are testing our Angular services thoroughly.

Let's learn how to write test scripts for testing our services. In order to test a service, let's first create a service using the ng command.

Run the following command in your terminal:

ng g service ./test-app/test-app

The preceding command will generate the test-app.service.ts and test-app.service.spec.ts files in the test-app folder.

Services are injectable, which means that we have to import them into their respective components, add them to the providers list, and create an instance of the service in the component constructor.

We modify test-app.service.ts and add the following code to it:

```
import { Injectable } from '@angular/core';

@Injectable()
export class TestAppService {

  getAuthorCount() {
    let Authors =[
      {name :"Sridhar"},
      {name: "Robin"},
      {name: "John"},
      {name: "Aditi"}
    ];
   return Object.keys(Authors).length;
  };
}
```

Note the following important things from the preceding code snippet:

1. We imported the injectable from Angular core.
2. We defined the @injectable metadata and created a class for our service--TestAppService.
3. We defined the getAuthorCount method to return the count of author.

We need to import and inject the service class into the component. To test the preceding service, we will write our tests scripts in the test-app.service.specs.ts file.

The way we write test scripts for testing services is similar to how we write for testing components.

Now, let's create the test suite for testing a service by adding the following code in the `test-app.service.spec.ts` file:

```
import { TestBed, inject } from '@angular/core/testing';
import { TestAppService } from './test-app.service';

describe('TestAppService', () => {
 beforeEach(() => {
 TestBed.configureTestingModule({
 providers: [TestAppService]
 });
 });

 it('Service should return 4 values', inject([TestAppService],
   (service: TestAppService) => {
     let countAuthor = service.getAuthorCount;
     expect(countAuthor).toBe(4);
 }));

});
```

An analysis of the preceding code is as follows:

1. We import the required modules, `TestBed` and `inject`, into the `spec` file.
2. We import the `TestAppService` service into the `spec` file.
3. Using **Dependency Injection(DI)**, we create the `service` instance of `TestAppService`.
4. We create a test case; we need to inject the service, invoke the `getAuthorCount` method, and assert whether the value matches to 4.

The following screenshot shows the output when we run the tests:

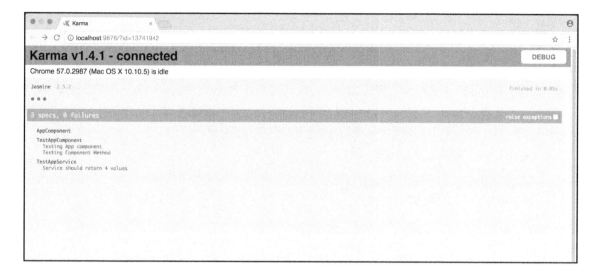

In this section, you learned about unit testing using Jasmine test scripts for Angular components and services.

We have to inject the service using DI in every test case.

Testing Angular services - Mocking backend services

In the preceding section, you learned how to write test scripts to test our Angular services. In this section, we will write a test script and learn how to mock backend services in real-time projects.

The following are the use cases we will writing our test scripts for:

1. Write a test script to test a method in service.
2. Write a test script to check whether the return value of the method contains a particular value.

3. Write a test script to mock the backend connection using `mockBackend` and also check whether the target URL is correct.

4. Write a test script to set the `mockResponse` for the request URL.

5. Finally, call a method written in `service` and map the response, which should be equal to the `mockResponse`.

Let's create our service `test.service.ts` file and add the following code to it:

```
import { Injectable } from '@angular/core';
import { Http } from '@angular/http';
import { Observable } from 'rxjs';
import 'rxjs/add/operator/map';

@Injectable()

export class TestService {
 constructor (private http: Http) {}
 getpublications() {
    return ['Packt', 'Packt PDF', 'Packt Video'];
  }

  getproducts() {
    return this.http.get('someurl1').map((response) => response);
  }

  search(term: string): Observable<any> {
    return this.http.get(
        'someurl'
    ).map((response) => response.json());
  }
}
```

The important things to note in the preceding code snippet are as follows:

1. We are importing the required module into the spec file, namely `injectable` from `Angular/core`.

2. We are importing the required module into the spec file, namely `Http` from `Angular/http`.

3. We are importing the required module into the spec file, namely `Observable` from `Angular/rxjs`.

4. We are creating the component class for `TestService`.

5. We are using the `@injectable` decorator, which will allow the service to be injected into any component or service.
6. In the constructor, we are injecting the `HTTP` service and creating an instance HTTP.
7. We are creating three methods: `getPublications`, `getProducts`, and `search`.
8. In `getProducts`, we are making an HTTP call, which, of course, we use to mock the server URL.
9. We are mapping the response of the HTTP request to the `response` variable.

Now that we have our service ready, we can start writing our test spec file to test the variables and methods.

Before we write our test scripts in the `spec` file, let's create a `beforeEach` method, which will have all the initiations, and we register the providers before each test script:

```
beforeEach(() => {
  TestBed.configureTestingModule({
    imports: [ HttpModule ],
    providers: [
    {
      provide: XHRBackend,
      useClass: XHRBackend
    },
    TestService ]
  });
});
```

Just as we defined the `beforeEach` method for testing Angular components, we define the `beforeEach` method for services. In the providers array configuration, we are registering the `XHRBackend` class.

 Since services have dependencies on other modules and require providers, we need to define and register the required services using `configureTestingModule`.

Let's analyze the preceding code snippet in detail:

1. We are defining a `beforeEach` method, which will be executed before each test script.
2. Using `TestBed`, we are configuring the test module using `configuringTestingModule`.

3. Since the parameters passed in configureTestingModule are similar to the metadata passed to the @NgModule decorator, we can specify providers and imports.

4. In imports, we import the HttpModule.

5. We are configuring the required dependencies--XHRBackend and TestService-- in the providers list.

6. We are registering a provider, XHRBackend with an injection token and setting the provider to XHRBackend, so that, when we request the provider, the DI system returns a XHRBackend instance.

Now we can create the spec file, test.service.spec.ts, and add the following code to the file:

```
import {TestService} from './test.service';
import { TestBed, inject } from '@angular/core/testing';
import { MockBackend, MockConnection} from '@angular/http/testing';
import { HttpModule,XHRBackend, ResponseOptions,Response, RequestMethod }
from '@angular/http';

const mockResponse = {
 'isbn': "123456",
 'book': {
    "id": 10,
    "title": "Packt Angular"
  }
};
const mockResponseText = 'Hello Packt';

describe('service: TestService', () => {
 beforeEach(() => {
    TestBed.configureTestingModule({
       imports: [ HttpModule ],
        providers: [
         {
           provide: XHRBackend,
           useClass: XHRBackend
         }, TestService]
    });
  });
  it('Service should return 4 publication values',
    inject([TestService, XHRBackend], (service: TestService,
      XHRBackend: XHRBackend) => {
        let names = service.getpublications();
        expect(names).toContain('Packt');
        expect(names).toContain('Packt PDF');
```

```
            expect (names) .toContain('Packt Video');
            expect (names.length) .toEqual(3);
    }));

    it('Mocking Services with Json', inject([TestService, XHRBackend],
        (service: TestService, XHRBackend: XHRBackend) => {
            const expectedUrl = 'someurl';
            XHRBackend.connections.subscribe(
                (connection: MockConnection) => {
                    expect (connection.request.method) .toBe (RequestMethod.Get);
                    expect (connection.request.url) .toBe (expectedUrl);
                    connection.mockRespond(new Response(
                    new ResponseOptions({ body: mockResponse })
                ));
            });
        service.getbooks() .subscribe(res => {
          expect (res) .toEqual(mockResponse);
        });
    }));
});
```

It's a long code snippet, so let's break it down for analysis:

1. We are importing the `TestService` service file into the `spec` file.
2. We are importing the required modules, `TestBed` and `inject`, from `@angular/core/testing`.
3. We are importing the modules, `MockBackend` and `MockConnection`, from `@angular/http/testing`.
4. We are importing the modules, `HttpModule`, `XHRBackend`, `ResponseOptions`, `Response`, and `RequestMethod`, from `@angular/http`.
5. We define a `mockResponse` variable, which has a temp `json` object.
6. We also define a `mockResponseText` variable and assign it a value.
7. We will use the `beforeEach` method we defined earlier, through which we will register all the providers and dependencies.
8. In the first test script, we are registering the `TestService` instance as `service` and the `XHRBackend` instance as `XHRBackend`.
9. We are calling the `service.getpublications()` method, which will return the array.
10. In the result names, we are asserting the values to contain the strings passed as test data.

11. In the second test script, we are creating connections using `mockBackend` and passing the requests `method` and `url` using `subscribe`.

12. Using the `mockRespond` connection, we are setting the response value as `mockResponse`.

13. We are also calling the `getbooks` method, mapping the response, and asserting the `toEqual` value to `mockResponse`.

Run the tests; we should see the output shown in the following screenshot:

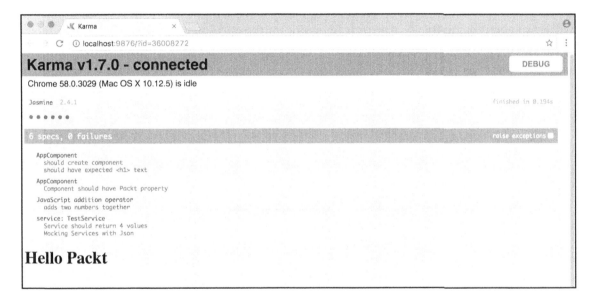

If you see the preceding screenshot, that's great.

So far, in this section, you have learned and explored the Jasmine framework and its built-in methods available for testing Angular components and services.

We discussed testing Angular components: testing the variables and methods. We also discussed how to write the `beforeEach` method to be executed before each test script and how to create an instance of the component and access its properties. We also covered testing Angular services using the Jasmine framework and testing Angular services and their properties: variables and methods.

For testing Angular services, you learned how to create a `beforeEach` method, which will be executed before each test script and will have the providers and dependencies created once before each test script.

You learned to test the backend services by mocking the services. This is really useful when you are independently developing Angular services and components.

In the next section, you will learn about using the Protractor framework for testing the end-to-end tests.

Introduction to Protractor framework

In the preceding sections, you learned about unit testing using Jasmine. In this section, you will learn about using the Protractor framework for the end-to-end testing of Angular applications.

This is how the official site explains Protractor:

> *Protractor is an end-to-end test framework for Angular and AngularJS applications. Protractor runs tests against your application running in a real browser, interacting with it as a user would.*

Protractor framework is packaged in the Angular CLI tool, and we can find the e2e folder created in our main project directory:

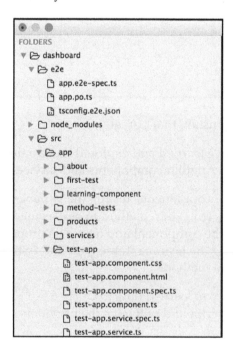

You will learn to write end-to-end tests for your Angular applications and keep them under the `e2e` folder.

> Remember that it's a best practice to create separate E2E scripts for each functionality or page.

Protractor - A quick overview

Protractor is a wrapper around Selenium WebDriver that provides a lot of built-in classes and methods, which we can use for writing end-to-end testing.

Protractor API exposes various classes and methods mainly around `Browser`, `Element`, `Locators`, and `ExpectedConditions`.

The Protractor supports the two latest major versions of Chrome, Firefox, Safari, and IE-- which means we can write our test scripts and run them on any/all of the leading browsers available.

For writing end-to-end tests, we will need to target the elements in the page, read their properties, update the attributes, and invoke methods attached to the elements or send and verify the data.

We will discuss various classes and methods available in the Protractor framework using which we can automate our application functionality by writing end-to-end testing.

Let's learn about the methods and classes available, which we can employ using the Protractor framework.

Protractor and DOM

In this section, you will learn about interacting with DOM elements in the page using Protractor.

Protractor API supports and exposes classes and methods for targeting element(s) in the page. We need to mention explicitly whether we need to target a specific element or if we are expecting a group of elements to be returned.

The `element` function is used to find HTML elements on your webpage. It returns an `ElementFinder` object, which can be used to interact with the element or get information about the properties and methods attached to it.

We will need to find, edit, remove, and add elements and their properties in the page dynamically. However, to implement these use cases, we need to first define and find the target elements.

We can define target element(s) using the following methods:

- `element`: This method will return a single/specific element:

```
element ( by.css ( 'firstName' ) );
```

- `element.all`: This method returns a collection of elements:

```
element.all(by.css('.parent'))
```

Using the aforementioned methods, we can target any and all elements in the page. In next section, you will learn about available methods we can use to find elements along with the `element` or `element.all` methods.

Some methods available to select element(s)

In the preceding section, we saw a list of the most frequently used methods to select or target an element or multiple elements in the page.

To use the previously discussed methods, you need to mention explicitly whether you need to target a specific element or if we are expecting a group of elements to be returned.

In this section, let's learn about available methods and ways to target/select elements in our test script. We can target one or more elements in one go.

We can use almost all attributes, properties, and custom directives to target specific elements.

Let's take a look at some of the ways we can target elements in the test script:

- `by.css`: We can pass the CSS selector to select a element(s):

    ```
    element( by.css('.firstName' ) );
    ```

    CSS `selectors` are the most commonly and frequently used method for targeting and selecting elements.

- `by.model`: We use this to select or target an element using the `ng-model` name bound to the element:

    ```
    element( by.model ( 'firstName' ) );
    ```

    Note that the official documentation still suggests using CSS selectors instead of model.

- `by.repeater`: We use this method to select elements displayed using the `ng-repeat` directive:

    ```
    element( by.repeater('user in users').row(0).column('name') );
    ```

- `by.id`: We use this method to select an element using it's ID:

    ```
    element( by.id( 'firstName' ) );
    ```

- `by.binding`: Use this to select elements associated with one-way or two-way Angular binding:

    ```
    element( by.binding( 'firstName' ) );
    ```

- `by.xpath`: Use this to select element(s) by traversing through `xpath`:

    ```
    element(by.css('h1')).element(by.xpath('following-
        sibling::div'));
    ```

- `first()`, `last()`, or specific elements: We use these methods to get elements at specific locations or indices:

    ```
    element.all(by.css('.items li')).first();
    ```

We learned about some of the methods we can use to target elements by using their properties and information. For a complete list of methods available, refer to the official documentation for Protractor on GitHub.

In the next section, you will learn about various built-in methods we can use to write test scripts to automate the application logic.

Exploring the Protractor API

In this section, you will learn about various built-in classes and methods available in the Protractor API, which we can use for writing our test scripts.

The Protractor API has a lot of predefined built-in properties and methods for `Browser`, `Element`, `Locators`, and `ExpectedConditions` support.

It provides a lot of built-in methods ranging from click events to setting the data for inputs forms, from getting text to getting URL details and much more, to simulate actions and events in the application page.

Let's take a quick look at some of the available built-in methods to simulate user interactions:

- `click`: Using this method, we can schedule a command to click on this element. The method is used to simulate any click events in the page:

    ```
    element.all( by.id('sendMail') ).click();
    ```

- `getTagName`: This gets the tag/node name of the element:

    ```
    element(by.css('.firstName')).getTagName()
    ```

- `sendKeys`: Using this method, we can schedule a command to type a sequence on the DOM element:

    ```
    element(by.css('#firstName')).sendKeys("sridhar");
    ```

- `isDisplayed`: Using this method, we can schedule a command to test whether this element is currently displayed in the page:

    ```
    element(by.css('#firstPara')).isDisplayed();
    ```

- `Wait`: Using this method, we can execute a command to wait for a condition to hold or promise to be resolved:

```
browser.wait(function() {
  return true;
}).then(function () {
  // do some operation
});
```

- `getWebElement`: Using this method, we can find the web element represented by this `ElementFinder`:

```
element(by.id('firstName')).getWebElement();
```

- `getCurrentUrl`: Using this method, we can retrieve the URL of the current application page. This method is used with the `browser` module:

```
var curUrl = browser.getCurrentUrl();
```

For a complete list of properties and methods, refer to the official documentation of Protractor on GitHub.

In this section, you learned about some of the available methods you can use for writing your test scripts and automating application workflows in the page.

We will learn to use some of the built-in methods in the following sections through examples. In the next section, we will start writing test scripts using Protractor.

Protractor - First steps

In this section, let's start writing test scripts using Protractor. We will make use of the methods that we saw earlier in the chapter and element targeting to write our test scripts.

A general syntax of a Protractor framework test suite is as follows:

```
describe("Sample Test Suite", function() {
  it("This is a spec that defines test", function() {
    // expect statement to assert the logic etc
  });
});
```

Analyze the preceding code snippet, and you will realize that it's very similar to the one we created for Jasmine test scripts. Bingo!

The test suites written for Jasmine and Protractor look similar. The major difference is that we make use of the `element` and `browser` modules through which we can target any specific DOM elements in the page.

Now, in the `app.e2e-specs.ts` file, we write our first end-to-end test script; add the following code snippet to the file:

```
import {element, by, browser} from 'protractor';

  describe('dashboard App', () => {
    it('should display message saying app works', () => {
      browser.get('/');
      let title = element(by.tagName('h1')).getText();
      expect(title).toEqual('Testing E2E');
    });
});
```

Let's analyze the preceding code snippet in detail. The subsequent steps have been followed:

1. We are importing the required modules, `element`, `by`, and `browser`, from the `protractor` library into our test script.
2. Using the `describe` statement, we assign a name for our end-to-end test specs and we write our `specDefinitions` for it.
3. We define a test script using the `it` statement, and in the function we use `browser` to navigate to the home page and checking the `<H1>` tag and value to be equal to `Testing E2E`.

We have defined our e2e test scripts; now let's run the tests using the `ng` command, as follows:

```
ng e2e
```

The preceding command will run, invoke the browser, execute the e2e test scripts, and then close the browser.

You should see the following results in the terminal:

```
E2ML1151As-MacBook-Pro:master Admin$ cd dashboard/
E2ML1151As-MacBook-Pro:dashboard Admin$ ng e2e
** NG Live Development Server is running on http://localhost:49152 **
Hash: c2e15de52b7ec7619119
Time: 17356ms
chunk    {0} polyfills.bundle.js, polyfills.bundle.js.map (polyfills) 166 kB {4} [initial] [rendered]
chunk    {1} main.bundle.js, main.bundle.js.map (main) 24.2 kB {3} [initial] [rendered]
chunk    {2} styles.bundle.js, styles.bundle.js.map (styles) 65.2 kB {4} [initial] [rendered]
chunk    {3} vendor.bundle.js, vendor.bundle.js.map (vendor) 3.67 MB [initial] [rendered]
chunk    {4} inline.bundle.js, inline.bundle.js.map (inline) 0 bytes [entry] [rendered]
webpack: Compiled successfully.
[00:10:54] I/update - chromedriver: file exists /Applications/MAMP/htdocs/MTproject3/master/dashboard/node_modules/protractor/node_modules/webdriver-manager/selenium/chromedriver_
2.29.zip
[00:10:54] I/update - chromedriver: unzipping chromedriver_2.29.zip
[00:10:54] I/update - chromedriver: setting permissions to 0755 for /Applications/MAMP/htdocs/MTproject3/master/dashboard/node_modules/protractor/node_modules/webdriver-manager/se
lenium/chromedriver_2.29
[00:10:54] I/update - chromedriver: chromedriver_2.29 up to date
[00:10:54] I/launcher - Running 1 instances of WebDriver
[00:10:54] I/direct - Using ChromeDriver directly...
Spec started

  dashboard App
    ✓ should display message saying app works

Executed 1 of 1 spec SUCCESS in 2 secs.
[00:10:58] I/launcher - 0 instance(s) of WebDriver still running
[00:10:58] I/launcher - chrome #01 passed
E2ML1151As-MacBook-Pro:dashboard Admin$ ▊
```

If you see all test scripts passed, all our E2E tests have passed. Congrats!

> The command needs to be run in the parent directory of the project directory.

Writing E2E tests using Protractor

In the preceding section, you learned to write your first test script using Protractor. In this section, we will extend our example and add more meat to it.

Let's take a look at the use cases we will automate in our example:

1. We will check whether our home page has the title `Testing E2E`.
2. We will check whether the element with the `firstPara` ID is displayed on the page.
3. We will assert that the `class` attribute of the element with the `firstPara` ID is equal to `'custom-style'`.
4. Finally, we read the current URL of the page and check whether it's equal to the value we pass in the assertion.

Let's now write our E2E spec for this. In the `app.e2e.spec.ts` file, add the following lines of code:

```
import { browser, by, element } from 'protractor';

describe('Form automation Example', function() {
  it('Check paragraphs inner text', function() {
    browser.get('/first-test');
```

```
    var s = element(by.css('#firstPara')).getText();
    expect(s).toEqual('Testing E2E');
  });

  it('Should check for getAttribute - class', function() {
    browser.get('/first-test');
    var frstPa = element(by.id('firstPara'));
    expect(frstPa.getAttribute('class')).toEqual('custom-style');
  });

  it('Should check element for isDisplayed method', function() {
    browser.get('/first-test');
    var ele = element(by.css('#firstPara')).isDisplayed();
    expect(ele).toBeTruthy();
  });

  it('Check the applications current URL', function() {
    var curUrl = browser.getCurrentUrl();
    expect(curUrl).toBe('http://localhost:49152/first-test');
  });

});
```

A breakdown and analysis of the preceding code are as follows:

1. We imported the required modules, `element`, `by`, and `browser`--from `protractor`.
2. We wrote a `describe` statement to create a test suite with the name `'Form automation Example'`.
3. For the first test script, we told `protractor` using `browser` to navigate to the `/first-test` URL using the method `get`.
4. We received the element with the `id` as `firstPara` and its text and checked whether the value is equal to `Testing E2E`.
5. In the second test script, we navigated to the URL `/first-test` using the `get` method and received the same element with the `id` as `firstPara`.
6. Using the `getAttribute` method, we now take the `class` attribute of the element and check whether its value matches to `'custom-style'`.
7. In the third test script, we told `protractor` using `browser` to navigate to the `/first-test` URL using the `get` method.
8. Using the `isDisplayed` method, we checked whether the element is displayed on the page or not.

9. In the fourth test script, we told `protractor`, using the `browser` method `getCurrentUrl`, to get the `currentUrl` of the page

10. We checked whether the `currentUrl` matches the value passed in the test script.

To run end-to-end tests, we will use the `ng` commands. In the project directory, run the following command:

```
ng e2e
```

The following screenshot shows the output that we will see once all the tests have passed:

How easy and simple is it to create and run tests, right?

This is good start, and we will continue to learn to write more test scripts using advanced techniques.

Go ahead and plug your logic, and write automated test scripts for your applications.

Writing E2E tests using Protractor - Advanced

So far, in earlier sections, we have covered installing, using, and writing test scripts using the Protractor framework. We have learned and implemented built-in methods and classes exposed by the Protractor API.

In this section, we will cover writing advanced test scripts, which will have interactions in the page, and test the elements thoroughly.

Take a look at the use cases that we will cover:

1. We will test our array values.
2. We will target our element using the class attribute.
3. We will check the heading of the page.
4. We will simulate the `click` event attached on a button and then verify the text changes of another element.

Let's get started with writing our test scripts.

We will need to first create our `test-app.component.html` file. Create the file, and add the following code to the file:

```html
<h3 class="packtHeading">Using protractor - E2E Tests</h3>

<input id="sendEmailCopy" type="checkbox"> Send email copy

<!-- paragraph to load the result -->
<p class="afterClick">{{afterClick}}</p>

<!-- button to click -->
<button (click)="sendMail()">Send mail!</button>
```

The analysis of the preceding code snippet is as follows:

1. We defined an `h3` title tag and assigned a `class` attribute with a value as `packtHeading`.
2. We created a `input` type `checkbox` element with an ID as `sendEmailCopy`.
3. We defined a paragraph `p` tag with a `class` attribute as `afterClick` and bound the value inside `{{ }}`.
4. We defined a `button` and attached a `click` event to call the `sendMail` method.
5. The purpose of the `sendMail` method is to change the text inside the `paragraph` tag.

Now that we have our template file defined, it's time for us to create our component file.

Create the `test-app.component.ts` file, and add the following code snippet to it:

```typescript
import { Component } from '@angular/core';
import { Component } from '@angular/core';
import { FormsModule } from '@angular/forms';
```

```
@Component({
  selector: 'app-test-app',
  templateUrl: './test-app.component.html',
  styleUrls: ['./test-app.component.css']
})

export class TestAppComponent {
  constructor() {}
  public myModel = "Testing E2e";
  public authorName = 'Sridhar';
  public publisherName = 'Packt';
  public afterClick = 'Element is not clicked';
  public hiPackt() {
    return 'Hello ' + this.publisherName;
  }
  public sendMail() {
    this.afterClick = 'Element is clicked';
  }
}
```

Let's analyze the preceding code snippet in detail:

1. We imported the `Component` and `Oninit` modules from `@angular/core`.
2. We also imported `FormsModule` from `@angular/forms`.
3. We created `Component` and associated the HTML and CSS files to `templateUrl` and `stylesUrl`, respectively.
4. We defined the `myModel`, `authorName`, `publisherName`, and `afterClick` variables.
5. We assigned values to the variables defined.
6. We defined a `hiPackt` method, which will display `Hello Packt`.
7. We defined a `sendMail` method, which when invoked will update the value of the `afterClick` variable.

So far, so good. Stay with me on this; we are going to write beautiful test scripts very soon.

Now, we got our template file defined and implemented our component file; we know the functionality of the component very well. It's time to get the testing part started.

Let's create the test spec `app.e2e.spec.ts` file, and add the following code snippet to it:

```
import {element, by, browser} from 'protractor';

describe('dashboard App', () => {
  beforeEach(function () {
```

```
    browser.get('/test-app');
  });

  it('should display message saying app works', () => {
   const title = element(by.tagName('h1')).getText();
   expect(title).toEqual('Learning Angular - Packt Way');
  });

  it('should display message saying app works', () => {
   element(by.tagName('button')).click();
   const title = element(by.css('.afterClick')).getText();
   expect(title).toEqual('Element is not clicked');
  });

  it('Should check is radio button is selected or deselected',
    function() {
      var mailCopy = element(by.id('sendEmailCopy'));
      expect(mailCopy.isSelected()).toBe(false);
      mailCopy.click();
      expect(mailCopy.isSelected()).toBe(true);
  });

  it('Check the applications current URL', function() {
      var curUrl = browser.getCurrentUrl();
      expect(curUrl).toBe('http://localhost:49152/test-app');
  });

});
```

Let's take a detailed look at what's happening in our test specifications:

1. We define a beforeEach method, which will be executed before the test script and will open the browser URL as defined.
2. We now write a test script to test the title value of the h1 tag using the assertion toEqual.
3. In the second test script, we get a button element using tagName and invoke the click method.
4. Since the method was clicked, the value of the paragraph has been updated.
5. We will retrieve the paragraph element using by.css and get the text value of the paragraph inside it.
6. We assert whether the newly updated value is equal to Element is clicked.
7. In the third test script, using the isSelected method we check whether the input element type checkbox was checked.

8. Using the `click` method, we now toggle the `checkbox` and check the value again. This test script is to show you how to play with form elements.

9. Finally, in the last test script, we get the URL of the current page using `getCurrentUrl` and check whether it matches to `/test-app`.

That's it, all done. Now, we have our template file in place, we have created the component, and we have our test spec file as well.

It's show time. Let's run the app, and we should see the output shown in the following screenshot:

In this section, you learned to write test scripts using the Protractor framework. We explored all the built-in available methods in the framework for us to use while writing scripts.

We noted that test scripts written are similarly to Jasmine test scripts. We also saw how to target a specific element or collection of elements using various methods, such as `by.css`, `by.binding`, and `by.id`.

We discussed event handling and bindings using the Protractor framework.

Summary

Testing is one of the most crucial and important aspects of application development. In this chapter, you learned how to use Angular CLI, Jasmine, and Protractor framework. Automation testing using Jasmine and Protractor can help you save time and effort.

You learned about writing unit test scripts for Angular components and services and also how to write E2E test cases for workflow automation testing. You explored in detail Jasmine framework and the Protractor framework methods and variables built-in to functions.

We delved into targeting specific elements as well as retrieving collections of elements together to read, update, and edit properties and values. Go ahead and automate your applications using these great testing frameworks.

In the next chapter, you will learn about design patterns in Angular. Typescript is an object-oriented programming language and, as such, we can leverage decades of knowledge on object oriented architecture. You will also explore some of the most useful object-oriented design patterns and learn how to apply them in an Angular way.

17
Design Patterns in Angular

TypeScript is an object-oriented programming language and, as such, we can leverage decades of knowledge on object-oriented architecture. In this chapter, we explore some of the most useful object-oriented design patterns and learn how to apply them in an Angular way.

Angular is, by itself, an object-oriented framework and it forces you to do most of your development in certain ways. For example, you are required to have components, services, pipes, and so on. Forcing upon you these building blocks contributes to building good architecture. Very much like what the Zend framework does for PHP or Ruby on Rails for Ruby. Frameworks are here to make your life easier and speed up the development time.

While the Angular way of designing things is way above average, we can always do better. I do not claim that what I present in this chapter is the ultimate design, and you will be able to use it to resolve anything from a one pager for a bakery to pagers to dashboards for the Mars One mission--such a design does not exist--but, it definitely improves your tool belt.

In this chapter, we will learn to use the following patterns:

- Model-View-Controller(MVC)
- Singleton
- Dependency Injection
- Prototype
- Reusable pool
- Factory
- Memento

Model-View-Controller (MVC)

Oh MVC, good old MVC. You served us well for many years. Now, people want you to retire, without fuss if possible. Moreover, even I can see how younger unidirectional user interface architectures can outsmart you and make you look like a relic from the past.

In this section, we will first describe what the MVC is, regardless of the programming language used to implement it, and then we will see the shortcomings of applying MVC for frontend programming. Finally, I will present a way to implement an MVC that makes sense with Angular regarding ease of implementation, maintenance, and performance.

MVC at large

The whole principle behind the MVC design pattern is fairly straightforward. Indeed, as shown in the following figure, it is composed of three blocks: Model, View, and Controller. More specifically, the intent of the MVC is to define a one-to-many dependency between objects so that when one object changes state, all its dependents are notified and updated automatically:

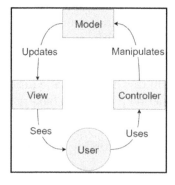

MVC overview

Let us analyze the preceding image block by block:

- The **Model** stores the data required by the application according to commands sent by the **Controller**.
- The **Controller** receives actions from the **User** (that is, a click on a button) and directs **Model** updates accordingly. It can also set which **View** is used at any given moment.

- The **View** is generated and updated every time the **Model** changes.

And that is it.

Let's see what a simple MVC implementation would look like in pure TypeScript.

First, let's define a `Movie` class like we did back in `Chapter 10`, *Material Design in Angular*. In this version of the `Movie` class, we have only two attributes, `title` and `release_year`, which are defined using a TypeScript constructor:

```
class Movie{

    constructor(private title:string, private release_year:number){}

    public getTitle():string{
        return this.title;
    }
    public getReleaseYear():number{
        return this.release_year;
    }
}
```

Then, we define a `Model` class that imports the `movie.ts` file, containing the `Movie` class, using the reference keyword. This `Model` class, which will be responsible for updating the view, has a movie array and two methods. The first method, `addMovie(title:string, year:number)` is public and appends a new movie at the end of the movies attribute. It also calls the second method of the class: `appendView(movie:Movie)` which is private. This second method manipulates the view as per the MVC definition. The view manipulation is rather simple; we append a new `li` tag to the `movie` element of the view. The content of the newly created `li` tag is a concatenation of the movie title and release year:

```
class Model{

    private movies:Movie[] = [];

    constructor(){
    }

    public addMovie(title:string, year:number){
        let movie:Movie = new Movie(title, year);
        this.movies.push(movie);
        this.appendView(movie);
    }

    private appendView(movie:Movie){
```

```
        var node = document.createElement("LI");
        var textnode = document.createTextNode(movie.getTitle() +
            "-" + movie.getReleaseYear());
        node.appendChild(textnode);
        document.getElementById("movies").appendChild(node);
    }

}
```

We can now define a controller for our pure TypeScript MVC. The Controller has a private `model:Model` attribute that is initiated in the constructor. Also, a `click` method is defined. This method takes a string and a number in parameters for the title and the release year, respectively. As you can see, the `click` method forwards the title and the release year to the `addMovie` method of the model. Then, the controller's job is done. It does not manipulate the view. You will also notice the last line of the `controller.ts` file: let `controller = new Controller();`. This line allows us to create an instance of the `Controller` class that View can bind to:

```
class Controller{

    private model:Model;

    constructor(){

        this.model = new Model();
    }

    click(title:string, year:number){

        console.log(title, year);
        this.model.addMovie(title, year);

    }

}
let controller = new Controller();
```

The last piece of our MVC implementation is the view. We have a bare-bones HTML form which, on submit, invokes the following: `controller.click(this.title.value, this.year.value); return false;`. The controller has been defined in the `controller.ts` file with let `controller = new Controller();`. Then, for the parameters, we send `this.title.value` and `this.year.value` where this refers to the `<form>`.

The title and year refer to the field for the title and the release year of the movie, respectively. We also have to add return false to prevent the page from reloading. Indeed, the default behavior of an HTML form, on submit, is to navigate to the action URL:

```html
<html>
    <head>
        <script src="mvc.js"></script>
    </head>
    <body>
        <h1>Movies</h1>
        <div id="movies">
        </div>

        <form action="#" onsubmit="controller.click(this.title.value,
            this.year.value); return false;">
          Title: <input name="title" type="text" id="title">
          Year: <input name="year" type="text" id="year">
         <input type="submit">
        </form>

    </body>
</html>
```

In the header, we add the mvc.js script generated by the following command: tsc--out mvc.jscontroller.ts model.ts movie.ts. The generated JavaScript looks like the following:

```javascript
var Movie = (function () {
    function Movie(title, release_year) {
        this.title = title;
        this.release_year = release_year;
    }
    Movie.prototype.getTitle = function () {
        return this.title;
    };
    Movie.prototype.getReleaseYear = function () {
        return this.release_year;
    };
    return Movie;
}());
/// <reference path="./movie.ts"/>
var Model = (function () {
    function Model() {
        this.movies = [];
    }
    Model.prototype.addMovie = function (title, year) {
        var movie = new Movie(title, year);
```

```
        this.movies.push(movie);
        this.appendView(movie);
    };
    Model.prototype.appendView = function (movie) {
        var node = document.createElement("LI");
        var textnode = document.createTextNode(movie.getTitle() +
            "-" + movie.getReleaseYear());
        node.appendChild(textnode);
        document.getElementById("movies").appendChild(node);
    };
    return Model;
}());
/// <reference path="./model.ts"/>
var Controller = (function () {
    function Controller() {
        this.model = new Model();
    }
    Controller.prototype.add = function (title, year) {
        console.log(title, year);
        this.model.addMovie(title, year);
    };
    return Controller;
}());
var controller = new Controller();
```

On the execution side, at loading time, the HTML page would look like the following screenshot:

MVC at loading time.

Then, if you use the form and add a movie, it will automatically impact the view and display the new movie as shown in the following image:

MVC after using the form.

MVC limitations for the frontend

So, why is the MVC pattern not used that often when it comes to Frontend programming supported by a framework such as Angular? First, if you are using Angular for an app that provides a service, you are likely to have a Backend with which you exchange some information. Then, if your Backend also uses the MVC design pattern, you will end up with the following hierarchy:

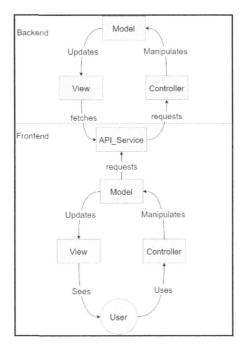

MVC Frontend and Backend.

In this hierarchy, we have an MVC implementation on top of another MVC implementation. Both implementations communicate with each other via an API service that sends requests to the Backend Controller and parses the resulting view. As a concrete example, if your user has to sign in to your app, they will see the sign in View on the Frontend that is powered by a User Model and a sign Controller. Once all the information (email, password) has been entered, the User clicks on the Sign-in button.

This click triggers a Model update and the Model then triggers an API call using the API service. The API service makes a request to the `user/signin` endpoint of your API. On the Backend side, the request is received by the User Controller and forwarded to the User Model. The Backend User Model will query your database to see if there is a matching User with the provided user and password. Finally, a View will be output, containing the user information if the login was successful. Going back on the Frontend, the API service will parse the produced view and return the relevant information to the Frontend User Model. In turns, the Frontend User Model will update the Frontend View.

For some developers, that many layers and the fact that the architecture is duplicated on the Frontend and the Backend just feels wrong even though it brings maintainability through a well-defined separation of concerns.

The dual MVC is not the only concern. Another problem is that the frontend models will not be pure models as they have to account for variables regarding the UI itself such as visible tabs, form validity, and so on. Hence, your Frontend Models tend to become a hideous blob of code where UI variables rub shoulders with the actual representation of your user, for example.

Now, as always, you can avoid these traps and harness the advantages of the MVC pattern. Let's see how in the next section.

Angular is MVC

In this section, I present an architecture for the MVC in Angular that has proved itself. I have used this architecture for the past eight months at `toolwatch.io` (web, Android, and iOS). Obviously, the features we propose on the web version or the mobile apps are the same and work the same way; what changes are the views and the navigation scheme.

The following figure presents the overall architecture:

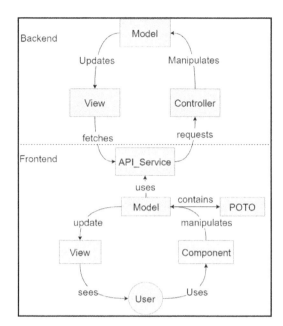

MVC for Angular.

From top to bottom, we have the Backend, the reusable pieces of the Frontend, and the specialized Frontend (that is, mobile or the web). As you can see, on the Backend, nothing changes. We have kept our traditional MVC. Note that the Frontend parts would also work with the non-MVC Backend.

Our Model will use that service to get, put, and delete a plain TypeScript object from the remote database through a hypothetic JSON API.

Here's what our user TypeScript object looks like:

```
export class User {

    public constructor(private _email:string, private _password:string){}

    get email():string{
        return this._password;
    }

    get password():string{
        return this._email;
    }
```

```
        set email (email:string){
            this._password = email;
        }

        set password (password:string){
            this._email = password;
        }


    }
```

Nothing too fancy here. Only a plain TypeScript object that contains two attributes: `email:_string` and `password:_string`. These two attributes are initialized in the Constructor using the TypeScript inline declaration style. We also leverage the getter/setter of TypeScript to access the `password:string` and `_email:string` attributes. You might have noticed that the TypeScript getter/setter look like C# properties. Well, Microsoft is one of the principal industrial investigators for TypeScript, so it makes sense.

I do like the conciseness of the writing, especially when combined with inline attribute declarations in the constructor. What I do not like, however, is the necessity to have underscored variables names. The problem is that, once again, this TypeScript will be transpiled to JavaScript, and in JavaScript, variables and function are a bit more abstract than, let's say, Java or C#.

Indeed, in our current example we could invoke the getter of the `user` class as follows:

```
user:User = new User('mathieu.nayrolles@gmail.com', 'password');

console.log(user.email); // will print mathieu.nayrolles@gmail.com
```

As you can see, TypeScript does not care about the type of the target it is calling. It can be a variable named email or a function named `email()`. Either way, it works, with different results, but it works. The underlying rationale behind this odd behavior, for an object-oriented program, is that, in JavaScript, it is acceptable to do:

```
var email = function(){
    return "mathieu.nayrolles@gmail.com";
}
console.log(email);
```

Consequently, we need to differentiate the actual variables of the function with different names. Hence the _.

Let's go back to our MVC implementation now that we have a full-proof user object to manipulate. Now we can have a `UserModel` that manipulates the user **Plain Old TypeScript Object (POTO)** and the needed variable for the graphical interface:

```typescript
export class UserModel{

    private user:User;
    private _loading:boolean = false;

    public constructor(private api:APIService){}

    public signin(email:string, password:string){

        this._loading = true;

        this.api.getUser(new User(email, password)).then(

            user => {
                this.user = user;
                this._loading = false;
            }
        );
    }

    public signup(email:string, password:string){

        this._loading = true;
        this.api.postUser(new User(email, password)).then(
            user => {
                this.user = user;
                this._loading = false;
            }
        );
    }

    get loading():boolean{
        return this._loading;
    }
}
```

Our model, named `UserModel`, receives an injection of an `APIService`. The implementation of the `APIService` is left to the reader as an exercise. However, it will be very similar to what we have seen in Chapter 9, *Advanced Forms in Angular 2*. In addition to the `APIService`, `UserModel` owns the `user:User` and `loading:bool` attributes. The `user:User` represents the actual user with its password and email. The `loading:bool`, however, will be used to determine whether or not a loading spinner should be visible in the view. As you can see, `UserModel` defines the `signin` and `signup` methods. In these methods, we call the `getUser` and `postUser` methods of the hypothetical `APIService` that both take a User in argument and return a Promise containing the said user synchronized via the JSON API. On receipt of the promises, we turn off the `loading:bool` spinner.

Then, let's have a look at the controller, which will also be a component in an Angular environment as Angular components control the view which is displayed, and so on:

```
@Component({
    templateUrl: 'user.html'
})
export class UserComponent{

    private model:UserModel;

    public constructor(api:APIService){

        this.model = new UserModel(api);
    }


    public signinClick(email:string, password:string){
        this.model.signin(email, password);
    }

    public signupClick(email:string, password:string){
        this.model.signup(email, password);
    }


}
```

As you can see, the controller (component) is simple. We only have a reference to the model, and we receive an injected `APIService` to be transferred to the model. Then, we have the `signinClick` and `signupClick` methods that receive user input from the view and transfer them to `model`. The last piece, the view, looks like this:

```
<h1>Signin</h1>

<form action="#" onsubmit="signinClick(this.email.value,
```

```
this.password.value); return false;">

    email: <input name="email" type="text" id="email">
    password: <input name="password" type="password" id="password">
    <input [hidden]="model.loading" type="submit">
    <i [hidden]="!model.loading" class="fa fa-spinner"
        aria-hidden="true">loading</i>
</form>

<h1>Signup</h1>

<form action="#" onsubmit="signupClick(this.email.value,
    this.password.value); return false;">

    email: <input name="email" type="text" id="email">
    password: <input name="password" type="password" id="password">
    <input [hidden]="model.loading" type="submit">
    <i [hidden]="!model.loading" class="fa fa-spinner"
      aria-hidden="true">loading</i>
</form>
```

Here, we have two forms, one for the signin and one for signup. Both forms are alike except for the `onsubmit` method they use. The sign-in form uses the `signinClick` method of our controller, and the sign-up form uses the `signupClick` method. In addition to these two forms, we also have, on each form, a Font Awesome spinner that is only visible once the user model is loading. We achieve this by using the `[hidden]` Angular directive: `[hidden]="!model.loading"`. Similarly, the submit buttons are hidden when the model is loading.

So, here it is, a functional MVC applied to Angular.

As I said at the beginning of this section, for me, the actual usefulness of the MVC pattern in Angular comes from its extensibility. Indeed, leveraging the object-oriented aspect (and what comes with it) of TypeScript allows us to specialize a controller and model for different Angular applications. For example, if you have an Angular website and an Angular mobile application, as I do with `toolwatch.io`, then you have business logic you can reuse on both sides. It would be a shame to have two sign-ins, two sign-ups, and two of everything to code and maintain over time when we could have only one!

At `toolwatch.io`, for example, the web application uses standard Angular, and we built the mobile applications using Ionic2 and Angular. Obviously, we have a lot a frontend logic shared between the mobile apps (Android and iOS) and the website. Ultimately, they tend to achieve the same purposes and functionalities. The only difference is the medium used to use those functionalities.

In the following figure, I loosely represent a complete way of leveraging the MVC pattern with a focus on reusability and extensibility:

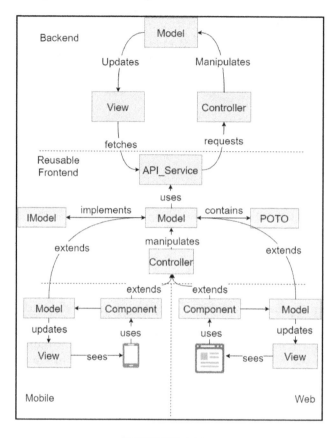

Reusable MVC for Angular.

Once again, the Backend stays as-is. We have the same MVC pattern there. As a reminder, the MVC pattern on the Backend is entirely up to you, and you could take advantage of the Frontend MVC pattern with a functional Go Backend, for example. What differs from the previous version of the MVC exposed here is the introduction of the Reusable Frontend part. In this part, we still have an API service in charge of consuming our JSON API. Then, we have a model that implements the `IModel` interface:

```
export interface IModel{

    protected get(POTO):POTO;
    protected put(POTO):POTO;
    protected post(POTO):POTO;
```

```
        protected delete(POTO):boolean;
        protected patch(POTO):POTO;


    }
```

This interface defines the `put`, `post`, `delete`, and `patch` methods that have to be implemented in the subsequent models. The `POTO` type that these methods take as parameters and return is the mother class for any domain model you have in your program. A domain model represents the synchronizable entity of your business logic such as the User we used before. The domain model and the model part of MVC are not to be confused. They are not the same thing at all. In this architecture, User would extend `POTO`.

The model (of MVC this time) contains a `POTO` also to implement the `IModel` interface. Also, it contains the variables and methods you need to update your views. The implementation of the model itself is rather straightforward as I have shown earlier in this section. However, we can kick things up a notch by leveraging the generic aspect of TypeScript and envision the following:

```
    export class AbstractModel<T extends POTO> implements IModel{
        protected T domainModel;

        public constructor(protected api:APIService){}

        protected get(POTO):T{
            //this.api.get ...
        };
        protected put(T):T{
            //this.api.put...
        };
        protected post(T):T{
            //this.api.post...
        };
        protected delete(T):boolean{
            //this.api.delete...
        };
        protected patch(T):T{
            //this.api.patch...
        };
    }

    export class UserModel extends AbstractModel<User>{

        public constructor(api:APIService){
            super(api);
        }
```

```
    public signin(email:string, password:string){

        this._loading = true;

        this.get(new User(email, password)).then(

            user => {
                this.user = user;
                this._loading = false;
            }
        );
    }

    public signup(email:string, password:string){

        this._loading = true;
        this.post(new User(email, password)).then(
            user => {
                this.user = user;
                this._loading = false;
            }
        );
    }
    //Only the code specialized for the UI!
}
```

Here, we have the generic `AbstractModel` that is constrained by `POTO`. It means that the actual instance of the `AbstractModel` generic class (known as a template in a language such as C++) is constrained to have a class-specializing `POTO`. In other words, only domain models such as `User` can be used. So far, the separation of concern is excellent as well as the reusability. The last piece of the reusable part is the controller. In our sign-up/sign-in example, it would look very much like this:

```
export class UserController{

    public UserComponent(protected model:UserModel){
    }

    public signin(email:string, password:string){
        this.model.signin(email, password);
    }

    public signup(email:string, password:string){
        this.model.signup(email, password);
    }

}
```

Now, why do we need an additional building block here and can't we use a simple Angular component as we did for the simpler version of the Angular MVC? Well, the thing is that, depending on what you use on top of your Angular core (Ionic, Meteor, and so on), the component is not necessarily the main building block. For example, in the Ionic2 world, you use pages that are the custom version of the classical component.

So, for example, the mobile part would look like this:

```
export class LoginPage extends UserController{

    public LoginPage(api:APIService){
        super(new UserModel(api));
    }

    //Only what's different on mobile!

}
```

If need be, you can also extend UserModel and add some specialization as shown in the figure of Reusable MVC for Angular. On the browser side, add this piece of code:

```
@Component({
    templateUrl: 'login.html'
})
 export class LoginComponent extends UserController{

    public UserComponent(api:APIService){

        super(new UserModel(api));
    }

    //Only what's different on the browser !

}
```

Once again you can also extend UserModel and add some specialization. The only remaining block to cover is the view. To my despair, there is no way to extend or add a style file for that. Hence, we are doomed to have a duplication of HTML files between clients unless the HTML file is the same between the mobile app and the browser app. From experience, this does not happen much.

The whole reusable frontend can be shipped as a Git submodule, standalone library, or a
`NgModule`. I personally use the Git submodule approach, as it allows me to have two
separate repositories while enjoying auto-refresh on the client I am working on when I do a
modification on the shared frontend.

Note that this MVC also works if you have several frontends hitting the same backend
instead of several types of frontend. For example, in an e-commerce setup, you might want
to have differently branded websites to sell different products that are all managed in the
same backend, like what's possible with Magento's views.

Singleton and Dependency Injection

Another handy pattern to use for frontend application is the singleton. The singleton
ensures that only one instance of a given object exists in your program. Moreover, it
provides a global point of access to the object.

Here's what it looks like in practice:

```
export class MySingleton{

    private static instance:MySingleton = null;


    //This constructor is private in order to prevent new creation
    //of MySingleton objects    private constructor(){

    }

    public static getInstance():MySingleton{
        if(MySingleton.instance == null){
            MySingleton.instance = new MySingleton();
        }            return MySingleton.instance;      }

}

let singleton:MySingleton = MySingleton.getInstance();
```

We have a class that has a `private static instance:MySingleton` attribute. Then, we
have a `private` constructor that makes the following fail:

```
let singleton:MySingleton = new MySingleton();
```

Note that it fails because your TypeScript transpiler complains about the visibility. However, if you transpile the MySingleton class to JavaScript and import it in another TypeScript project, you will be able to use the new operator as the transpiled JavaScript has no visibility at all.

The problem with this fairly simple implementation of the singleton pattern is concurrency. Indeed, if two processes hit the getInstance():MySingleton at the same time, then we will have two instances of the MySingleton on the program. To be sure that does not happen, we can use a technique called early instantiation:

```
export class MySingleton{

    private static instance:MySingleton = new MySingleton();

    private constructor(){

    }
}

singleton:MySingleton = MySingleton.getInstance();
```

While you can implement your singleton in Typescript, you can also leverage the Angular way of creating a singleton: services! Indeed, in Angular, services are only instantiated once and injected to any components needing them. Here's an example of a service and injection via the NgModule we have seen before in this book:

```
// ./service/api.service.ts
import { Injectable } from '@angular/core';

@Injectable()
export class APIService {

    private increment:number = 0;

    public constructor(){
        this.increment++;
    }

    public toString:string{
        return "Current instance: " + this.increment;
    }
}

// ./app.component.ts

@Component({
```

```
  selector: 'app-root',
  templateUrl: './app.component.html',
  styleUrls: ['./app.component.css'],
})
export class AppComponent {

    public constructor(api:APIService){
        console.log(api);
    }

}


// ./other.component.ts

@Component({
  selector: 'other-root',
  templateUrl: './other.component.html',
  styleUrls: ['./other.component.css'],
})
export class OtherComponent {

    public constructor(api:APIService){
        console.log(api);
    }
}

//app.module.ts

import { BrowserModule } from '@angular/platform-browser';
import { NgModule } from '@angular/core';
import { FormsModule, ReactiveFormsModule } from '@angular/forms';
import { HttpModule } from '@angular/http';
import { NgbModule } from '@ng-bootstrap/ng-bootstrap';
import { APIService } from './services/api.service'

import { AppComponent } from './app.component';
import { OtherComponent } from './other.component';

@NgModule({
  declarations: [
    AppComponent,
    OtherComponent
  ],
  imports: [
    BrowserModule,
    FormsModule,
    HttpModule,
    ReactiveFormsModule,
```

```
        NgbModule.forRoot()
    ],
    providers: [APIService],
    bootstrap: [AppComponent]
})
export class AppModule { }
```

In the preceding code, we have:

- `APIService` displays the `@Injectable()` annotation that makes it, well, injectable. Also, the `APIService` has an `increment:number` attribute that is incremented every time a new instance is created. The `increment:number` being static, it will tell us exactly how many instances there are in our program. Finally, the `APIService` has a `toString:string` method that returns the current instance number.
- `AppComponent` is a classical component that receives an injection of the `APIService`.
- `OtherComponent` is another classical component that receives an injection of the `APIService`.
- `/app.module.ts` contains our `NgModule`. In the `NgModule`, most of the declarations shown here have already been discussed in this book. The novelty comes from the `providers: [APIService]` part. Here, we declare a provider for the `APIService` itself. As the `APIService` does not do anything too crazy, it can be provided by using a reference to the class. More complex services that, for example, require injection need custom-tailored providers.

Now, if we navigate to these two components, the result is:

```
Current instance: 1
Current instance: 1
```

This proves that only one instance has been created and the same instance has been injected to both components. Hence, we have a singleton. However, this singleton, while convenient, isn't safe. Why, you ask. Well, the `APIService` can also be provided at the component level, like so:

```
// ./app.component.ts

@Component({
    selector: 'app-root',
    templateUrl: './app.component.html',
    styleUrls: ['./app.component.css'],
    providers: [APIService],
})
```

```
export class AppComponent {

    public constructor AppComponent(APIService api){
        console.log(api);
    }

}

// ./other.component.ts

@Component({
  selector: 'other-root',
  templateUrl: './other.component.html',
  styleUrls: ['./other.component.css'],
  providers: [APIService],
})
export class OtherComponent {

    public constructor OtherComponent(APIService api){
        console.log(api);
    }
}
```

In such a case, two separate instances would be created, resulting in the following output:

```
Current instance: 1
Current instance: 2
```

Consequently, using Angular services, you cannot enforce the singleton pattern contrary to its plain TypeScript counterpart. Also, the plain TypeScript would be an order of magnitude faster than the Angular services as we skip the injection process altogether. The exact number depends heavily on the CPU/RAM of your machine.

The only question left to answer in the case of a singleton is when to use it. A singleton enforces only one instance of a given class in your program. Consequently, it is a very good fit for any sort of communication with a backend or any hardware access. For example, in the case of communication with a backend, it might be desirable to have only one APIService handling API keys, API limits, and CSRF tokens across the board without having to make sure we pass the same instance of the service throughout all our components, models, and so on. In the case of hardware access, you might want to be sure that you have only one connection open to the webcam or the microphone of our users so you can properly release them when you are done with it.

Prototype and reusable pool

Object-oriented developers looked at ways to reduce the cost of creating objects, especially, when those objects are expensive to create because they require, for example, a database pull or complex mathematical operations. Another reason to invest in reducing the creation cost of a particular object is when you create a lot of them. Nowadays, backend developers tend to disregard this aspect of optimization as on-demand CPU/memory have become cheap and easy to adjust. It will literally cost you a few bucks more a month to have an additional core or 256 MB RAM on your backend.

This used to be a big deal for desktop application developers too. On a client desktop, there is no way to add CPU/RAM on demand, but fairly cadenced quad cores and a *ridiculous* amount of RAM for consumer PCs made the issue less problematic.

Nowadays, only game and intensive analytics solutions developers seem to care. So, why should you care about the creation time of your object after all? Well, you are building something that is likely to be accessed from old devices (I still use an iPad 1 for casual browsing on the kitchen or the couch). While a desktop application developer can publish minimum and recommended configurations--and enforce them by refusing to install itself-- we, as web developers, don't have this luxury. Now, if your website does not behave properly, users will not question their machines but your skills. Ultimately, they will not use your products, even when on a capable machine.

Let's see how to use the `Prototype` design pattern. The `Prototype` design pattern allows an object to create customized objects without knowing their class or any details of how to create them. The intent is to create new objects by copying this prototype rather than actually instantiating a new object. First, we will need a `Prototype` interface as so:

```
export interface Prototype{

    clone(): Prototype;
}
```

The `Prototype` interface only defines a `clone` method that returns a `Prototype`-- compliant object. You will have guessed it, the optimized way of creating objects is to clone them when needed! So let's say you have an object `Movie` that, for some reason, takes time to build:

```
export class Movie implements Prototype {

    private title:string;
    private year:number;
    //...
```

```
    public constructor();
    public constructor(title?: string, year?: number);
    public constructor(title?: string, year?: number) {
    {
        if(title == undefined || year == undefined){
            //do the expensive creation
        }else{
            this.title = title;
            this.year = year;
        }
    }

    clone() : Movie {
        return new Movie(this.title, this.year);
    }
}

let expensiveMovie:Movie = new Movie();
cheapMovie = expensiveMovie.clone();
```

As you can see the override function in TypeScript is different from most languages. Here, the two signatures of the constructor are on top of each other and share the same implementation.

Moreover, that is it for the `Prototype` pattern.

One other pattern that often goes with the prototype pattern is the object pool pattern. While working with expensive-to-create objects, cloning them sure makes a difference. What can make an even bigger difference is to not do anything at all: no creation, no cloning. To achieve this, we can use the pool pattern. In this pattern, we have a pool of objects ready to be shared by any clients or components in the case of an Angular application. The pool implementation is simple:

```
export class MoviePool{

    private static movies:[{movie:Movie, used:boolean}];
    private static nbMaxMovie = 10;
    private static instance:MoviePool;

    private constructor(){}

    public static getMovie(){

        //first hard create
        if(MoviePool.movies.length == 0){

            MoviePool.movies.push({movie:new Movie(), used:true});
```

```
                return MoviePool.movies[0].movie;


        }else{

            for(var reusableMovie of MoviePool.movies){
                if(!reusableMovie.used){
                    reusableMovie.used = true;
                    return reusableMovie.movie;
                }
            }
        }

        //subsequent clone create
        if(MoviePool.movie.length < MoviePool.nbMaxMovie){

MoviePool.movies.push({movie:MoviePool.movies[MoviePool.movies.
            length - 1].movie.clone(), used:true});
            return MoviePool.movies[MoviePool.movies.length - 1].movie;
        }

        throw new Error('Out of movies');
    }

    public static releaseMovie(movie:Movie){
        for(var reusableMovie of MoviePool.movies){
            if(reusableMovie.movie === movie){
                reusableMovie.used = false;
            }
            return;
        }
    }
}
```

First and foremost, the pool is also a singleton. Indeed, it would not make much sense to have this costly object as a reusable design if anyone can create pools at will. Consequently, we have the `static instance:MoviePool` and the private constructor to ensure that only one pool can be created. Then, we have the following attribute:

```
private static movies:[{movie:Movie, used:boolean}];
```

The `movies` attribute stores a collection of movies and a Boolean used to determine if anyone is currently using any given movie. As the movie objects are hypothetically taxing to create or maintain in memory, it makes sense to have a hard limit on how many such objects we can have in our pool. This limit is managed by the private `static nbMaxMovie = 10;` attribute. To obtain movies, components would have to call the `getMovie():Movie` method. This method does a hard create on the first movie and then leverages the prototype pattern to create any subsequent movie.

Every time a movie is checked out of the pool, the `getMovie` method changes the used Boolean to true. Note that, in the case where the pool is full and we do not have any free movies to give away, then an error is thrown.

Finally, components need a way to check their movies back to the pool so others can use them. This is achieved by the `releaseMovie` method. This method receives a checked out movie and iterates over the movies of the pool to set the according Boolean to false. Hence, the movie becomes usable for other components.

Factory pattern

Let's assume that we have a `User` class with two private variables: `lastName:string` and `firstName:string`. Also, this simple class proposes the method hello that prints `"Hi I am", this.firstName, this.lastName`:

```
class User{
    constructor(private lastName:string, private firstName:string){
    }
    hello(){
        console.log("Hi I am", this.firstName, this.lastName);
    }
}
```

Now, consider that we receive users through a JSON API. Most likely, it will look something like this:

```
[{"lastName":"Nayrolles","firstName":"Mathieu"}...].
```

With the following snippet, we can create a `User`:

```
let userFromJSONAPI: User =
JSON.parse('[{"lastName":"Nayrolles","firstName":"Mathieu"}]')[0];
```

Until now; the TypeScript compiler doesn't complain, and it executes smoothly. It works because the parse method returns `any` (that is, the TypeScript equivalent of the Java Object). Sure enough, we can convert the `any` into `User`. However, `userFromJSONAPI.hello();` will yield:

```
json.ts:19
 userFromJSONAPI.hello();
                 ^

TypeError: userFromUJSONAPI.hello is not a function
    at Object.<anonymous> (json.ts:19:18)
    at Module._compile (module.js:541:32)
    at Object.loader (/usr/lib/node_modules/ts-node/src/ts-node.ts:225:14)
    at Module.load (module.js:458:32)
    at tryModuleLoad (module.js:417:12)
    at Function.Module._load (module.js:409:3)
    at Function.Module.runMain (module.js:575:10)
    at Object.<anonymous> (/usr/lib/node_modules/ts-node/
      src/bin/ts-node.ts:110:12)
    at Module._compile (module.js:541:32)
    at Object.Module._extensions..js (module.js:550:10)
```

Why? Well, the left side of the = statement is defined as `User`, sure, but it will be erased when we transpile it to JavaScript.

The type-safe TypeScript way to do it would be:

```
let validUser =
JSON.parse('[{"lastName":"Nayrolles","firstName":"Mathieu"}]')
 .map((json: any):User => {
     return new User(json.lastName, json.firstName);
 })[0];
```

Interestingly enough, the `typeof` function will not help you either. In both cases it will display `Object` instead of `User` as the very concept of `User` does not exist in JavaScript.

While the direct type-safe approach works, it is not very expansible nor reusable. Indeed, the map `callback` method would have to be duplicated everywhere you receive a JSON user. The most convenient way to do that is with the `Factory` pattern. A `Factory` is used to create objects without exposing the instantiation logic to the client.

If we were to have a factory to create a user; it would look like this:

```
export class POTOFactory{

    /**
     * Builds an User from json response
     * @param  {any}  jsonUser
     * @return {User}
     */
    static buildUser(jsonUser: any): User {

        return new User(
            jsonUser.firstName,
            jsonUser.lastName
        );
    }
}
```

Here, we have a static method named `buildUser` that receives a JSON object and takes all the required values inside the JSON object to invoke, with the right attributes, a hypothetical `User` constructor. The method is static as are all the methods of such a factory. Indeed, we do not need to save any states or instance-bound variables in a factory; we only encapsulate away the gruesome creation of users. Note that your factory will likely be shared with the rest of your POTOs.

Memento pattern

The memento pattern is a really-really useful pattern in the context of Angular. In Angular-powered applications, we use and overuse Two-way Data Binding between domain models such as `User` or `Movie`.

Let's consider two components: one named `Dashboard` and the other one named `EditMovie`. On the Dashboard component, you have a list of movies displayed in the context of our IMDB-like application. The view of such a dashboard could look like this:

```
<div *ngFor="let movie of model.movies">
    <p>{{movie.title}}</p>
    <p>{{movie.year}}</p>
</div>
```

This simple view owns a `ngFor` directive that iterates over the list of movies contained in a model. Then, for each movie, it displays two p elements containing the title and the release year, respectively.

Now, the `EditMovie` components access one of the movies in the `model.movies` array and allow the user to edit it:

```
<form>
    <input id="title" name="title" type="text" [(ngModel)]="movie.title" />
    <input id="year" name="year" type="text" [(ngModel)]="movie.year" />
</form>
<a href="/back">Cancel</a>
```

Thanks to the Two-way Data Binding used here, the modifications were to the movie title and year will directly impact the dashboard. As you can notice, we have a cancel button here. While the user might expect that the modification is synchronized in realtime, he/she also expects that the Cancel button/link cancels the modifications that have been done on the movie.

That is where the Memento pattern comes into play. This pattern allows you to perform undo operations on objects. It can be implemented in many ways, but the simplest one is to go with cloning. Using cloning, we can store away one version of our object, at a given moment, and if need be get it back. Let's enhance our `Movie` object from the `Prototype` pattern as follows:

```
export class Movie implements Prototype {
    private title:string;
    private year:number;
    //...
        public constructor();
            public constructor(title?: string, year?: number);

            public constructor(title?: string, year?: number) {

            if(title == undefined || year == undefined){
            //do the expensive creation
            }else{
            this.title = title;
            this.year = year;
            }
        }

    clone() : Movie {
            return new Movie(this.title, this.year);
    }
    restore(movie:Movie){
            this.title = movie.title;
            this.year = movie.year;
    }
}
```

In this new version, we added the `restore(movie:Movie)` method that takes a `Movie` as an argument and sets the local attributes to the values of the received movie.

Then, in practice, the constructor of our `EditMovie` component could look like this:

```
import { Component } from '@angular/core';
import { Movie } from './movie';
@Component({
  selector: 'app-root',
  templateUrl: './app.component.html',
  styleUrls: ['./app.component.css']
})
export class AppComponent {
  title = 'app works!';

  private memento: Movie;

  constructor(){
    this.memento = new Movie("Title", 2015);
    let movieTmp = this.memento.clone();
    this.memento.setTitle("Another Title");
    //Prints Another title
    console.log(this.memento.getTitle());
    this.memento.restore(movieTmp);
    //Prints Title
    console.log(this.memento.getTitle());
  }
}
```

What's interesting is that you are not limited to one memento over time; you can have as many as you want.

Summary

In this chapter, we learned how to use some of the classical object-oriented patterns that are applicable, and useful, for reusable and easy-to-maintain/extend real-world applications. The MVC was adapted to Angular and expanded to enable highly reusable business logic between different applications. Then, we saw how to control the creation of our object with the singleton with and without Dependency Injection and the prototype coupled to a pool to limit the number of expensive objects in the system. Finally, we learned how to use the factory patterns to avoid the traps in JSON-to-TypeScript automatic (and partial) object conversion and saw how to perform *undo* operations with the memento pattern.

If you want to learn even more about patterns to improve your performance, operations costs, and maintainability, you can check out the upcoming *Angular Design Patterns and Best Practices* book by Packt Publishing. This book goes in-depth into patterns and their implementation to find the best fit your application.

Index

Made in the USA
Monee, IL
12 August 2021